T0381949

WILD GRACE

WILD GRACE

—

The Untamed Women of Modern Dance

—

SARA VEALE

faber

First published in 2025
by Faber & Faber Limited
The Bindery, 51 Hatton Garden
London EC1B 8HN

Typeset by Faber & Faber Ltd
Printed and bound by CPI Group (UK) Ltd, Croydon, CR0 4YY

A CIP record for this book
is available from the British Library

ISBN 978–0–571–36856–3

2 4 6 8 10 9 7 5 3 1

To my luminous family

CONTENTS

CONTENTS

PROLOGUE
State of grace

Where I'm from, in the American South, grace is a virtue, and not just the religious kind. It's about courtesy, dignity, decency, control. Staying cool and keeping the peace. It's smoothing over the cracks, even when – especially when – you're burning to prise them open.

As a dance critic, I find grace in suspended leaps and liquid poses, in lines that bend to the rhythm of a ragged primal scream. My own days as a dancer showed me how to take something alive and whip it back on itself, uncovering its elegant pulse. Dancerly grace, in its stillest moments and its stormier ones too, brings order to the wild topography of the body. It's an organising of self that requires immense discipline.

Outside of the studio, though, away from the stage, grace can take on a different complexion, losing some of its warm animal potential. It's mainly expected of women, in my experience, part of a broader pressure we face to stay composed in a world where flared tempers are reserved for important men in important meetings. Every day we're asked to abide, appease and accommodate. To make ourselves smaller and less needy. To avoid giving anyone cause to think we are, even for just a second and in this one small way, difficult.

Our deepest reserves come into play as the elemental collapses into the systemic. For me, this means not self-combusting when I fathom women's marginalisation in nearly every seat of influence, from government to tech to Hollywood. Four billion of us expected to swallow our own sidelining and go smilingly on our way. Even

I

in the dance sphere, where women crowd the student, teacher and performer ranks, the directors and choreographers – the decision makers – are usually men.

I've always admired women who resist this cool exterior, voicing the unease we're told is unseemly. It's a radical act in a society that urges submission in the name of civility, a clutch at justice that's as personal as it is political. See, it has a serious shrinking effect, all this indulging and obliging and taking in stride. It's a chisel to your core, notching away steadily until you wake up one day and there's a hole where your heart used to be.

I've gathered the subjects of this book as unbridled voices who defied the mindset that self-possession requires compliance and capitulation. As dancers and dancemakers, they channelled their disquiet into an explosive new art form championing fresh perspectives and unsung histories. They did this knowingly and incidentally, loudly and subtly, using their choices onstage and off to challenge expectations about the way they looked, behaved and created. Between them are classically trained graduates and self-styled soloists, grade school dropouts right up to PhDs, ambassadors for Black, white, Jewish and immigrant experiences. Together with hundreds of other innovators zipping around their orbit, these dancers redefined the meaning of grace in their art and their lifestyles, conveying vital truths about what it means to walk the world as a woman.

————

The story of modern dance is a story of subversion – of forms challenged and hierarchies toppled in the pursuit of blazing artistic integrity. Starting in the 1890s, first-generation wavemakers rejected the aerial, symmetrical sensibilities of classical ballet in favour of 'free' dancing that revelled in its own iconoclasm. Early moderns flouted the usual hallmarks of stage-friendly femininity – from fluffy tulle to dainty *port de bras* – with a ferocity that cost them as many admirers as it gained them.

Over the next sixty years, their successors codified these raw, gravity-bound gambols into a range of techniques that could be taught, challenged and evolved. These varied hugely in tone and style, but were unified by an expressionist momentum and a resolve to reveal the effort so often disguised onstage. The moderns strove to find truth in the way we move through space and everyday life. With every technical reinvention came a conscious confrontation of the body and its social ramifications, including the long-held image of dancers as ornaments rather than creatives in their own right.

Throughout its lifespan,* modern dance flew the flags of originality, autonomy and egalitarianism. The same spirit of defiance that awoke the movement guided its practical evolution – who determined its boundaries, whose visions were indulged. Before the moderns came along, male directorship was the mainstay of the concert stage. By conceiving and performing their own work, the female spearheads of modern dance upended the ranks of creative influence, a gear shift with an indelible impact. They made it possible for women to dictate the terms of their art as dancers, creators and educators alike.

These schisms had powerful reverberations in the wider world, echoing and shaping new ideas around permissibility, especially for women. Isadora Duncan's embrace of short, thin tunics at the turn of the century, for example, was a pushback against the Victorian-era policing of female bodies – 'the warp and woof of

---

* The broad bookends of the modern dance movement are generally considered to be the 1890s and the 1960s, making the term 'modern dance' something of an anachronism. Many of the techniques, works and companies from this era survive today, but the movement itself is historical.

New England Puritanism', in her words.[1] She performed braless and barefoot at a time when corsets reigned supreme, challenging a stricture that bound women onstage and beyond. It's one of many details in modern dance's storied history that saw a break from custom call attention to women's emancipation.

Duncan was at the vanguard of a brigade of moderns who helped instigate critical conversations around the politics of womanhood – dress codes and beauty standards, anxieties around female sexuality, the rights of women as workers, activists and citizens of the world. Some tackled these issues in their studio practices, using their platform to push the dance world towards diversity and inclusion; others positioned themselves as storytellers of the female experience, intent on broadening their audiences' world view. Themes, techniques, costumes and casting all came into play, helping steer modern dance into a salient critique of the status quo. The language of their art, and the subjects they explored, united in powerful consonance to rewrite cultural narratives about power, agency and a woman's place.

———

Each of the nine women I've profiled in *Wild Grace* pushed boundaries in her own questing way, finding inspiration within herself and the wider spheres she inhabited. It was a heady integrity that propelled Isadora Duncan towards a bespoke language of dance at the turn of the twentieth century – a bone-deep conviction that a new vocabulary was needed to convey the truths of existence. For her contemporaries Loie Fuller and Maud Allan, it was the pull of the theatrical, visions of concert halls ablaze with fresh marvels of form. Second-generation moderns Martha Graham, Anna Sokolow and Sophie Maslow harnessed their own impassioned urges to rewrite the dance chronicle in the interwar years, roused by the frictions of a fast-changing world; and come the mid-century,

Katherine Dunham, Pearl Primus and Pearl Lang broke centuries-old ancestral chains with their own creative reckonings. These trailblazers dedicated their careers to recasting the contours of performance, each stirred by an intuition that the yelps and gasps in her heart were not incompatible with life on the stage. Their recognition of the progressive possibilities of dance – the way it can, in the brilliant words of Agnes de Mille, serve 'as recompense for all [we] find insupportable in woman's traditional lot'[2] – triggered a tectonic shift in dance history, rocking the canon with a bold new genre that embraced the wilds of womanhood.

Of course, these are just some of the players who helped change take root. Modern dance owes a debt to a vibrant ensemble of both men and women who introduced dynamic movement theories and radical subjects to the stage, not least Ruth St Denis, Ted Shawn, Mary Wigman, Doris Humphrey and Merce Cunningham – heavyweights I've only glanced upon here but who were essential to the movement's genesis and evolution. There were also bold fringe actors whose contributions amount to so much more than the quick references I've offered, especially in charting new courses of femininity, from Olga Desmond, who insisted on the dignity of the naked female form, to Noami Leaf Halpern, a bard for her Jewish foremothers' triumphs. These changemakers encompassed a marvellous variety of methods, mantras and geographies, using the transcendent nature of dance to challenge the hard-bodied here and now.

While some of my subjects would relish the feminist aura I've invoked, I can imagine a few rejecting it out of hand – Duncan in particular, a 'wild voluptuary', as de Mille once admired,[3] with a habit of bucking the labels foisted upon her. I chose their stories for their colour and vim, and the pressing way they sit on my chest. They remind me that autonomy isn't a given, and that progress is neither linear nor inevitable; that I'm able to quibble the particulars of inequality because others before me have shown its prevalence in the first place. 'Don't let them tame you!' Duncan implored an audience in 1922, flashing her breast in defiance.[4] It was a roar of vexation, a middle finger to oppressive expectations of female obedience. Untamed, she and her fellow moderns transformed the lifeblood of grace.

———

This book came together during a period of immense change in my life. I was pregnant with my first child when I decided on the bones of it, and the final draft emerged shortly after my second arrived. My body had awed me with its wherewithal each time, assuming, and in turn producing, a life of its own with very little input from me. I found the inexorability of it all both frightening and energising.

Stumbling through the fog of new motherhood, wondering if I'd ever find my way back to 'before', or if I even wanted to, I found a soul-steadying affinity with these dancers who spun their womanhood into their art, wielding their bodies as junctures of power, resistance, debate, even existence itself. Dancers and dance lovers know the life force of a body at work. It's our 'first and last garment', as Martha Graham put it,[5] home to integrities that can't be shaken.

With new currents of feminism come new questions around applying a contemporary lens to past narratives, especially ones that involve rebellious women. The pages that follow don't salute defiance as an asset in its own right, but they do celebrate the gumption of my subjects and consider, with all that we know and can infer today, the social climates that spurred them on – the heyday of suffragism, for example, and the trials of war, racism and urbanisation. The gap between now and a century ago doesn't yawn as widely as you'd expect. In a world where fathers are still praised for 'babysitting' their own children, where the word 'slut' continues to sting, where more women have been to space than choreographed for some of the world's biggest stages, we need radicals to grab us by the throat and stir us from complacency.

It's been decades since even the youngest of the moderns graced the stage, but their legacies are alive and pulsing. In their refusal to conform, we can find urgent lessons for today. How we raise and regard women, how our self-conception influences our other identities, the power and duty of art to address the questions that keep our hearts beating – and the mettle it takes to do this when the whole world is urging you to keep quiet.

ACT 1, CURTAIN
Dismantling the Cult of Domesticity

Cast

ISADORA DUNCAN
LOIE FULLER   MAUD ALLAN

with

RUTH ST DENIS
MARY WIGMAN
CLOTILDE VON DERP
HERTHA FEIST

and

DANCE COMPANY

As far as insurrections go, the advent of modern dance was more of a freewheeling fringe effort than some slick *coup d'état*. Discontented with classical ballet, the cornerstone of the concert stage in the late-nineteenth century, droves of dancers – mainly soloists – began investigating alternative approaches to dance, from intriguing sculpturesque techniques to intrepid interpretations of mythology. Their ascent from the wings to centre stage was reactive, not directive, yoked by creative idealism rather than shared convictions about form or aesthetic. Taken together, though, their efforts sparked a blazing revolution. Like their modernist counterparts in painting and literature, these renegades stormed the establishment and upended its conventions in search of a more socially focused perspective. Ignited by the energy of dancers pounding away on beaches and grassy knolls, in parlours, studios, galleries and cabarets, a vivid new dance movement flared into action.

Elevated by its Renaissance roots and buffed by the rigours of imperial Russian pedagogy, the ballet stage the early moderns squared off against was decorated and haute, often with the couture to match.* This finery was a robust framework for the fairy-tale

* In Europe, at least. In the United States, ballet was mostly treated as a foreign art in the nineteenth century, a novelty act absorbed into the wider world of variety theatre.

fantasies that continue to dominate the ballet canon today: dolls coming to life and sleeping beauties awaiting true love's kiss. Multi-act grand ballets – particularly the confections emerging from St Petersburg's theatres in the second half of the nineteenth century – were the pinnacle of repute for the dancers of the day.

This Russian inflection was actually a newish development at the time. The ghostly themes and soft, floaty footwork of French dance-makers like Jules Perrot had dominated the ballet circuit for much of the 1800s, in step with a wider cultural lust for all things Romantic, but by the time the *fin de siècle* bounded into frame, a bolder, more broad-chested technique had unseated this trend, thanks in large part to the ballet master Marius Petipa, whose tenure at the influential Imperial Russian Ballet steered the genre towards new heights of athleticism. As the new century approached, the willowy saunters of ballets like *Giselle* and *La Sylphide* gave way to the spectacular leaps and spins of *Swan Lake*. Serge Diaghilev's touring troupe, the Ballets Russes, also raised the stakes with a string of sensational avant-garde productions in the 1910s.

The budding crop of moderns were mostly uninterested in these distinctions, however. At best, they found ballet a detached style of performance – inaccessible in both form and content – while the most strident among them deemed it a dance of pretension and degeneration, of 'living death', by Isadora Duncan's reckoning.[1] Duncan aimed her ire at ballet's aerial preoccupations and responded by leaning into the swerves of gravity – a U-turn from the gliding pointe work and taut postures of classical technique. Meanwhile, her contemporaries Loie Fuller and Ruth St Denis questioned the exclusive standards of the ballet stage, and the presumption that less codified styles couldn't achieve a similar gravitas, joining Maud Allan and other artists around Europe and the United States in integrating elements of popular theatre into their work, including vaudeville and burlesque. Costuming became a locus of experimentation for all these trailblazers. There was Fuller with her shape-shifting dresses, Duncan bare-legged in gauzy tunics, Allan and St Denis revealing their midriffs in daring two-piece ensembles. Working in the margins were iconoclasts like Clotilde von Derp and Hertha Feist, who pushed the spectrum to even further extremes with respective cross-dressing and nudist ventures.

While it would be some time before philosophies formalised and techniques coalesced, one vital concern in this bright, burning dawn was scaling towards a higher plane of emotional expression. Dance should be driven by sensations, impulses and cravings, this first generation felt; it should be a rousing declaration of feeling and verve. 'It might very well be that I love the dance so immensely because I love life, because of its metamorphoses and elusiveness,'[2] Mary Wigman, an innovator of German expressionist dance, wrote towards the end of her life. Death and dreams became important motifs; so did desire and *joie de vivre*. Dancers started to look to mythology and mysticism to unlock the enigmas of the human spirit. With their eyes to the sky, these pioneers set to carving out a corner of the dance world where humanity wasn't an abstract notion but a bodily concern, where quivering souls might find a voice through a brave new grammar of motions and poses.

Breaking from the traditions of ballet meant embracing independence and conflicting inner drives. The spirit of individuality underpinning modern dance means it's sometimes best defined by what it wasn't. But one key commonality among its early figureheads was the pro-woman tenor of their art – the way they used new forms of dance to key into their vision of themselves as modern women. Unbound by pointe shoes and the trappings of male ballet masters, Duncan and company emerged as the marquee names of a new genre created not just for but by women.

Much of the thinking that shored up the foundations of modern dance came out of Europe in the nineteenth century. French singer and orator François Delsarte, gripped by the gulf he perceived between emotional and physical expression in the arts, was instrumental in encouraging a generation of performers to link sentiments with gestures, inner with outer. His theories lived on well after his death in 1871, trickling into the practices of first-wave modern dancers internationally, from Rudolf Laban and Mary Wigman, pillars of Germany's experimental *Ausdruckstanz* (expressionist dance) scene, to North American trendsetters like Ruth St Denis, Ted Shawn and Isadora Duncan. Swiss composer Émile Jaques-Dalcroze also had a role to play with his development of eurythmics, a pedagogy that influenced the way many artists approached rhythm and movement in the late nineteenth century.

Between the 1890s and 1910s, modern styles of dance cropped up across the world: in national schools in Hungary and Russia, where they'd evolved out of rhythmic gymnastics and philosophical movement theories; in bohemian pockets of Switzerland and Germany, riding the waves of expressionism and *Köerperkultur* (body culture); and in vaudeville houses across the United States, where skirt dancing and other dramatic visuals flourished. Animated by a mounting social gusto for physical activity, and by the turn-of-the-century appetite for artistic innovation, dancers probed creative new courses of movement. The United States and Germany, lacking the deep-rooted ballet traditions of France and Russia, were especially fertile ground for experimentation.

By the 1910s, the hallmarks of modern dance had burrowed into the cultural consciousness: a break from classical footwork and upright movement vocabularies, a rejection of conventional costuming, a shift towards figurative, dynamic imagery, and an elision of the creator and performer roles. In this blossoming sphere, the dancers themselves decided the stories they would tell.

These artists looked to dance to give shape and meaning to a world where agriculture was yielding to manufacturing, countryside to cityscape, Enlightenment philosophies to modernist experimentation. The new century promised a sea change for women in particular. With social, political and economic opportunities bubbling around the globe, female enterprise became increasingly prominent, including in the world of dance, where women were grabbing the reins, no longer content to reprise ready-made styles. These were modern dancers, modern women, emboldened to reshape their place in society. Duncan anticipated their impact with characteristic romanticism: '[The dancer of the future] will realize the mission of woman's body . . . From all parts of her body shall shine radiant intelligence, bringing to the world the message of the thoughts and aspirations of thousands of women. She shall dance the freedom of woman.'[3]

———

When the British writer Sarah Grand published 'The New Aspect of the Woman Question' in 1894, a polemic ridiculing men's inclination 'to howl down every attempt on the part of our sex to make the world a pleasanter place to live in',[4] she gave a piquant voice to a feminist ideal emerging in the Victorian *fin de siècle*: the New Woman. Independent, educated and career-focused, the New Woman came to represent an archetype for women disenchanted with the prescriptive marriage/motherhood route and set on widening their prospects beyond the home, whether that meant rejecting domesticity altogether or reshaping it to allow them to build a professional profile or explore new romantic experiences. Her remit was both personal and political, broadening the boundaries of womanhood by staking a claim in male-governed spheres, from employment and academia to leisure and courtship. The thought of an entire generation of young women flagrantly defying tradition caused as much titillation as it did derision in the early days of New Woman discourse. A self-determinant woman – a dangerous prospect!

The first generation of modern dancers plugged into the New Woman zeitgeist with gusto. In sync with this groundswell of female self-reckoning, dancers began examining their agency in the canon, sidestepping the patriarchal rubric of ballet – with its swaggering impresarios and demure ballerinas – in favour of self-led endeavours. Sensual stagewear, provocative scenarios and democratic forms of teaching materialised; movement styles developed to defy the image of women as passive and fragile. 'Modern dancer' now came with several implicit slashes: performer/choreographer/producer, even lighting designer, all in one. This contingent redefined how female dancers could dress and think and be and be seen – and not just onstage. Bohemian travels and passionate affairs, sometimes lesbian, abounded among the early moderns. They both reflected and fashioned the changing script of womanhood.

I think it's a testament to the New Woman's radicalism that she first found prominence as a fictional archetype. Bold, ambitious female characters populated novels, plays and stories in the 1870s and 1880s, reflecting a variety of outlooks on the shifting sands of female sovereignty. There were triumphant heroines, like Mary Erle of Ella Hepworth Dixon's *The Story of a Modern Woman*, who strikes out on her own and carves a successful career as a writer, as well as tragic figures, like Sue Bridehead of Thomas Hardy's *Jude the Obscure*, doomed to a morbid form of divine retribution after she refuses to marry her children's father. Henrik Ibsen's *A Doll's House* was especially influential, offering a compelling portrait of a housewife oppressed by the 'sacred duties'⁵ of her marital role. For many authors, fictive catastrophe – dead children, suicidal wives, annihilated marriages – became a mast for pinning their philosophical colours. Where Kate Chopin, a forerunner of twentieth-century feminist fiction, used unhappy conclusions to highlight the injustice of narrow-minded gender roles, Henry James employed them as cautionary tales, warning women off nonconformity with illustrations of righteous comeuppance.

Soon, the New Woman's renown migrated from narrative to non-fiction, with thinkers like Olive Schreiner and Mona Caird parsing her principles on the page and in the drawing room, to similarly divisive effect. For every essay or anecdote lauding her promise, there were others decrying her threat of degeneration. Artists also debated her significance around this time. Political cartoonists caricatured the New Woman as vulgar and delinquent – flighty mothers who leave their hard-working husbands to cope with crying children and dirty dishes – while illustrators for popular women's weeklies celebrated her with images of scintillating ladies about town. The American photographer Frances Benjamin Johnston paid homage with portraits of liberated women enjoying customarily 'male' activities: drinking, smoking, exercising. In the modern dance sphere, twin threads of romanticism and darkness emerged: Isadora Duncan, for example, hailed independent womanhood with dreamy arcadian frolics, while Mary Wigman styled herself as a witch in one of her best-known roles, a daring probe into the dark side of the soul.

This range of interpretations speaks to the dynamism of the New Woman as both an abstract concept and a real-life figure. Her qualities were malleable in consonance with class, capital and agenda, revealing stirring new entrées into womanhood. As women began channelling New Woman credo both in and outside the home,

17

her incarnations multiplied: there were dedicated reformers and workaday professionals, political activists and studious co-eds, avid athletes and socialites. The visibility of these factions sharpened as the nineteenth century gave way to the twentieth, with public reactions continuing to diversify. The New Woman was, depending on who you asked, tenacious, unhinged, ladylike, mannish, self-empowered, slutty, militant, enlightened. In any case, she defied the Victorian paradigm of the 'True Woman', whose femininity hinged on domesticity and sexual purity. By dating, socialising, studying for degrees, joining the workforce, founding new associations, creating art, even simply cycling around city streets, these women became a living prototype for independence, hugely influencing perceptions of femininity in the decades to come.

———

A confluence of fast-moving social, cultural and political developments at the turn of the twentieth century fuelled the emergence of the New Woman and her push for autonomy, especially in terms of sexuality. Ladies' magazines endorsed fresh new expressions of femininity; debate kindled around family planning; suffragists campaigned vigilantly for women's right to vote. Divorce, property and employment laws progressed, and universities around the world began opening their doors to women – developments that hugely improved women's ability to lock down financial security and social respectability outside of marriage.

The air was thick with possibility, priming women for paths outside the Victorians' glorified 'Cult of Domesticity': living alone, raising children outside of marriage, forgoing them altogether, even experimenting with casual and same-sex relations. This proliferation of choice was central to the New Woman cause. The objective wasn't to erase the roles of wife and mother, but to dethrone them from the pantheon of pre-eminent female identities. For many, this meant shedding the moralistic baggage these roles carried in their traditional incarnation. As the activist Mary Heaton Vorse quipped in 1913: 'I am trying for nothing so hard in my own personal life as how not to be respectable when married.'[6]

Defiance in the marital sphere was a sticking point for the early moderns, few of whom were matriarchs in the traditional sense. Ruth St Denis declined to exchange rings or include any talk of obedience in her wedding vows when she married fellow dancer Ted Shawn, while Isadora Duncan loudly opposed the institution of marriage altogether. Maud Allan and Mary Wigman each opted for career over nuptials, the latter once boasting that she explicitly instructed her students to 'give an impression that every man should enthusiastically call out: "I would not like to be married to any one of them!"'[7] Loie Fuller even lived semi-openly as a lesbian in her later life. Rejecting the standard marriage plot – and its precepts of women as either virginal or maternal – was essential to their autonomy, both privately and artistically.

Consider Fuller, who developed a rapturous, otherworldly aesthetic; Duncan, attuned to the politics of a revealing costume; Allan, a purveyor of erotic moves and characterisations. Each of these displays was at once a roiling expression of self and a radical subversion of the status quo. Just as New Woman culture braced these dancers to confront patriarchal expectations, it primed audiences to be receptive to their rebellion, especially the maverick lens they brought to costuming, choreography and expressions of independent womanhood.*

---

* Some other early moderns reshaping the standards of the stage for women at this time include Carmen Tórtola Valencia, Adorée Villany, Valéria Dienes, Rita Sacchetto, Katja Wulff and Olga Desmond.

By stepping into the spheres of production and directorship, these pioneering artists dismantled a centuries-old pecking order, reconfiguring the cartography of dance to include critical new pathways. They stretched conceptions of what dance was and could be, tracing a continuum between free-spirited dance forms and offstage liberties, between self-willed dancemaking and agency in their own futures. Individually and collectively, they established modern dance as a salient force for change, including vital new appraisals for women's dress, sexuality and professional potential.

ACT 1, SCENE 1

The church that Isadora built

A baptismal moment in modern dance happened on an August evening in 1908, when a few hundred New Yorkers headed to Manhattan's Criterion Theatre to see a thirty-one-year-old Isadora Duncan debut a set of Greek-inspired solos. The concert was her first show stateside after nearly a decade abroad, and promised a glimpse of the distinctive performance style that had earned this American expat feverish acclaim around Europe since she began touring the Continent as a self-styled 'free dancer' in 1900. A drip-feed of transatlantic dispatches over the years had teased details of an idiosyncratic 'dance poetess'[1] who performed barefoot and gave searing speeches about the life-affirming promise of art. Special cables reported on her diaphanous costumes, which had provoked the censors in Paris and Berlin. An American critic following Duncan's European ascent hyped her stage presence with epic metaphor: 'an Ancient Greek Bas-Relief Come to Life'.[2]

On the stage of my mind, the crowd at the Criterion lights the match of Ezra Pound's electric city, with its 'squares after squares of flame, set up and cut into the aether'[3] – a mass of bodies ignited by some red-hot yearning for modern dance. In reality, patrons of New York's Theater District were used to light, jangly fare like ragtime musicals. Duncan's audience probably drifted in on a cloud of late-summer languor. Either way, her showing – a montage of avant-garde dances to Christoph Gluck's pounding *Iphigenia* suite, performed in a short, wispy Hellenic tunic – was a startling spark in the night.

Knees bent and arms swinging, Duncan rippled with liquid plasticity, swishing her torso in a fluid spiral. She crouched, arching backwards to raise her chest to the sky; she sloped off balance, a gauzy skirt rustling her bare knees as she draped herself on the floor. The mythic episodes she referenced – maidens playing ball games, warriors assembling for battle – were stripped to their sentiments and sculpted into something silver-smooth. In the closing number, she emulated the maenads' legendary dance for Dionysus, tilting her throat back in a skysong of ecstasy.

Consciously minimalist, with no glittering set or climactic narrative, her performance was weightier than the upbeat variety acts often seen on Broadway and the pirouetting ballet productions of the nearby Metropolitan Opera House, where Duncan would soon reprise her work. She performed alone on a dimly lit stage; her costume was simple and loose, eschewing the frills normally adorning female dancers – bodices that produce hourglass waistlines, slippers that contour feet into perfect crescents. In doing so, she presented a bold vision of femininity that rejected artifice and surged with autonomy. 'If my art is symbolic of any one thing,' Duncan would tell the press in later years, 'it is symbolic of the freedom of woman and her emancipation from the hidebound conventions that are the warp and woof of New England Puritanism.'[4]

Back to my imagined stage, where the curtain falls on a rip-roaring ovation, the crowd bellowing in appreciation of her soul-swinging timbre. The actual response was underpowered: a smattering of polite applause, according to a reviewer from *Variety*, who praised Duncan's 'gliding grace' but suggested her abstract solos were 'a rather flimsy foundation' for a full ninety-minute show: 'It is a fairly safe venture that a goodly percentage of the Criterion's audience who lent their applause to the none too plentiful gaiety of the evening did so because they thought that it was the proper thing to do and not because they found real delight in Miss Duncan's performance.'[5] You can sense the writer's uncertainty in trying to place this 'tremendously studious effort', with its Continental laurels and French-flecked programme, in the context of a zippy Broadway theatre.

You wouldn't know it from this write-up, but alongside the agnostics in the crowd that night were some instant converts to the Church of Isadora, including the conductor Walter Damrosch, who invited Duncan to perform with his New York Symphony Orchestra that autumn – an engagement that inspired the rapturous response she'd grown accustomed to in Europe. She found another early disciple in the poet William Carlos Williams, who wrote a letter to his brother calling her performance at the Criterion 'the most perfect, most absolutely inspiring exhibition I have ever seen . . . I could see all our future before us in her dancing and I came away alive as I have rarely been to the exquisite beauty of simple perfect truth.'[6]

This idea that Duncan was modernity incarnate, the embodiment of a bright, brave way forward for America, would soon draw her acolytes around the country, and is a colourful part of her legacy as the 'Mother of Modern Dance'. The America of 1908 was urbanising, industrialising; it was the year of the Ford Model T and the skyscraping Singer Tower. 'Anything, everything, is possible,' Thomas Edison told the nation.[7] The marvels continued on the dance stage, where performers tapped, jigged and twirled in shimmering spectaculars.

Then came Duncan, thundering in with a theatre built on the intensities of nature, not glitz. She presented the female body as an altar for the human condition, introducing a new paradigm for performance to a nation with none of the Renaissance legacies that elevated fleshly concerns. She personified the freedoms – social, creative, moral, professional – the tide of social change promised women in her homeland as the twentieth century flickered into action.

Most biographies of Duncan sketch her as a precocious, artsy child, a portrait gleaned from her memoir, *My Life*, published in 1927, the year she died. An early section recounts her efforts as a six-year-old to start a 'school of the dance'[8] for other neighbourhood children, noting that her enterprising instincts joined a lofty desire to forge a new art form to rival classical ballet. The memory is magnified with a grandiosity present in most of Duncan's prose: 'I dreamed of a different dance. I did not know just what it would be, but I was feeling out towards an invisible world into which I divined I might enter if I found the key.'[9]

Fact and what were probably dashes of fantasy conjure a bohemian family home in San Francisco, helmed by a restless mother who taught her children to scorn possessions in favour of art and adventures – the fabled origin site of this 'different' dance. Duncan wrote of experimenting fireside while her mother tinkled away on the piano, a young Isadora swivelling her body in a sinuous rebuke to the stiff ballet lessons she'd endured at the suggestion of a family friend. She framed these private ventures as the driver behind her decision to leave school at age ten to teach dance full-time with her sister, but her father's abandonment, which shook the family's already precarious finances, almost certainly played a role too.

Classes with Miss Duncan typically involved improvising to well-known poems and songs, her students encouraged to interpret the lyricism through motion – an anguished dash here, a gleeful string of skips there. As they moved into their teens, Duncan and her siblings started creating their own works and even staging them at small concerts along the Californian coast. 'We were all very emotional and refused to be repressed,' as she described it.[10]

Adolescence retreated, adulthood approached, and Duncan's ambitions swelled to include world-class performer, à la Sarah Bernhardt, the celebrated French actress and muse to several of the day's biggest playwrights.* In 1896, just shy of nineteen, she moved to Chicago, where she ad-libbed 'peppery'[11] dances in upmarket clubs and music halls, knocking out high kicks to jaunty popular jingles. Desperate for something more highbrow, she reached out to the theatre mogul Augustin Daly and managed to secure a spot in his upcoming pantomime in New York City. In *My Life* she describes the production as 'very stupid and quite unworthy of my ambitions and ideals',[12] and adds similarly uppity remarks about the next role Daly offered, a prancing fairy in *A Midsummer Night's Dream*. She cut ties as soon as her contract allowed.

Truth and authenticity were the keystones of Duncan's modus vivendi. She saw theatrical acts like Daly's as hollow whimsies – a 'bitter disillusion'[13] of 'skirts and frills and kicks'.[14] Ballet fell even lower in her esteem. 'I am an enemy to the Ballet, which I consider a false and preposterous art,'[15] she decrees with characteristic grandiloquence in her book, deeming it 'ugly',[16] 'affected', 'mechanical',[17] 'vulgar',[18] and 'against every artistic and human feeling'.[19] She took particular offence at its gravity-defying aesthetic (contrived, in her opinion) and its staunch, upright alignment ('giving the result of an articulated puppet'[20]). She also rejected its sugary visage of femininity, in which female dancers are stylised 'more like a lovely bird or butterfly than a human being'.[21]

Duncan, by contrast, longed to dance 'not in the form of nymph, nor fairy, nor coquette, but in the form of woman in her greatest and

---

* 'The Divine Sarah', as Bernhardt was known, was beloved by many early moderns, including Duncan, Loie Fuller and Maud Allan, all of whom admired her sensuous approach to movement.

purest expression'.[22] It's easy to scoff at her sense of self-importance, especially her tendency to present herself as a redeemer of a way-ward world, but there's a formidable grit to her mission, especially the target she set on puritanical ideas around chastity. Duncan saw the potential for dance to articulate the aspirations of the independent woman and judged it a moral imperative – an uphill climb at a time when in some American states women could still be arrested for wearing trousers or using contraception.

Fed up with 'trying to amuse the public with something which was against my ideals',[23] Duncan began devising her own routines, invoking the melodies of heavyweight composers like Wagner and Chopin to help 'express the truth of my Being in gesture and movement'.[24] She had a silken sense of musicality, spinning drama from curving notes. In 1899 she travelled by cattle steamer to London, convinced its buzzing beau monde would lend 'intelligent sympathy'[25] for her ideas. The capital's stages were saturated with male directors at the time, but Duncan found a foothold among the society crowd and quickly got her first taste of creative satisfaction. The actress Mrs Patrick Campbell – George Bernard Shaw's original Eliza Doolittle – was instrumental in introducing her to theatre moguls who could offer lift-off for her experimental dances.

Fast-forward a few years, and London's theatres were opening their doors to the wave of modern dancers Duncan heralded, from Isadora imitators to pioneers such as Ruth St Denis and Maud Allan. The Savoy Theatre, normally a showcase for Gilbert and Sullivan operas, hosted the breakout British choreographer Margaret Morris in 1910, shortly after she met Duncan's brother Raymond and learned some of the dancer's technique under his tuition. Morris's choreography for a production of *Orpheus and Eurydice* – which adapted Duncan's naturalist poses – wowed West End audiences: 'nothing like it has ever been seen on the London stage', declared an early review.[26]

Duncan's splash in London swiftly led to engagements in Paris, where Loie Fuller's electric creations were powering a shining interest in modern dance, as well as Berlin, Munich, Vienna, Budapest and beyond, her profile given an extra boost thanks to a brief tour with Fuller's company. Between 1900 and 1908, Duncan performed in gardens and along waterfronts, in the shadow of the Parthenon, on opera house stages to full-size orchestras and sold-out audiences that demanded encore after encore. She insisted on stages dressed in ocean-blue draperies, and toured with admiring flocks of young dance students in tow. A chorus of praise trailed her, transforming from gossip to gospel the story of a dancer who drove people to delirium. Fanciful op-eds imagined her showered in roses and carried through the streets, cries of adulation springing loose from her followers' throats.

Fellow creatives adored Duncan and played a major role in cementing her cult status. She won them over with stirring scenes onstage and hot-blooded parlour debates about dance as a language of deliverance. In return, they memorialised her in statues, paintings, poems, photographs, crafts and more. Auguste Rodin sketched her fleet-footed prances in charcoal; Antoine Bourdelle and Maurice Denis inscribed her likeness in the bas-relief and murals of Paris's Théâtre des Champs-Élysées; and Charlotte Perkins Gilman lauded her in verse: 'Mother of happiness! Mother of beauty!'[27] For a time, Duncan had the eyes, ears and hearts of the dance world, from fellow moderns like Ruth St Denis and José Limón to ballet icons like Michel Fokine, Frederick Ashton and Marie Rambert. 'When she appeared, we all had the feeling . . . that God was present,'[28] the sculptor Josep Clarà recalled, shoring up her messianic reputation. With their tributes and eulogies, Duncan's devotees celebrated the radical new art form she'd developed and her tenacious faith in its power to lift humanity.

The dancing Duncan awed with was a floaty, harmonious succession of walks, skips and runs, sprinkled across supple phrases that ignored the sharp boundaries of ballet. She let her feet hang naturally instead of pointing them and rarely kicked her knees higher than the hip. She married rhythms to the push and pull of gravity, devising falls that would take her to the ground and then back to her feet within a neat upward spring. The uninhibited air of her movement – the way it appeared to be impulsive and organic – often gave the impression of spontaneity, though she rarely improvised.

A striking photograph taken around 1916 captures her reclining with her right leg bent and right arm outstretched, a mirror image of Michelangelo's Adam as he receives the spark of life. Duncan spoke frequently of the relationship between dance and the soul, and of her conviction that 'true movements are not invented but discovered',[29] positioning her naturalist aesthetic as an excavator of something arcane and momentous.

When Duncan organised her practices into a formal technique, she gave prominence to the solar plexus, the network of nerves located in the abdomen, declaring it 'the central spring of all movement'.[30] Duncan technique saw every motion start at the centre of the torso and radiate outwards, coursing across the body like a crackle of electricity. It was a major departure from classical ballet, where the base of the spine is the axis for alignment, and gave the sense of a dance originating within the dancer instead of one foisted on her – a powerful reverb of Duncan's wider philosophy around liberation and self-determination.

The commanding centrifugal force of this technique intensified the passion of Duncan's uplifting frolics as well as her darker pursuits. In 2020 I interviewed the ballerina Viviana Durante about her restaging of 'Dance of the Furies', a clawing solo from 1905 that

Duncan later reworked into a group dance. Performed to a section of Gluck's *Orfeo ed Euridice*, it animates the vengeance deities who guard the Underworld, casting them in a creepy, contorted mould, all wrenched fingers and heaving chests.

'What's fascinating is the femininity that runs through that,' Durante said.[31] 'The most beautiful women experience anger, drama, the darkest side of the soul that you go to. This is what [Duncan] meant. People were shocked by it, and that's probably why some thought she was slightly mad.' This fiery temper fortified Durante's restaging, a hurling spiral of motion that framed fury not as some distant torch for heroes on quests but something that blazes inside us all.

Duncan performed her work without shoes or stockings, wearing short, loose tunics that freed her figure rather than 'enforcing [its] deformation'[32] – another memo to articulate her vision of the liberated woman. Her tunics were sometimes sheer enough to catch a glimpse of her breasts, a tack that vexed gatekeepers for two decades, even after scantier styles became a familiar sight on the concert stage. Pushback mainly came from officials scandalised by what they saw as a high-minded attempt to legitimise prurience, like the American minister who branded Duncan a 'jumping Jezebel'.[33] A police order barred her from performing in a Berlin bar in 1906 on grounds of obscenity, and the mayor of Indianapolis instructed constables to stand in the wings during a 1922 show at the city's opera house to ensure her costume complied with 'ideas of propriety'.[34] 'I have had about as much chance this winter in America as Christ had before Pilate,'[35] she griped after the latter episode.

While Duncan never allied herself with any formal streams of feminism, her rebellious brand of artistry amplified the uprising of progressives around the world, from the suffragists to the Gibson Girls. Her stagewear, in particular, echoed the defiant spirit of the dress reform movement, a Victorian-era revolt against corsetry that continued to reshape silhouettes well into the twentieth century in line with growing demands for practicality and equality. Her grasp at agency carried through to her technique, which championed independent self-expression in its very mechanics. That she created and performed her choreography herself, and eventually passed it on to a new generation of dancers in Europe and the United States, was also revolutionary, subverting the male-dominated performance culture that had stymied her at the start of her career.

Together these elements made Duncan a standard-bearer for an emerging breed of women who embraced impropriety in their work and in their lifestyles, unlacing independence from its chauvinist girdles. This notion of reclamation was central to the New Woman cause. As one advocate wrote playfully in 1885:

As 'New Woman' she is known.
'Tis her enemies have baptised her,
But she gladly claims the name;
Hers it is to make a glory,
What was meant should be a shame.[36]

Duncan flaunted her 'shames' – revealing outfits, explosive emotions, even three unwed pregnancies – on the world stage, reframing them as rights to be celebrated. Her insubordination sanctified progressive new approaches to femininity and self-possession, flipping the idea of indecency on its head.

———

Soon after moving to London in 1899, Duncan began giving private recitals in the drawing rooms of the capital's cultural elite, performing short, colourful set pieces inspired by antiquities and Renaissance art she'd spotted in the British Museum. Some of these early solos, including *Spring Song* and *Ophelia*, exemplified the organic textures and cadences that root her technique; others, like *La Primavera* and *Bacchus and Ariadne*, captured the 'rhythms of the feet and Dionysiac set of the head'[37] she admired in the paintings of Botticelli and Titian.

She debuted these latter two works at a 1900 function at London's New Gallery called 'Dance Idylls from Fifteen Century Masters' [*sic*], dancing between readings on music, painting and mythology. A reviewer from the *Evening Telegraph* praised her 'grace and spirit', and noted her emphasis on expressionism over athleticism: 'Miss Duncan has both the elevation and the muscular strength of the dancer, but she makes it her chief aim to develop the pictorial side of the dance, and leaves feats of limb to others.'[38]

Duncan graduated from the salon to the stage as soon as she began travelling the Continent. Her repertoire bloomed like a hothouse rose, and she began selling out prestigious concert halls for weeks at a time. Swaying along to the momentous notes of Wagner, Strauss, Gluck, even the great Beethoven, she captured the drama and intensity of a woman moving through the modern world, relishing its pleasures and battling its barricades.

Sands of feeling shifted inside her, from the spry to the stately. *The Blue Danube* (1902) saw her fling her weight in exhilaration, a triumph over oppression. In *Dance of the Scythes* (1903) she conjured the vigour of the Amazons, the female warriors rumoured to be men's equals; in *Ballspiel* (1901) she danced on the margins of adolescent joy and electric adult affairs. These nuanced portraits of womanhood – performed in an era when the perimeters of femininity were in unprecedented flux – captivated audiences around Europe and drew droves of female fans in her early years.

The pro-woman register of Duncan's art matured as her career progressed and waves of activism crested behind the scenes, especially

when she returned to America in 1908, where feminism was starting to stand for something bigger than voting reform. Marriage
and divorce laws had progressed to give women more rights; a
pink-collar workforce was fast flourishing. In 1904 the influential
writer Winnifred Harper Cooley declared that 'The new woman,
in the sense of the best woman . . . has come to stay.'[39] Increasingly,
Duncan's onstage avatars took on a tenor of prerogative – agents of
their own destiny vested to seek out art, education, self-reflection
and even sexual pleasure.

'Bacchanal', the closing number to the *Iphigenia* dances Duncan
showed with the New York Symphony in 1908, was one of her most
vocal bids for women's sexual empowerment. Like 'Dance of the
Furies', the routine started as a solo and later evolved to include
a small ensemble, this time channelling the sybaritic sprees of the
female cult that worshipped Dionysus.

Reconstructions show the group version as a graceful, rippling
ceremony that intensifies with Gluck's quickening notes. The dancers wave their hands, then their torsos, rocking back and forth; they
skip and twirl, working up to a whirling tumult before collapsing in
a heap – a metaphor for orgasm. The frenzy summons something
erotic and alive, but there's no menace. These aren't sirens of the sea
moss or the vampires puncturing the pages of gothic fiction, ancient
horrors with dangerous appetites. In this universe, desire is a sacred
expression of life.

In *My Life*, Duncan recounts several self-mythologising anec-
dotes of mysterious strangers predicting her grand fate, leading
her to conclude that it was her destiny 'to bring about a great
renaissance of religion through the Dance, to bring the knowledge
of the Beauty and Holiness of the human body through its expression of movements'.[40] Imbuing her dancing with this theological
purpose became a way to present female desire as something

34

organic and innate, linked to a divine primal tempo.*

'It is a prayer, this dance,' she told a crowd in Berlin in 1903. 'Each movement reaches in long undulations to the heavens and becomes a part of the eternal rhythm of the spheres.'[41] She was speaking about 'the dancer of the future', an ideal she imagined would 'realize the mission of woman's body and the holiness of all its parts', awakening 'womankind to a new knowledge of the possible strength and beauty of their bodies'.[42] Her creed resisted objectification and embraced individuality. It held a potent disruptive promise on an artistic and civic scale alike.

Duncan eventually built up her repertoire to include motifs as wide-ranging as Romantic poetry, transcendentalist philosophy and communist politics, but her Greek dances of the early 1900s remain some of her best-known works, encapsulating her lifelong veneration of classical imagery – the suggestive flutter of a wind-kissed tunic, the earth-rumbling romance of mythic wars and arcadian adventures. She saw these vivid dances as a concentrated effort to 'reach back over two thousand years to a beauty not perhaps understood by us, or understandable by others'.[43]

Her reverential view of antiquity harmonised with the modernist literary lions who roared in Duncan's later years – T. S. Eliot, James Joyce, Ezra Pound and Virginia Woolf, who all called on myth to

---

* Third-generation Duncan dancer Andrea Mantell Seidel offers some brilliant personal insight into this subject in *Isadora Duncan in the 21st Century: Capturing the Art and Spirit of the Dancer's Legacy*, describing 'Bacchanal' as 'a model for young women that empowers their sexuality and identity as women without commodifying or externalizing their sense of self' (p. 173). She restaged the piece for the Isadora Duncan Dance Ensemble in 1995, an experience she felt 'gave the company an opportunity to explore and impart mature, healthy concepts of female sexual identity . . . I believe that they learned that sex in the context of love is sacred, and that the sensuality of the body is worthy of reverence, not objectification and commodification' (p. 176).

lend meaning to the uncertainties of modern life. Just as individual New Women adapted feminist principles to suit their personal agendas, Duncan borrowed variants from the ancient world that fitted her unique vision of emancipation. She envisaged women divesting themselves from narrow-minded mores, goddesses free to celebrate their sacred bodies. She found exceptional inspiration in Botticelli's *Primavera*, with its eddy of naked feet and floral garnishes: 'I felt that so far life had been a bungle, and blind seeking; I thought, if I can find the secret of this picture, I may show others the way to richness of life and development of joy.'[44]

Some of the dancers who trained with Duncan in the early 1900s went on to perform with her and later spread her teachings to the next generation of moderns. A handful of legacy companies still exist today to safeguard and showcase her technique – its soft, rippling arm flourishes and elastic calibrations of weight and lyricism. To dance Duncan technique is to rejoice in your own inimitable existence in the world. The visionary theatre practitioner Edward Gordon Craig, the father of Duncan's first child, recalled the singularity of her craft when he first saw her perform in 1904: 'She was speaking her own language, not echoing any ballet master, and so she came to move as no one had ever seen anyone move before.'[45]

———

A hundred years before body positivity went from fringe concept to global movement, there was a dancer who proudly likened her frame to 'the hardy physique of a farm-servant'[46] and viewed her 'ample figure' as a creative asset, not a snarl to be unstitched. Photos of Duncan from the 1920s show soft thighs and heavy breasts, the cartography of a body that savoured and indulged.

The Edenic repose captured in film belies the ugly words that came her way as she approached middle age and continued to preach the sanctity of the naked human form. After seeing her perform in the early 1920s, a young George Balanchine offered a crude appraisal: 'it was absolutely unbelievable – a drunken, fat woman who for hours was rolling around like a pig.'[47] In 1922 the *Philadelphia Inquirer* expressed astonishment at Duncan's ability to attract her then partner, the twenty-five-year-old Sergei Yesenin, dedicating an entire spread to an investigation of 'How the Celebrated Barefoot Dancer Was Won by the Young Russian Poet, Who Found Her Growing Fatness Adorable Enough to Sing About Instead of Something To Be Laughed At or Pitied.'[48]

For me, one of Duncan's most inspiring acts was refusing to indulge this spite. Dancers spend hours in front of mirrors, scrutinising lines and silhouettes; the dance world has never not glorified the slender integrity of a sylph. Duncan, however, was unapologetic about her broad stature, even as the flapper craze of the 1920s ushered in a fixation on gamine tautness, embracing her body as her instrument throughout its evolving guises. Brandishing it on stage, she quite literally asserted visibility in a sphere that prizes slightness, revealing a new dimension of her naturalist credo, which imagined a world where 'thinness [is] not equivalent to spirituality'.[49] Here she was, the dancer of the future that she'd prefigured in Berlin: 'the free spirit, who will inhabit the body of new women; more glorious than any woman that has yet been; more beautiful than all women in past centuries: The highest intelligence in the freest body!'[50]

From her early days in London until her death in Nice in 1927, Duncan lived itinerantly, wafting between Europe, the Soviet Union and the United States with the changing winds of her career. She took a string of male and female lovers, including the philanthropist Paris Singer (married at the time) and the poet Mercedes de Acosta, and had three pregnancies, all by different men, proudly continuing to perform while expecting and after her children's births. She opened dance schools wherever she could, starting in Grunewald, Germany, home to her most famous batch of protégées, fondly known in the press as the 'Isadorables'. In 1922, age forty-four, during a period of heavy drinking in Russia, she met and married Yesenin, a bolshie young poet who shared her ideas about the need to revolutionise classical art.

In *My Life*, Duncan calls marriage 'an absurd and enslaving institution',[51] tracing her opposition to her parents' unhappy divorce and describing how her hostility sharpened when she read George Eliot's *Adam Bede* at the age of twelve. 'Deeply impressed by the injustice' meted out to its protagonist, an unwed mother convicted of infanticide after abandoning her child out of shame, 'I decided, then and there, that I would live to fight against marriage and for the emancipation of women and for the right for every woman to have a child or children as it pleased her, and to uphold her right and her virtue.'[52] A contrarian to the core, Duncan maintained, even during her brief union with Yesenin, that she was 'absolutely, unutterably and vehemently opposed to all legalized marriage'.[53] (Her own, she insisted, was a mere prerequisite 'to get my husband past [American] customs officers'[54] and palatable solely due to the Soviet Union's relaxed approach to annulment: 'Such a marriage is the only convention to which any free-minded woman could consent.'[55]). Her original bitterness would come full circle after a turbulent year of booze-fuelled arguments and trashed hotel rooms. In the summer of 1923 she left Yesenin, using the about-face to once again denounce matrimony: 'I never believed in marriage, and now I believe in it less than ever.'[56]

Rewind ten years to witness the great tragedy of Duncan's life, which gives some insight into her exhibitionism and the feverish pitch it reached in her later years, when her reputation for drinking and proselytising began to overshadow her triumphs onstage. On 19 April 1913, her children, two-year-old Patrick and six-year-old Deirdre, were drowned in Paris, along with their nanny, when a car accident sent their vehicle into the River Seine. The following year, after begging an acquaintance to help her have another baby, Duncan suffered a stillbirth. She plunged into a blistering depression, weighed down by the unbearable memory of 'little cold hands that would never again press mine in return'.[57]

In the decade following her children's deaths, Duncan hit the gas pedal on her push to found dance schools and legacy ventures; she even adopted all six of the Isadorables and gave them her surname. Her peers would describe a diametric resistance to moderation and a consumptive drive to find pleasure in any person or dogma that might offer it. She dallied in brash socialist politics and intensified her obsession with the ancient Greeks, who had an allegory for everything, including a woman deprived of her children in retaliation for her hubris. 'Like Niobe turned to stone, I sat and longed for annihilation in death,' Duncan wrote of the days following the accident.[58] In 1923 she channelled her grief into a slow, weighty solo called *Mother*, clasping a slice of empty space in her arms.

'Art is greater than life' was the mantra that saw Duncan into and beyond the years of the First World War, when 'even the artists said, "What is Art?"'[59] She harnessed the war's 'marvellous message of defiance'[60] to create gallant dances of militarism and nationalism, including 1916's *La Marseillaise*, an ode to 'bleeding, heroic France'[61] that she performed in a crimson cloak. In 1917, the subjugation behind the Russian Revolution inspired a staggering vaunt to Tchaikovsky's *Marche Slave*, Duncan casting herself as a browbeaten serf.

The tenor of these war-inspired works shifted from celebration to agitation when Duncan toured them in America in 1922 with

Yesenin by her side, suggesting Bolshevist sympathies at a time when anxieties around communism were rocketing in the West. The panic of America's first Red Scare spurred rumours of nefarious political plots, including a supposed scheme between socialists and feminists to undermine the social order. Ironically, Duncan, while sympathetic to aspects of both these causes, was uninterested in formal activism and never committed herself to either. Her taste for subversion moved to its own tempo.

A show in Boston that autumn, shortly after she'd been detained by immigration authorities suspicious of her Soviet ties, provoked one of the biggest scandals of her career, when Duncan exposed her breast in a burst of passion during a curtain-call speech. 'This is red! So am I!' she shouted, ripping open her top and waving a crimson scarf. 'It is the color of life and vigor. You were once wild here. Don't let them tame you!'[62] The mayor of Boston banned her from performing in the city, and the press scrambled to cover the fallout, with the brash-talking evangelist Billy Sunday labelling Duncan a 'Bolshevik hussy'.[63]

Before leaving the city, she challenged her detractors' moral distress: 'Why should I care what part of my body I reveal? Why is one part more evil than another? Is not all body and soul an instrument through which the artist expresses his inner message of beauty?'[64] Reflecting on the incident a few months later, she chalked up their criticism to weakness of character and lack of imagination: 'The curse of my country is its slavishness, mental and physical ... [Boston in particular] is in rigor mortis because of its fearful conception of life and culture.'[65]

Duncan gave her final performance in the summer of 1927, at the Théâtre Mogador in Paris, aged fifty. While her barefoot antics and heated speeches had lost much of their novelty by this point, her larger-than-life fame, including her grip on Europe's cognoscenti, still gave an impression of untouchability – a pretext that made her death two months later an extraordinary shock. On 14 September 1927, a long scarf Duncan was wearing wound itself around the wheel of a friend's speeding convertible in Nice, breaking her neck.

According to witnesses, her last words before stepping into the car were: 'Farewell, my friends. I go to glory' – a dramatic, probably apocryphal epitaph that invited the world to characterise the fiasco as a fitting display of exhibitionism. 'Isadora's end is perfect,' her erstwhile collaborator Jean Cocteau declared.[66] While tremendously dehumanising, there's a morbid sort of sense to his decree. It was inconceivable that such a huge personality would go out with a whimper; it had to be a bang.

History has rehewn Duncan's image many times over, kneading her personal turbulence and artistic prodigy into one explosive persona. To admire her is to entertain ego and contradictions; to overlook problematic stances, including her racialised distinctions between the sexuality of her own art and the 'primitive savage' nature (her words) of popular dances like jazz.[67] It's an act of tethering, a string around all the towering philosophies and pronouncements that pulls them earthside and asks us to consider, for better or worse, the human behind the cult figure – a person who desired, demanded and suffered. Idolatry levelled into something truer and sounder.

The irony of Duncan's extravagance is that it was both her making and her undoing. She lived in an age of aspiration and possibility, and so she made her own myths, using dance to celebrate herself and all she knew she could be. She sensed menace in submission and called on her audiences to join her in confronting the institutions that expect us to assent: the sexist architecture of the dance world, the oppression of girdles and dowries, the exploitation of shame as a tool for keeping women in line. Her exhibitionism makes us uncomfortable because it exposes something about the way we expect women to behave. You can celebrate yourself as long as you do it quietly. For all her self-importance, Duncan embodied a voluble chorus, not an insular solo. She refused to shut up and be grateful, and the world is better because of it.

ACT 1, SCENE 2

Our Loie of Ascension

There's a poster of Loie Fuller in my bathroom that I admire whenever I step out of the shower. It's an illustration by Jules Chéret advertising the American dancer's 1892 debut at the Folies Bergère, the hot-ticket Paris cabaret. Perched in a loose arabesque, her lips a come-hither bloom, she's swept up in a vortex of purple, orange and yellow swirls – a fire-walker in the sunrise of the now. The air of sensation exemplifies Fuller's tenure as 'the toast' of *fin de siècle* Paris. She was a spectacular performer who manipulated light, fabric and motion to conjure luminous imagery, from the earthly to the celestial.

The pillar of Fuller's portfolio was her 'Serpentine Dance', a solo technique that involved vivid light projections and dizzying waves of silk. Rippling a billowy dress using rods sewn into her sleeves, Fuller summoned the contours of flowers, butterflies, waves and snakes, uplighting this imagery with iridescent effects she devised herself. In one illustrious dance she was a lily, wafting in a velvet pink haze; in another she materialised as a red-hot flame. Her technicolour act was a hit at the Folies and fast-tracked Fuller from middling Midwestern vaudevillian to international dance marvel in just a few weeks. The press dubbed her 'La Loïe', a 'priestess of pure fire'[1] who lit up the stage with her blazing iconography.

Fuller's glamour didn't stem from her personal appearance, which she characterised as waiflike, but from her magnetic stage presence. Haloed in a rainbow of beams, whipping up fizzing whirlpools of fabric, she elevated beauty from a passive characteristic to a mutable force – something you could wield and develop for your own self-expression. With feminism and femininity often seen as competing interests in turn-of-the-century France, Fuller's theatrics strike me as radical in more than just a visual sense. Here was a woman staging her image on her own terms – recasting what usually feels fixed, ignoring 'should' and embracing 'could'. The poster in my bathroom captures just one of the many incarnations she adopted in a career that thrived on imagination and metamorphosis.

Henri de Toulouse-Lautrec and other spearheads of Europe's art nouveau scene joined Chéret in capturing Fuller's sinuous bodywork in lithographs, sculptures, watercolours and even a set of bronze table lamps by François-Raoul Larche. These artworks bubble with the brio of the belle époque, channelling the oomph of Fuller's dancing, the way she manoeuvred along a single breathless continuum, splendour unspooling in the sweep of her wingspan. Their plasticity deepens the longer you spend with them; it's clear that her shape-shifting wasn't just inspiration to these artists but a living expression of their ideals, marshalling the dynamism of art nouveau with its curvaceous sense of movement and bouquet of lithe, natural forms.

As a performer fuelled by instinct rather than classical training, Fuller drew a patent correlation between dancing and the natural world: 'motion has been the starting point of all effort at self-expression, and it is faithful to nature,' she wrote in her memoir, published in 1908.[2] This was an avant-garde take on the role of movement within dance – Fuller was one of the first high-profile performers to consider it an expressive force in and of itself, more so than theme, narrative or music – and has prompted some historians to question whether her output should even be considered dance at all. As it happens, Fuller was likewise on the fence, calling it dance 'for want of a more appropriate title'.[3]

But questions of classification stand miles apart from the heart-swelling resonance of her artistry. While Fuller's work is usually defined by its striking aesthetic, it also sounds the depths of a deeply emotive well. In 2019, London's Barbican Centre held an exhibit on cabaret culture in the dawn of modernism, with a room dedicated to Fuller's prismatic productions. I can still remember the vim radiating off an 1897 film clip of her serpentine technique on display (performed in the clip by an unnamed woman). Swathed in diaphanous silks, the dancer windmilled and zigzagged her arms, morphing her silhouette with the swish of a bonfire shadow. The tilt of her head laced rapture and wit; her body hummed with the promise of flight. When she swooped her arms to strike the five-point star of a monarch butterfly, her figure ribboned in pastel sunbursts, it seemed entirely possible that the next frame would show her floating into the rafters.

Even through a gritty reel, even with a different dancer brandishing the silks, you can sense the hunger in Fuller's shimmering compositions – for mystery, drama, ascension. An eagerness to present a spectacle that transcends the fraught experience of possessing a female body in this world. This is what self-determination looks like, her work says to me. She definitely set out to channel something poignant onstage, even if her words on the subject are muted: 'In the dance . . . the human body should, despite conventional limitations, express all the sensations or emotions that it experiences.'[4] A tide in shy retreat, the sincerity of the light at six in the morning – a body on the move can reveal uncharted colours and moods.

Exactly which sensations Fuller sought to express was usually left up to her audiences to interpret, a quality that put her right in step with her artistic climate, especially the turn-of-the-century Symbolism movement, powered by imaginative forays into our intuitions and inner lives. Writers over the years have called Fuller a projection screen for her viewers' fantasies, including the founding father of Symbolism himself, Stéphane Mallarmé, who praised her for evoking 'the virginity of un-dreamt of places' in an 1893 essay on her influence.[5] Her fluctuations of form, of self, allowed audiences to intuit possibility, opportunity and beauty outside of the usual bounds. Where fashion magazines like *La Mode* vaunted hourglass figures, Fuller basked in billowing fabric; as society moved towards a sharper, crisper understanding of the future, she softened her visage with lustrous rays and glistening projections. Her femininity existed on its own plane, asserting its visibility beyond the contemporary social order – a powerful notion, then and today.

––––––

If Isadora Duncan dominates the modern dance masthead, Loie Fuller can be found in the producer credits. She choreographed more than a hundred works between the 1890s and 1920s, and though this catalogue died with her, it was hugely important to the rise of modern dance. We have Fuller to thank for championing gravitas in non-technical dancing and introducing mixed-media choreography that widened the ways performance could look and feel. Crucially, she invented a range of pioneering lighting effects that reimagined the aesthetic potential of dance and theatre, from star-bright colour wheels to canny apertures for illuminating the stage from below.

Fuller's run at the Folies clenched her career just a few years after another defining crossroads: her turn in a melodrama called *Quack M.D.* The child of musicians, and a performer herself from the age of four, back when she was Mary-Louise of Fullersburg, Illinois, she'd spent most of her youth touring the United States with small stock companies and vaudeville attractions, including Buffalo Bill's bootstrapping Wild West Show. In her twenties, she took up a skirt-dancing gig in London and soon had the chance to put these swaying moves to work back in the United States in *Quack M.D.*

Fuller, playing a woman under hypnosis, was tasked with her own costuming and choreography. Enveloping herself in an Indian silk robe she'd been gifted in London, she improvised a gliding dance set against a row of green lamps, her elbows furled into wings, light and motion in glossy synthesis. The production was a flop, critically and commercially, but several reviewers singled out Fuller's scene, admiring the originality of her stagecraft. 'The newspapers were in agreement in announcing that I had a remarkable string to my bow – if I only knew how to make the most of it,' she noted.[6]

She began experimenting with her robe, placing a mirror against her living-room window and spiralling into slices of sunlight refracting off the glass. 'Golden reflections played in the folds of the sparkling silk, and in this light my body was vaguely revealed in shadowy contour,' Fuller recalled of these sessions of 'great discovery'.[7] She was on the verge of an idea, its profile inchoate but its concerns deep-rooted and affecting. She spent the coming months whittling down a dozen 'characteristic motions'[8] – bodily thrusts that sent her skirt flying – and using them to create twelve twisting dances inspired by natural phenomena: an orchid, a cloud, a butterfly, a flame. A designer as much as a performer, she devised vivid colour schemes for each dance, aside from her finale, which she planned to reveal in darkness, a single streak of amber ripping into the black.

Fuller debuted this vision – branded 'The Serpentine' by an enterprising manager, who suggested she set it to 'Au Loin du Bal', a catchy contemporary waltz – in the spring of 1892, between the acts of a comedy called *Uncle Celestin*. The producers declined to use her bespoke lighting design for the early weeks of the tour, but they worked it in ahead of the show's New York City premiere, a much-anticipated event for Fuller, who sensed that this particular performance would be pivotal to her transition from entertainer to artiste.

It took an oversized crew of technicians to illuminate her vision, which involved oceanic swells of silk and spectral projections of the moon, but the effort paid off: Fuller provoked a wildly enthusiastic response, with one critic extolling her 'unique, ethereal, delicious' visage[9] and another declaring her performance 'infinitely more artistic than the toe-dancing of the greatest prima ballerina'.[10]

With its whimsical complexion and arcing use of fabric, Fuller's act was an evolution of the skirt dancing she'd learned in England. Between the 1870s and the 1890s, the skirt dance was a staple in the Victorian music hall, that knees-up hotspot, appearing alongside folksy singalongs as well as specialty acts like juggling and acrobatics. The style took off in London in the early 1870s when Kate Vaughan, star of the Gaiety Girls chorus line, drew crowds with an elegant new step dance she performed in a lacy floor-skimming slip.

The fetching image of a woman swizzling her hemline caught fire internationally, with skirt-swishing routines soon cropping up in musicals, plays, pantomimes and burlesques on both sides of the Atlantic. In England and the United States, skirt dancing veered towards poised and demure, while French dancers spiced things up with bloomer-revealing high kicks and jump splits. Vaughan's popularity prefigured a string of breakout soloists in the run-up to the twentieth century: you had Letty Lind pinwheeling in accordion pleats, Katie Seymour serving a whirling dervish of rapid-fire footwork, Lottie Collins warbling her hit song 'Ta-ra-ra Boom-de-ay', ruffling her petticoat to big up the 'boom'.

And then there was Fuller, whose take on the skirt dance exaggerated the role of costume so much that it became a new style unto itself. The robes she favoured involved far more fabric than her forerunners' outfits: they weren't skirts so much as sails, with a diameter that could gust up to twenty feet above her head, a shell of silk scalloping around her.* 'Head, hands and feet followed the evolutions of the body and the robe,' as she described it, emphasising that her costume was fundamental to her technique, not just complementary.[11]

Fuller was fond of sprightly modern scores, especially Claude Debussy's experimental 'symphonic sketches' – an unusual choice for soloists at the time, who typically veered towards classical arrangements or popular songs. In combination with her atmospheric lighting designs, her act became a pulsing sensory experience, swirling together the latest in sound, colour and dance. She wasn't averse to performing it in popular venues like music halls, with their carousing crowds, but she was determined for people to see it as serious and imaginative, not cheap showbiz.

Fuller's sway was sharp and swift. Her New York City stint spawned a spate of imitators eager to try their hand at her sailing moves, prompting her to seek a US copyright for her Serpentine Dance in late 1892, though this was eventually declined on the basis that the choreography was too abstract to copyright. By the end of the 1890s, serpentine dancing, complete with fluttering veils and glowing lights, had become a generalised style. A cottage industry even sprung up of impersonators claiming to be Fuller: during her tours around Europe and beyond, to Japan, Mexico, Cuba, Russia and South America, she occasionally discovered that 'there, too, Loie Fuller had been ahead of me'.[12]

But in the summer of 1892, her commercial success was still waiting in the wings. A payment dispute over her *Uncle Celestin* contract spurred a falling-out with her manager, who was quick to

---

* Fuller's costume for her *Lily Dance*, from 1895, was said to contain five hundred yards of silk, with the hem measuring around a hundred yards.

replace her with another dancer, certain that her talents were interchangeable. Frustrated by his short-sightedness, and by her failure to secure a legal injunction against the substitute performing what Fuller saw as her intellectual property, she ditched the States for Europe, imagining it as somewhere 'educated people would like my dancing and would accord it a place in the realm of art'.[13]

The starry lights of Paris beckoned, and after a few months in Germany – where financial woes and contractual obligations required her to perform in a lowly circus attraction, slotted 'between an educated donkey and an elephant that played the organ'[14] – Fuller headed to the 9th arrondissement to audition for Édouard Marchand, director of the famed Folies Bergère.

In a twist that seems impossibly postmodern, Marchand revealed that there was a version of the Serpentine Dance already on the bill, danced by an imitator who'd seen Fuller perform in New York. It was a roller-coaster reckoning for Fuller, who despaired at the irony of it all – how the only thing standing in the way of her fame was her own fame. At the same time, the incident reinforced her conviction that her technique was a rare double threat: envied in form and inimitable in execution.* Marchand agreed, offering Fuller her own slot immediately after seeing the real deal. In a further dash of irony, she performed under the imitator's name for the first two nights of her run before debuting under her own.

Fuller was thirty years old when she signed with the Folies; the world of theatre glimmered before her like a moonstruck horizon. In November 1892, she debuted a quartet of dances – *The Serpentine*,

---

* As Fuller recalled: 'Instead of further upsetting me the sight of her soothed me. The longer she danced the calmer I became . . . My imitator was so ordinary that, sure of my own superiority, I no longer dreaded her. In fact I could gladly have kissed her for the pleasure that her revelation of inefficiency gave me' (*Fifteen Years*, p. 54).

The Violet, *The Butterfly* and what fans dubbed *The White Dance* – to breathless reviews. Talk of La Loïe and her kaleidoscopic concerts boosted ticket sales, which in turn prompted additional performances, the fame machine chugging away to swell her initial engagement into a marathon three-hundred-performance run, with Fuller eventually headlining the revue.

The rest of the decade fizzed by in a spritz of doting fans and international tours, new dances and new devices to illuminate them, culminating in the 1900 Exposition Universelle, where Fuller – the only woman with her own pavilion – was as much a marvel as the steam-powered technologies on display. Jean Cocteau, tastemaker du jour, pronounced her the expo's most exciting attraction: 'Let us all hail this dancer who . . . created the phantom of the era.'[15]

It was around this time that Fuller met Isadora Duncan and invited the starlet to join her upcoming European tour. Both would be remembered as soloists who built their reputations by flouting the conventions of the stage, though an important distinction is that Fuller did so with far less controversy. Whether she was liked personally is up for debate – in her memoir she laments that 'my personality counts for nothing'[16] – but her newfangled stage creations never inspired the pearl-clutching that Duncan's did. Fuller wasn't seen as an irreverent disruptor so much as an intriguing innovator.

A keystone of Fuller's appeal, and of her exceptionalism, was her genius in the lighting sphere. She invented a range of cutting-edge devices for the stage, including angled mirrors, glass pedestals and lantern projectors with slides painted in liquified gelatin, obtaining patents for many of these, as well as several chemical compounds she developed to illuminate the fabric of her costumes. Extinguishing the house lamps and draping the stage in black – itself a groundbreaking step – Fuller crafted a spellwork of light that was equal parts artistic and technical, informed by 'a play of colours in the draperies [of her costume] that could be mathematically and systematically calculated'[17] (her words).

In 1896 *Scientific American* wrote about 'the wonderfully beautiful effects' of this approach, focusing on Fuller's 'startling' *Fire Dance*, which used a lantern embedded in the stage floor to send crimson beams shooting upwards: 'The filmy veil is pure white, but as the dancer approaches the opening in the stage floor the veil turns to a fiery red and the flames wave to and fro as if they were being blown by the wind.'[18] W. B. Yeats admired this imagery in more lyrical terms in his 1932 poem 'Byzantium': 'An agony of trance / An agony of flame that cannot singe a sleeve.'[19]

To Fuller, 'the question of illumination, of reflection, of rays of light falling upon objects' was a source of profound intrigue. She found it baffling that turn-of-the-century society was 'still in the infancy of art, from the standpoint of control of light'. Her early days in Paris featured frequent visits to Notre Dame to drink in 'the marvellous glass of the lateral rose windows' and 'the rays of sunlight that vibrated in the church, in various directions, intensely coloured, as a result of having passed through these sumptuous windows'. She made pilgrimages to the Louvre and London's British Museum and National Gallery too, eager to witness the tawny beams spangling through their glass roofs.[20]

Her curiosity was as academic as it was soulful. Despite just a few years of formal education, Fuller taught herself enough science to start experimenting with chemical compounds, and eventually set up a small laboratory in Paris, a site of obsessive research into new sources of illumination, from dyes to phosphorescent salts: 'Every penny I earn goes to that. I do not save for my old age. I do not care what happens then. Everything goes to my laboratory.'[21] Her experiments weren't without hazard: after one explosion too many, she was evicted from her original premises and had to re-establish them elsewhere.

In 1904 Fuller wrote to the physicists Pierre and Marie Curie about their Nobel Prize-winning discovery of radium, asking if it might be possible to harness the element onstage as a lighting effect. They responded with a firm no, explaining its health hazards, but were intrigued by Fuller's curiosity and invited her to perform some of her work at their home – the start of a long-running friendship.[22] She later dedicated *Radium Dance* to the couple, working fluorescent salts into a black gauzy dress to create the illusion of stars flickering around her as she swept across a shadowy stage.

Fuller was also acquainted with the astronomer Camille Flammarion, who sponsored her membership into the French Astronomical Society, and even crossed paths with Thomas Edison, inspiring the inventor to produce a hand-tinted film of her Serpentine Dance. Her foothold in the world of science came full circle in 1924, when the Louvre held a retrospective on her technical achievements in lighting and costuming.

Fuller's work as an inventor both enriched and complicated her identity as a performer. 'I suppose I am the only person who is known as a dancer but who has a personal preference for Science,' she reflected, calling this 'the great scheme of my life'.[23] I'm struck by the word 'scheme' here, with its connotations of stealth and deceit. It picks up on an enduring social hitch that encourages women – in the name of modesty, humility, femininity – to frame our achievements as exceptions to the rule. In accomplishing something, we've managed to get away with something.

The belle époque acquired its name in retrospect; people didn't realise it was a golden age until the First World War thundered into view. Fuller's multimedia vision swam in the same sea of vitality that buoyed this era of prosperity – the race towards modernity and the halcyon optimism behind it, the bright-eyed belief in progress that made it possible to fuse art and technology in unparalleled forms, rearranging their bones into a higher order. But maybe, without foresight of her own legacy, Fuller saw her scientific aspirations as something of a ploy. Writing in *Le Temps* in 1907, the theatre director Jules Claretie praised 'her footlights, her electric lamps, all this visual fairyland which she has invented and perfected, which has made of her a unique personality, an independent creator, a revolutionist in art', noting that 'had she not been so well known she would have been taken for an anarchist'.[24] Dancer, scientist, both, neither – she was a major force any way you slice it.

In true avant-garde style, Fuller's boundary-pushing went beyond the aesthetics of her field to influence the structures around it. Take the Folies Bergère, which was 'transformed' by her tenure, in Édouard Marchand's words,[25] hailing unprecedented profits and a new generation of audiences. Marchand had shaped the venue into a hotbed of female talent after taking up his directorship in 1886, focusing on lively, often risqué talents – from soubrettes to snake charmers – that mostly drew working-class crowds. With La Loïe on the bill, though, the intelligentsia and the aristocracy also descended on the stalls. From here, her celebrity trickled into the social fabric of Paris itself, inspiring perfume ads and figurines, streetwear, even Loïe-themed cocktails. She boosted the city's cabaret scene and went on to scale its ladder of theatres, from the jazzy Théâtre des Champs-Elysées to the revered Paris Opera.

There's a chapter in Fuller's memoir dedicated to the 'many persons of distinction' she performed for as her sphere of influence went global in the early 1900s, including Alexandre Dumas (*fils*), Princess Marie of Romania and West Africa's King of Jolof.[26] Something about the new century aligned affluence with creative resolve. Neon could ignite the cityscape, and pictures could beam onto a screen. Vaccines would protect us from disease, and aeroplanes would carry us into the sky. A fiddler's daughter could invent a new dance style and tour the world on a paintbox cloud, her vision alive in Bon Marché beauties and sculptors who begged to cast her in bronze. She heard the cry of the future and rushed to meet its clarion call.

————

'The other evening I had, as it were, a vision of a theatre of the future, something of the nature of a feministic theatre,' Jules Claretie wrote in his aforementioned article for *Le Temps*. He was attending a rehearsal for Fuller's new *Salome* routine, an update on her 1895 solo by the same name, and recognised this 'wonderful impresaria', with her 'miracles of light', as a key player in a changing urban economy:

> *Women are more and more taking men's places. They are steadily supplanting the so-called stronger sex. The court-house swarms with women lawyers. The literature of imagination and observation will soon belong to women of letters. In spite of man's declaration that there shall be no woman doctor for him the female physician continues to pass her examinations and brilliantly. Just watch and you will see woman growing in influence and power; and if, as in Gladstone's phrase, the nineteenth century was the working-man's century, the twentieth will be the women's century.*[27]

The New Woman paradigm was often tethered to the political aims of first-wave feminism, but her resonance in France, and Paris in particular, had less to do with formal reform than personal ventures that took women outside of the home. The cityscape was gaining a new texture thanks to 'femmes modernes' fashioning new futures across the arts and sciences. Women's magazines played a vital role in embedding the idea of independent enterprise – either professional or recreational, from reading to writing to theatre – as a feminist endeavour. You didn't have to be part of a shared resistance to subvert the system.

You can see in Fuller's dancing certain New Woman ideals – her technique was spirited, creative and forward-thinking – but it's the context around it that yokes the innovative shades of her career to the subversive ones. By producing her own shows and taking charge of their tech, she blurred the usual masculine/feminine binary of theatre-based roles. And without a homestead to manage or children to raise, her art could take precedence. The closest Fuller got to conventional domesticity was her brief marriage to Colonel William Hayes, a nephew of the US President Rutherford B. Hayes, in 1889, a union of convenience that quickly ended in divorce. It's understood that Gab Sorère – a lesbian French film-maker Fuller lived with for some thirty years – was her actual life partner. Her sexuality hummed with the same quiet mystery as her silks, shadowing her pivots, unfixed by convention or obligation.

Writers today often claim Fuller as a queer icon, challenging historical characterisations of her as an unfortunate spinster. Discussions of her physique, on the other hand, remain stubbornly hoary. Admirers past and present tend to pile on the pejoratives when describing Fuller's everyday appearance: 'plump', 'plain', 'frumpy', 'pudgy', 'dowdy', even 'sausage-fingered'. Eve Curie, daughter of Drs Marie and Pierre, recalled her as 'an odd, badly dressed girl' with 'a shapeless figure',[28] while Jean Cocteau fathomed 'a fat, ugly American woman with glasses atop a pedestal maneuvering great waves of supple silk'.[29] I'm guessing the intention was to draw a distinction between her on- and offstage personas, highlighting the intrigue of a woman with zero showgirl glamour turning heads from Paris to Tokyo,* but to me this description underscores how

---

* Something Fuller herself occasionally did – see, for example, her proud

obsessed we are with attractiveness, and how difficult we find it to talk about women's looks in a neutral way. The stakes are especially high in dance, with its emphasis on poise and slenderness. When your body is your instrument, your appearance quickly edges into political territory.

It's true Fuller was older and stockier than the women who usually performed at the Folies, and her personal style was distinctly frills-free, an impression she entrenches in her memoir by sketching herself as a scrappy, dishevelled child and proclaiming that '[as an adult] I have likewise continued not to bother much about my personal appearance'.[30] In a later passage, reflecting on a botched attempt to treat cloth with phosphorescent salts, she conjures the image of a mad scientist: 'Part of my hair was blown off in an explosion while I was experimenting in my laboratory, and it made a great sensation in the neighborhood. The people called me a witch, a *sorciere*. My hair will not all grow again, but I do not care.'[31]

You don't see this in artwork like Jules Chéret's, where she's portrayed as lissom and svelte, with a tumble of red curls, or in the florid nicknames the media lavished on her: 'Fairy of Light', 'Magical Princess of Pearly Tints'. 'Before our very eyes she turned to many coloured, shining orchids, to a wavering, flowing sea flower, and at length to a spiral-like lily, all the magic of Merlin, the sorcery of light, colour, flowing form,' Isadora Duncan said after first seeing her peer perform,[32] using the same language of enchantment that many of Fuller's contemporaries reached for when describing her phantastic dancing visage. It was like they had to offload her from this dimension to compute her attractiveness. It's telling that

---

recollection of a child who rushed to meet her in her dressing room after a performance only to shrink away: 'That isn't her . . . This one here is a fat lady, and it was a fairy I saw dancing.' (*Fifteen Years*, pp. 141–142)

in praising Fuller, many of her fans erased her as a person altogether, referring to her in evanescent terms, a dreamy apparition of light and motion, building on a lofty declaration from Stéphane Mallarmé: '[a dancer] is not a woman ... but a metaphor'.[33]

But I'd argue that her transfigurations enabled her to inhabit her womanhood more deeply, not less. Instead of playing characters, Fuller tended to portray herself in a state of ascent – someone who could spark light from dusk, casting spells of silk that swept away the grief of the day. Her radiant lighting designs and sculpturesque costumes freed her from usual markers of prettiness in dancers – the tiny waistlines and slender ankles – and empowered her to channel a higher plane of brilliance. In her incandescent singularity, she questioned what we see as comely, along with the admiration and virtue tied up in female beauty. The literary critic Frank Kermode, reflecting on Fuller's cultural impact in a 1976 essay, put it bluntly when he wrote of her 'dehumanization' by the likes of Mallarmé: '[That was], and this we ought to expect, rooted in the terror and joy of the obscure primitive ground from which modern poets draw strength for their archaic art'.[34]

Here was a woman who toured with a pack of 'muses', helped launch the careers of dance giants like Duncan and Japan's Ohta Hisa, and rang in the 1914 summer solstice by performing on top of the Eiffel Tower, aged fifty-two. Fuller was still creating and producing in her sixties, just a few years before her death, giving her final performance in London in 1927. If she was a metaphor, it was for the lustre we deny women who don't fit prescriptive beauty standards. 'Loie Fuller modelled form out of a dream,' Sorère wrote in her diary the first time she saw Fuller perform. 'She *is* the butterfly, she *is* the fire, she is light, heaven, the stars.'[35]

We begin in darkness, heavy enough to steal your eyesight and stash it for safekeeping. A few seconds of black, then a gust of electric blue. The night unlocks to greet a cerulean spectre who swivels, arcs, ripples and bends, vanishing in her own undulations. Silks swish; violins judder. A sunrise blooms in the spectre's folds, orange and pink petals of dawn.

This isn't a glimpse of Fuller dancing but the actress Soko in the 2016 film *The Dancer*, performing a version of Fuller's *Lily Dance* pieced together by choreographer Jody Sperling, one of just a few dancemakers today to create live reconstructions of Fuller's dances. Despite launching a small school in 1908, she never passed on her choreography or lighting designs; and while she inspired at least eight early filmmakers to capture her signature style on-screen, there's no known footage of Fuller herself performing it, only stand-ins lit by basic hand-coloured effects. Viewing her work, as opposed to reading about it, is an act mired in filtration and construal. There are no stage notes to thumb through or student testimonies to observe. Even the best-researched revivals are several degrees of separation from their source, devised on projections and leaps of faith.

One vivid reference point for Fuller is the artwork she inspired, especially the lithographs that papered the street lamps of 1890s Paris, though there's an irony to using static imagery to access a performer so defined by fluidity. To isolate just one shape of her dazzling technique is to reduce an action to a pose. You're looking at an interruption, an ember. And while we have Fuller's own reflections, of course, these are sifted through the lattices of time and ego. For me, looking inward feels like the truest course to charting her resonance: considering the personal echoes of her writings, the way her story kindles memories and stokes a sense of self. If she's a projection screen, what am I projecting?

I first encountered modern dance as a teenager in the early 2000s, an era of tight, toxic fashion that goaded girls into seeking out attention while insisting we hated ourselves for wanting it. The more I learned about the moderns, the more I understood that interpretations of bodies and beauty are in constant flux; they resist conclusion and often defy rationale. I grasped at the talents of the greats, for whom nothing was static, not form or flair and definitely not ambition. They looked beyond the fads for something timeless and authentic, confident that brilliance would emerge in the hard truth of their spines.

Enter Fuller, whose idea of making herself beautiful was swallowing her body in fabric and creating dynamic new silhouettes for herself. Her confident individuality was, and continues to be, a powerful invitation for women to sidestep the narrow templates of the day; to ignore the ever-shifting goalposts and write our own terms; to shed any obligation to terms at all. She was a walking, spinning, whizzing reminder that affirmation is available outside of the male gaze. In the same way that her dancing transcended the traditional forces of narrative, Fuller herself sidestepped the usual provisos of fashion and sexuality. I see assertion in her eccentricity, an understanding that beauty isn't some lottery ticket dispersed at random. It's ours for the taking – or the rejecting.

Conversations about femininity continue to take in ever more granular dialogue about gender identity, sexual fluidity and the future of feminism. We're rewriting the stories of womanhood, and Fuller has an important place in the canon, propelling us towards a deeper and harder-hitting register.

ACT 1, SCENE 3

Of vice and virtue

Around the time that Isadora Duncan was casting her charms in New York's Criterion Theatre, London was warming up to a new modern dance luminary. The Canadian dancer Maud Allan enjoyed an intense burst of fame in Edwardian England thanks to a wildly popular solo called *Vision of Salome* that bust the British box office with a 265-show run over 1908 and 1909, catapulting her to momentary prominence as one of the era's most in-demand performers.

Allan created the dance in 1906 and toured it extensively, in concert halls and exclusive soirées, drawing fans across the globe, including King Edward VII, who enjoyed a private performance in Marienbad in 1907. Her career wound down in the 1920s, skimming well below the heights of Duncan's, but her acclaim as the iconic 'Salome dancer' lasted well into the twentieth century.

Allan was inspired to create her solo after watching a performance of Oscar Wilde's 1891 play *Salomé*, which imagines the titular biblical princess as a seductress who exacts revenge on John the Baptist for rejecting her advances. A drama of lust and temptation, *Salomé* had a complicated history in buttoned-up Britain. Shortly after production had begun on the play's world premiere as part of Sarah Bernhardt's London season in 1892, British officials banned it from the English stage on the grounds of blasphemy. Their outcry stemmed from the play's erotic centrepiece, the 'Dance of the Seven Veils', which sees Salome beguile her stepfather, King Herod, with a sensual dance in exchange for John's execution.

Gripped by the inner conflict she envisaged Salome pondering in the wake of John's death, Allan reworked this scene into a stand-alone routine about sexual awakening. She axed the male characters, making Salome's emotional journey the focus, and dressed herself in bejewelled, belly-baring chiffon – an erotic visage that she cranked up with sensual body rolls and odalisque poses. The curtain closed on her kissing a wax replica of John's severed, bleeding head. Her bold display drew her a feverish flock of female fans, including socialites who dressed up in veils and tried their hand at the snaking torsions they'd seen onstage. Sensing freedom in Allan's daring mien, they seized on her as a cipher for experimentation – momentary liberation from the era's strict dress codes and drawing-room decorum.

While *Vision of Salome* was Allan's career-defining work, it was actually an outlier in her broader portfolio, which mainly comprised what she called 'impressionistic mood settings' that reflected her interest in bringing music alive in new forms.[1] An accomplished pianist and impassioned aesthete, Allan shared her fellow moderns' rejection of ballet and threw herself into supple, free-flowing dances, from solemn waltzes to upbeat twirling frisks.

The form and feel of her dancing took its cue from whatever score she had at hand; she never developed a consistent vocabulary or unifying mantra for her choreography. 'How I dance, and why, and what is my intention in my dance, no one can say for certain,' she teases in the intro to her memoir, published at the height of her fame.[2] For this reason, she tends to be remembered as a beautiful performer but not an innovator of substance. She's rarely mentioned as one of the early enterprisers of modern dance.

For me, though, Allan's cultural capital can't be denied. There's a lot to admire about her both professionally and personally: the new links she forged between established and emerging dance forms; her independence as an unmarried female artist; the breadth of her repertoire, which included some fifty solos by the end of her career. She was an ambassador for experimental barefoot dancing, helping communicate its creative and cultural possibilities, especially in Edwardian England, where strait-laced scruples ruled.

Allan's most dynamic contribution was opening eyes to progressive new ideas around female propriety on both the stage and the street. *Vision of Salome* reclaimed a female archetype conceived by men and flagged Allan as a bold voice in evolving conversations about sexual mores, a biting dialogue in a society where women were expected to be indifferent to their own desire. The work made its mark across five continents; it was censored in several cities and even sparked a high-profile court case that drew to a head vicious double standards around virtue and vice. It was more than a brazen bit of showbiz; it was a radical reference point for early twentieth-century culture at large.

———

Maud Allan wasn't the only performer to bring Salome to the stage in the belle époque, or even the first. Around the same time that Loie Fuller debuted her own dance depiction of Salome in Paris in 1895, Salome skits began cropping up in vaudeville circuits around America, part of a wider vogue for glamorous, Eastern-inspired aesthetics and artefacts. None of these routines had the potency of Allan's, however. When Fuller reworked hers in 1907, a year after Allan started touring *Vision of Salome*, it became a distinctly sultrier iteration: the Allan effect had begun to take hold.

Within a year of Allan's debut, showgirls like Gertrude Hoffman, Eva Tanguay, Vera Olcott and Lotta Faust began emulating her moves to cheeky, occasionally scandalous, effect. The Ziegfeld Follies premiered a Salome number in 1907, and the following year Follies darling Mademoiselle Dazie opened a school in New York City to teach the routine to aspiring vaudevillians. The ballet sphere wasn't immune to the craze, a phenomenon the press dubbed 'Salomania'. In 1908 Ida Rubinstein, a soon-to-be soloist with the Ballets Russes, delivered a daring private performance in Paris that saw her disrobe entirely. Other ballerinas got in on the action too – including Bianca Froelich, who danced in the American premiere of Richard Strauss's *Salomé* opera in 1907 – and moderns like Ruth St Denis, who summoned an evocative spiritual air in her 1909 interpretation.

Salome's evolution from the submissive daughter described in the New Testament to the murderous temptress who enthralled the Salomaniacs is a winding, well-documented road. Highlights along the way include fifth-century Christians drawing associations between Salome's dancing and her sexuality, medieval painters depicting her as a symbol of seduction, and exponents of Europe's late-nineteenth-century Decadent movement fantasising about her destructive supremacy as a femme fatale – 'the symbolic incarnation of world-old Vice', in the words of the novelist Joris-Karl Huysmans.[3] Oscar Wilde's play was the apotheosis, concocting a heretical brew of incest, carnality and manipulation. Wilde's imprisonment for 'gross indecency' in 1895, following the exposure of his romantic relationship with the poet and author Lord Alfred Douglas, further entrenched its profane associations.

Aware of the play's scandal-scorched reputation, Allan cloaked her retelling in a figurative haze she hoped would ease its irreverence. *Vision of Salome* opens after Salome has danced for King Herod and received John the Baptist's head in reward. Shocked and titillated by her role in his death, she (in Allan's words) 'lives again the awful moments of joy and of horror which she has just passed through', re-enacting the dance in a reverie of sexual awakening.[4] 'What passes in those few moments through this excited, half-terror-stricken, half-stubborn brain makes of little Salome a woman!'[5] Allan enthused in 1908. While this layering didn't quell the story's predatory undertones, it did reframe it as an emotional *Bildungsroman* – a progressive take on a myth cloaked in misogyny, and one that would forever distinguish her interpretation.

Allan set her choreography to a winding piano arrangement by Marcel Rémy, and costumed herself in a pearly headdress, beaded bralette and sheer, shimmering skirt. (As a reporter would comment at a 1908 London performance: 'This is no dance of the seven veils. It is a dance of only one veil, and not much of a veil at that. She does not take it off. She does not need to.'[6]) Allan was booked to debut the routine at Vienna's Court Opera House in December 1906, but it ultimately premiered at the city's Carltheater after the Court, perturbed by her costume, insisted she wear something more modest. She refused, and the debacle made it into the press, alerting the public to a steamy new act from a promising interpretive dancer. Invitations from Europe's biggest impresarios poured in.

Allan spent a year touring *Vision of Salome* around the Continent, from Paris to Budapest to Munich, usually performing it as the finale in a suite of self-choreographed solos. Critics delighted in her 'piquant lack of costume',[7] and artists clamoured to capture her eroticism on canvas. A trio of oil paintings by Franz von Stuck, which Allan modelled for in 1906, depicted a topless Salome grinning beside a decapitated John the Baptist, crystallising impressions of the dancer and the princess as the same ruthless siren.

Vision of Salome enjoyed its most enthusiastic reception in London, in 1908, where an early review declared Allan the 'artistic sensation of the hour'.[8] The odd dissent cropped up – 'London has never seen such a glorification of the flesh!' bellowed the *Labour Leader*[9] – but these were balanced out with admiring op-eds avowing that her work was 'absolutely free from offense' and 'none but the most prurient could see the slightest appeal to any sense but that of beauty of motion and pose'.[10] Her small waist and serene, wide-set eyes helped lend a halo of purity, while the regular presence of dignitaries in the audience – from the Duke of Westminster to the Prince of Wales – reinforced the impression of a high-society event, not tawdry entertainment. Within a few months, Allan had become one of the West End's highest-paid performers. Unflagging demand stretched her initial two-week run at the Palace Theatre of Varieties into an eighteen-month engagement, a vote of confidence that helped her secure aristocratic patronage, a lavish apartment overlooking Regent's Park and a string of high-flying commissions, including a performance at the 1908 London Olympics.

Female theatregoers, thrilled by Allan's transgressive portrait of womanhood, were responsible for keeping her numbers up at the Palace. The *Daily Chronicle* noted that at one 1908 performance, more than 90 per cent of the audience appeared to be women: 'It might have been a suffragist meeting.'[11] Allan never associated herself with the suffrage movement – in her memoir she criticises the tactics of English suffragettes and claims, somewhat elliptically, that 'the ballot will be given [to woman] when she is ready to receive it'[12] – but her private politics were immaterial next to the ideological sheen that radiated around her, intensifying the charge of her routine, with its subtext of rebellion and self-determination.

The Palace eventually added special smoking-free matinees to accommodate Allan's eager female fans, among them a teenage Diana Cooper, who would later cite Allan's influence on carving out her own stage career. Allan was a true innovator in this respect, marrying celebrity and high art in a way that resonated across different social classes and age brackets. Soon her shapely likeness came to grace figurines, postcards, cartoons, greeting cards and statues – a commercial register of stardom usually reserved for actresses rather than dancers.

Allan's West End audiences were the most devoted of her career, showering her with fan mail and lobbying the capital's dance schools to add theatrical dancing to their curricula. They saw her show as an energising site of escapism – a safe, respectable space to experience an erotic daydream free from judgement or shame. Her influence even spilled into the home, where women swapped garden fetes for zesty 'Maud Allan parties'. Her performance was an event that lasted long after the curtain fell.

————

Beulah Maude Durrant was born in Toronto in 1873, eight years after the American Civil War and as many ahead of the European scramble to colonise Africa. It was a Gilded Age for some and a war-torn toil for others. Her childhood witnessed the surge of industrialisation responsible for feats like the Transcontinental Railroad, an engineering marvel that hummed a steady back-beat in San Francisco, where Allan lived with her parents and brother, Theodore, from the age of six to twenty-two. Her mother, Isabella, steered her children towards books and music, and both excelled academically and went on to pursue further education after high school.

A talented pianist, Allan studied under Eugene Bonelli at the San Francisco Grand Academy of Music before heading to Berlin in 1895 to join the acclaimed Hochschule für Musik, where she was tutored (and possibly romanced) by the maestro Ferruccio Busoni. During term breaks, Allan taught English for extra money and travelled the Continent with her mother, soaking up Swiss valleys and French villages, Italian cities sculpted by wind-whipped lake-shores. 'No girl with high ambitions can enter into a glorious life of art without a knowledge of the world as it is revealed in books,'[13] she proclaims in her memoir.

Germany, a turn-of-the-century hotbed for performing arts, was the site of Allan's migration towards dance, although it was tragedy rather than initiative that spurred this. The autumn after she arrived in Berlin, her brother was charged in a high-profile murder case involving two women mutilated in the San Francisco Baptist church where the Durrant family worshipped. He was later hanged for the murders, at which point his sister changed her name, abandoned her studies and shifted focus to dance. From now on, she would be Maud Allan, international artiste, a persona she adopted with the same aplomb that would come to character-ise her stage presence.

Despite her belief in her brother's innocence, Allan severed all ties to the man forever maligned as the 'Demon of the Belfry' and threw herself into her new profession abroad. Locking the trauma in a box somewhere deep and dark, she remained fiercely tight-lipped about her private life throughout her career, even when aspects of it spilled into the public arena, taking care to present herself as a respected and respectable woman. Commemorative postcards and other pictures of Allan in her streetwear show a wispy-haired beauty in high-necked dresses with pretty floral accents – a demure foil to her sinuous Salome persona.

Compared to the exacting strictures of the piano, Allan found the body an instrument of organic rhythms and infinite tessella-tions. She sidestepped formal training and instead explored her own experimental brand of dance in which music took a seat ahead of movement. 'The art of dancing, as understood by the great masses, is a series of regular rhythmical movements requiring a certain music; not so in my work,' she later explained to the press. 'What one usu-ally only vaguely feels when listening to beautiful music I am trying, through movement and mimicry, to express clearly and deeply – the thought which seems to hover on the wings of the melody.'[14]

Her melodic dexterity helped her develop her ambition, as did her working relationship with Marcel Rémy, a Belgian composer who encouraged her to research historical forms of dance and expression and try out new ways to visualise these.

Though it would prompt criticism throughout her career, Allan's amateur dance credentials had the advantage of distinguishing her from other early moderns, including Isadora Duncan, who stormed Europe the same decade that Allan entered the scene. It's unclear how much notice the pair gave each other, but the press wasted no time manufacturing a rivalry, pitting Duncan's 'inventive subtle mind' against Allan's 'inimitable grace of manuflection'.[15] Sensing that the borders of dance were shifting and that her musical talents might slot into a lucrative niche, Allan leaned into the image of a pretty, self-taught ingénue. The soft, smiling disposition she sported in public belied the enterprising persona who fiercely networked her way into Europe's prestigious concert hall circuit.

Allan's first works for performance were abstract solos danced to established classical compositions, including staples of the piano repertory, like Edvard Grieg's *Peer Gynt* suite. Early reviews describe her moving with lightness and poise, occasionally improvising as she moulded one plasticine pose into another. Her lissom medleys reflected influences as diverse as the Victorian *tableau vivant* craze and Delsartian movement principles, and represented an attempt, in her words, to 'express in movement the emotions and thoughts stirred by melody, beautiful pictures and sculpture'.[16] As she scaled the ranks of critical recognition, she became known for her elegant calligraphy of hand and finger gestures.

Allan's earliest solos weaved in the striking imagery she'd encountered during her European sojourns: vibrant Renaissance paintings, Etruscan pottery, vivid memories of women on the banks of the Arno who 'bore themselves like goddesses on springing, elastic feet'.[17] She also found inspiration in the charismatic Sarah Bernhardt, a source of creative rapture for Allan since her schooldays, when she saw the 'glorious' actress perform in San Francisco: 'I think the turning point in my career came from my first sight of that great woman,' she reflected in her memoir. 'She inspired me to express my thoughts in another manner.'[18]

Allan had a special affinity with Hellenic and Eastern motifs, and viewed dance as an ancient, once-pure form of expression that had been warped through codification. 'The moment that dancing becomes bound by rules and conventions it loses the very rationale of its existence,' she wrote in 1908.[19] Ballet was offensive to her for this reason. 'I pondered over the question of the truthfulness of such dancing. Was it dancing as dancing ought to be, and as dancing was originally conceived? I came to the conclusion it was not!'[20]

This attitude, in concert with her penchant for bare feet and gauzy dresses, usually prompts the canon to dismiss her as an imitator of Duncan. But while the two drew similar links between antiquity and integrity, I see Allan as a pioneer in her own right, just on a smaller scale. It wasn't the mechanics of her dancing so much as her choice of subject that set her apart, particularly when it came to *Vision of Salome*. In using the crown jewel of her portfolio to explore a topic as loaded as female sexuality, she showed the explosive social potential of modern dance. Like Loie Fuller, she also built new bridges between popular variety show entertainment and the more refined fare associated with concert halls and opera houses, helping broaden the movement's visibility and audience base.

Allan gave her first professional dance performance at the age of thirty on Christmas Eve 1903, at Vienna's Conservatory of Music, captivating the city's upper crust with a programme that included 'mood settings' of Franz Schubert's *Ave Maria*, Anton Rubinstein's *Valse-Caprice*, Felix Mendelssohn's *Spring Song* and

Frédéric Chopin's *Marche funèbre*. Her free-flowing stagewear stirred as much interest as her novel creations in these early days. 'Miss Maud Allan is no doubt the least dressed dancer of our time,' proclaimed one reviewer after seeing her perform in one of her signature frocks[21] – short, sleeveless numbers she modelled after ancient Greek undergarments. Like Duncan with her iconic tunics, Allan had her eyes on the past as well as the future, prefiguring the soft civilian silhouettes couturiers like Paul Poiret would begin fashioning in the 1910s.

Her Salome costume, by contrast, was striking and edgy, studded with scarlet jewels that traced circles around her breasts. She added metallic jewellery, dark eyeliner, bright nail varnish and a sheer, ankle-skimming skirt with a sling of beads carefully arranged across the crotch. When the press probed Allan on her déshabillé, she explained that concealing her 'instrument' (as she referred to her body) 'would be as foolish as to close and cover a piano and sculpture instead of opening the first and unveiling the latter'.[22] She was frustrated to find that accusations of indecency stemmed from women as often as men: 'It was one of my own sex, a nameless princess in a nameless city, who threatened to withdraw her patronage from a certain opera house if "a young person with naked feet" were allowed to dance there.'[23]

When *Vision of Salome* hit the West End, salacious details about Allan's personal life swept the capital, including whispers that she took both men and women as lovers. In London, the hearsay heated up interest in her work, but the climate was frostier outside of the city. Officials in Manchester and Preston censored her show, deeming it too blasphemous for public consumption, and her costume prompted at least one personal complaint to the Archbishop of Dublin. With her rocketing fame came accusations of obscenity, though Allan ploughed ahead with her provocative portrait of seduction, confident that her nuanced framing would show the complex, surprising nature of female sexuality. The consternation she encountered, however, was an early wind in the storm to come.

———

In 1910, Allan embarked on a world tour that lasted seven years, taking in Russia, the United States, Australia, New Zealand, South Africa and India, plus a pit stop in London for another run at the Palace. Though *Vision of Salome* remained her calling card, she created a great deal of work during this period, relying on these new dances, as well as gentler works like *Spring Song*, to balance out the sensual pitch of her signature routine.

In 1918, the West End beckoned again: Jack Grein, an Anglo-Dutch impresario, suggested she rework *Vision of Salome* for his upcoming production of Oscar Wilde's *Salomé*, due to open in the spring. While Allan had started to grow tired of the routine, Grein had a reputation for backing provocative plays like Henrik Ibsen's *Ghosts* and George Bernard Shaw's *Widowers' Houses*; she was hopeful his latest show, sure to cause a frisson, might offset the mixed reception she'd recently received in New York, where a critic called her dancing 'an art, no longer new, that depends on its novelty for popularity'.[24] It would also be a chance for Allan to assume a role once designated for Sarah Bernhardt, 'the one woman in the world I wanted to rival.'[25] After a few days of deliberation, she signed on to the production.

By 1918, *Salomé* had become a familiar text in Europe and the United States, thanks in part to the success of Richard Strauss's opera. It didn't have much of a presence in England, though, where the 1892 ban on the play was still in place. Familiar with the reach of the theatre censor, Allan and Grein sidestepped this by organising special 'subscription' showings that counted as private, rather than public, performances. Enter Noel Pemberton Billing, a right-wing politician and self-appointed morality warden infuriated at the thought of the play's revival. After hearing about Allan's involvement, he published a disparaging newspaper item about her titled 'The Cult of the Clitoris'. The provocative article married two of Billing's pet phobias: German treachery and the 'infiltration' of homosexuality into British society. In it, he insinuated that Allan was a lesbian accomplice to a prurient German extortion plot involving same-sex seduction. Within days, she sued Billing for obscene and defamatory libel in one of London's strangest causes célèbres.

Probably owing to his flimsy claim-to-evidence ratio, Billing had self-published his article in *The Vigilante*, a weekly journal he'd founded as a communiqué for his 1916 parliamentary campaign. The paper was a platform for invectives about the ills of immigrants, Jews, pacifists and gay people. Unsubstantiated exposés were a specialty, such as a 1918 article 'revealing' a German scheme to conquer Britain via an army of STD-riddled prostitutes. As a foreign woman with a liberal attitude towards sexually charged art, Allan was a natural target for *The Vigilante*'s spewage. Billing watched with glee as she launched her lawsuit, relishing the opportunity to broadcast his thoughts in a public forum. 'I'm a libeller,' he admitted in a press interview after the case went to trial. 'I have libelled public men for the past two and a half years … and if you think I am going to keep quiet as a public man while men are being killed at the rate of nine a minute to make a Sodomite holiday, I am not.'[26]

The litigation that ensued was ugly and sensationalist, its spectacle intensified by a war-weary public eager for a distraction from the fighting on the Western Front. British media outlets of all size and disposition reported on the affair, and newspapers across Europe and the United States too. Official proceedings began in April 1918 at Bow Street Police Court, where 'a queue some fifty yards long' assembled in the rain to watch Allan file her suit,[27] and when Billing's five-day trial started the next month at the Old Bailey, reporters and spectators raced to secure seats in the gallery.

Billing represented himself, using his platform to further malign Allan as 'a lewd, unchaste and immoral woman'[28] – someone unscrupulous enough to be an accomplice to treason. He unearthed the details of her brother's murder conviction, implying dissolution by association; suggested that her student days in Germany had coloured her political sympathies; and claimed that her dance with John the Baptist's head amounted to necrophilia. He also subjected her to humiliating personal questions – did she, for example, know what a clitoris was? When she answered yes, Billing held this up as proof of her depravity, insisting that only medical students and perverts had reason to be familiar with the term (himself notwithstanding).[29]

Finally, he drafted in witnesses to testify to Allan's 'performances of obscene and indecent character',[30] including a doctor who 'confirmed' the perversions of anyone who took part in or watched productions like *Salomé*. One of the most damning deponents was Harold Sherwood Spencer, assistant editor of *The Vigilante*, who called Allan's Salome 'a representation of a diseased mad girl', denouncing the dancer herself as 'a very unfortunate hereditary degenerate'[31] – catnip for the drama-hungry press. The fact of Spencer's recent discharge from the British army on the grounds of paranoid delusional insanity rarely made it into their dispatches.

With the right framing, Billing was able to transfigure Allan from a cosmopolitan artist who'd charmed the British elite into a crooked foreigner who'd infiltrated the aristocracy. Some journalists used their column inches to discuss the cynicism of his crusade, including Lucy Schwob, who, writing under the pen name Claude Cahun for the literary journal *Mercure de France*, noted that 'one will find [within his libel] the thesis of those Puritans who wish to snatch, under the guise of moral reform and invoking the state of the war, all freedom from the artistic expression of thought'.[32] Most, however, busied themselves with breathless reports of Allan's appearance and creative descriptions of her supposed iniquities (since the majority of outlets refused to print the words 'clitoris' and 'lesbian').

It's important to understand that the nervous national climate of Britain's war years gave Billing's narrative a foothold it would never have found a few years before or after them. The First World War was decimating the nation's identity as an infallible empire. Politics and economics had narrowed; morale had shuddered as the brutality of rationing, conscription and air raids came right to citizens' doorsteps. With nearly a million deaths on the books and a flu pandemic promising many more, the exhilaration that gripped Britons in the early days of the war had deadened. For those looking to rationalise the violence, Billing's rhetoric, however fringe, however reaching, made a convoluted sort of sense.

Allan's elusive sexual orientation was the final brushstroke in Billing's portrait of the 'menacing other'. His use of the word 'clitoris' in his article was an allusion to a long-held, cartoonishly misguided belief that lesbians and other 'lascivious' women could be identified by their oversized genitalia – a coded jab to out and shame Allan. That he coupled it with 'cult' added an edge of witch-hunt to his moral panic, deepening its gendered subtext. To me, these connotations focalise the misogyny of the case, magnifying its cultural footprint. Anxieties around emasculation hit a fever pitch during Britain's war years; the klaxon for feminist reform, sounding louder than ever in response to British women's extraordinary contribution to the war effort, strained against roars for them to know their place. This wasn't some forgettable tabloid squabble but a watershed moment for a society starting to open its mind to new gender norms and expressions of sexuality.

Two key cultural events bracketed the Billing affair, thrusting it into pole position as a socio-political weathervane in 1918. First was the release of Marie Stopes's *Married Love*, published a few months before Allan launched her lawsuit. The book sold out multiple printings in just a few weeks, captivating the country with its persuasive argument for the recognition of women's sexual desire. The second came just as the case went to trial: Parliament passed the inaugural legislation giving women the right to vote. Allan's fight for freedom of expression – artistic, personal, sexual – was absorbed into this wider reckoning over women's behaviour and independence. The suffragist through lines she'd seeded a decade earlier rooted themselves even deeper.

Surprisingly, Billing wasn't an opponent of women's suffrage; he even endorsed it in an early edition of *The Vigilante*. But if women's voting rights didn't perturb him, evolving ideas about their social enfranchisement certainly did. From this point of view, Allan posed the biggest threat of all: the unruly woman, empowered to parlay her deepest desires into reality. It was more than just her name on the line; it was her very humanity.

———

Allan was busy rehearsing for her role in Jack Grein's production when the vulgarities of 'The Cult of the Clitoris' made it into print. The pair persevered with the show as the litigation came underway, hopeful the kerfuffle might boost public interest, but it had the opposite effect. Originally scheduled to show at London's Prince of Wales Theatre, and then the Kennington Theatre, the run hurriedly shifted to the Royal Court Theatre at the last minute after its former homes disavowed it, fearing its mounting notoriety.

At least one performance took place, on 12 April 1918, and reviews were unkind. Foreshadowing the language of pathology that would later enter testimony, the *Morning Post* dismissed the show as a 'bizarre melodrama of disease', calling it 'an atmosphere people who are healthy and would desire to remain so would do well to keep out of'.[33] (Incidentally, the paper was endorsing Billing's upcoming parliamentary campaign and arranged for the review to be published on the same day as one of the preliminary hearings.) *The Stage* also took a harsh tone, judging the 'gaudy harlotry' of the show 'very impure'.[34] Instead of sending ticket sales soaring, these incendiary write-ups became the death knell to Allan's Salome chapter.

A month later Allan took to the stand to defend her artistic choices. 'I wish the Jury to understand that Salome lived in the Eastern world at a time when our rules were not in vogue,' she told the court. 'Salome was not a perverse young woman; therefore Mr Billing has no right to talk about sadism.' She steadfastly maintained that 'I cannot be responsible for what other persons read into [the performance]'.[35] Later she'd grieve over Billing's intrusive questioning: 'Never in my whole life have I spent such a hellish time as I did during those slow dragging hours at the Old Bailey,' she recalled. '[He's] the worst man that ever was.'[36]

On 4 June 1918, after deliberating for two hours, the jury acquitted Billing of all charges. Before dismissing the court, the judge offered some personal comments on the morality of 'actresses in almost nothing at all'. In his opinion, 'those who have the power – or believe they have the power – to prevent improper dances from being danced or such costumes worn on the stage . . . ought to exercise their powers most stringently and put a stop to that kind of performance.'[37] He'd also betrayed other prejudices too, referring to Oscar Wilde offhandedly as 'a great beast'[38] during the trial and allowing Alfred Douglas – Wilde's former lover – as a surprise witness for the defence. Despite authoring the English translation of *Salomé*, Douglas used his time on the stand to pronounce Wilde (dead for almost two decades at this point) 'the greatest force of evil that has appeared in Europe in the last 350 years.'[39]

Papers from the time report that the judgment inspired roaring applause from the gallery, and that a throng of ecstatic spectators gathered outside the courtroom to throw confetti in celebration of justice served. Cynthia Asquith, daughter-in-law of Prime Minister Herbert Henry Asquith, lamented this cheerful display in her diary: 'One can't imagine a more undignified paragraph in English history . . . It is such an awful triumph for the unreasonable.'[40] The nation's broadsheets drew a similar conclusion in the days to come. 'A weak judge, a feeble counsel, and a bewildered jury combined to score for the defendant a striking and undeserved success,'[41] the *Daily Mail* noted. For the *Daily Telegraph* the trial was 'A Deplorable Scandal . . . the sooner this is recognised and some steps are taken to make its repetition forever impossible, the better it will be for the welfare of the kingdom and the honesty of that public life, the credit of which has been so severely impugned.'[42] Impassioned as they were, though, these reflections focused on the consequences of the case for polite society, not the message it sent to artists, women in general or Allan herself.

The verdict marked the start of a slow, steady career descent for Allan. She retired *Vision of Salome* permanently and withdrew from the stage for several months, partly out of self-preservation and partly because she'd been shunned by the British theatre establishment. For a few years, she turned her attention to teaching dance, first in England, then California, but the urge to perform crept in, and in 1920 she embarked on a tour of South America – the first of an intermittent series of international circuits over the next decade that also took in Asia, North Africa and the United States.

In 1923 Allan created her first new work in half a decade, and this kick-started a small creative renaissance, with five new dances materialising in a single twelve-month period, and another handful over the next three years, including several more passes at Eastern-inspired reveries. Little is recorded about how these were received, a mark of her fade-out from the sphere of celebrity. The fanfare that had once sent women on dizzy hunts for Maud-stamped merchandise was long gone. Her shows no longer sold out, her relationships with the British nobility faded, and the dawn of the flapper gave women a new icon to emulate at their parties. Allan started a romantic relationship with her secretary, Verna Aldrich, and settled into a quiet life in London punctuated by the odd acting role, including a small turn in Max Reinhardt's *The Miracle* in 1932. She gave her final performances in 1934 and eventually returned to California, where she lived until her death in Los Angeles in 1956.

The particulars of Allan's station as an artist – the lack of details around her choreography, the predominance of a single routine over her portfolio, the defining stain of the Billing affair – complicate her place in modern dance history. So does the orientalist aesthetic of *Vision of Salome*, which represents short-sighted fantasy at best and sexist ethnic stereotyping at worst. But I think she deserves credit as an experimental artist, committed, in her words, to 'ever thinking, ever trying, ever rejecting'.[43] Like Ruth St Denis and many other early moderns, she held a genuine, if misguided, enthusiasm for the 'wizardries' of the East – for the 'night winds breathing over Syrian deserts [that] whisper to the pitying stars the story of Salome'.[44] She unearthed new dimensions of a previously one-note figure, repositioning her as an advocate for sexual expression in a society where female pleasure was demonised. However evasive her views on feminist causes like suffrage, Allan understood the need for ammunition against the men who greeted her work with 'a little sneer . . . "Oh, yes, of course! You're a woman."'[45] She empowered herself and the thousands of women who watched her dance.

When I first encountered Allan's story, I laughed at the outlandishness of Billing's claims against her – the holes in his rationale and the obvious contempt fuelling it. I saw him as a harrumphing relic of yesterday's world. But the unreasonable and the regressive still triumph regularly, boosted by the holler of people who fear equality because they think it means they'll be sidelined the way they sideline others. You can't scoff away the driving force of dread.

In her memoir, Allan recounts a historical anecdote about a Roman politician, Sallust, reproaching a constituent 'with the taunt that she danced with too much skill for a virtuous woman'.[46] Rankled by this gendered conflation of dancing and morality, she defied it from her earliest days as a performer, even before Billing became the Sallust to her dancing lady. She did it by refusing to confine herself to stockings or restrictive hemlines; by rejecting Victorian precepts in favour of classical ideals about beauty and nudity; and by embracing an image of lust that flew in the face of purity and propriety. Allan had the gumption to imagine a future in which virtue wasn't judged on sexual appetite. She set out to reshape her corner of the art world and ended up challenging a far wider status quo.

ACT 2, CURTAIN
Beyond the ballot box

Cast

MARTHA GRAHAM
ANNA SOKOLOW   SOPHIE MASLOW

with

DORIS HUMPHREY
HANYA HOLM
HELEN TAMIRIS
JANE DUDLEY
MARGARET BARR

and

DANCE COMPANY

The world wars of the twentieth century bookended a pulsing second chapter in modern dance history. The dancers making waves between the mid-1920s and mid-1940s confronted a world cleaved by calls of duty and shifting alliances, stock market twists that turned grasslands to dust. It was an era of trauma and adventure, fragmentation and resolve, traces of shell shock amid heady infusions of social change. The roar of the 1920s never quite drowned out the blare of boys in trenches. Modern dancers, like many artists in these years, questioned society and their place in it. They showed a huge interest in the body as an instrument of political expression, and migrated towards formal movement systems that could give shape and structure to new understandings of the world around them.

The cohort that rose to prominence in the interwar years boosted the scenes their forerunners had established and nurtured fresh ones too. Apostles of Isadora Duncan found new footholds in Britain, Denmark and Finland, while Mary Wigman's alumni deepened inroads across Germany, tapping into the elan of Weimar culture. European teachings trickled outwards, diffusing and re-emerging on the stages of Hong Kong, Tel Aviv, Chicago and beyond.*

* Especially vibrant exponents include Maggie Gripenberg, Asta Mollerup, Madge Atkinson, Ruby Ginner, Leslie Burrows-Goossens, Kurt Jooss, Dai Ailian, Gertrud Kraus, Gurit Kadman, Yardena Cohen, Harald Kreutzberg, Yvonne Georgi, Zohra Sehgal and Gret Palucca.

Some of the biggest names to emerge in this period were graduates of the renowned Denishawn school in Los Angeles, which collaged together an eclectic curriculum mingling Eastern 'oriental' dances (a speciality of co-founder Ruth St Denis) with ballet, ballroom and even hula and sword dancing. Some Denishawn dancers thrived on this medley and embraced it in their own careers; others ricocheted in unique directions, underscoring the reactive and protean nature of modern dance, where every rebellion spurred its own rebellion. For Martha Graham, Doris Humphrey and Charles Weidman, the school's most prolific alumni, bespoke new forms of dance were the way forward, with a focus on art inspired by American culture rather than foreign influences. Together with Hanya Holm, Wigman's pre-eminent protégée, these innovators – aka the 'Big Four' – were responsible for some of the most electric innovations of the era. By the mid-1930s, their booming companies had positioned New York City as the epicentre of modern dance experimentation.

Inspired by their predecessors' affinity with barefoot naturalistic dancing, many next-gen moderns embraced the basic pillars of human movement – walking, running, breathing – as a springboard for their own practice. Keen to dispel any lingering notions of modern dance as amateurish or improvisational, they built formal techniques that required diligent training to master. Fluidity and softness still had a role to play, but some dancers started striking out with sharp, oblique shapes and rhythms – slanted shoulders and hips askew, sloping delineations of body and space. Like the work of fellow avant-gardes, from Stravinsky to Picasso, these experimental ventures sometimes irritated as many audiences as they thrilled.

Second-wavers married these new forms to pensive themes, leaning into the here and now of what it means to be a person with fears, needs and ambitions. Human behaviour, both conscious and instinctive, was a coursing font of inspiration, especially for

Graham and two of her brightest associates, Anna Sokolow and Sophie Maslow. One of Sokolow's most acclaimed works explored the irony of loneliness in a crowded city, while Graham's forte was charting the inner drive of women. The latter called each of her dances 'a graph of the heart',[1] keying into a wider sense of introspection and subjectivity that suffused the age of modernism.

Mysticism was another thematic draw as dancers reached for new filters for the ambiguities of life. In sync with their counterparts in literature and the visual arts – from Paul Klee and Henri Matisse to Samuel Beckett and Henry Moore – many dancers explored primitivism too, intrigued by its evocation of primal simplicity and *tabula rasa*. Folk idioms held a similar spark, inspiring performers to rework allusive customs around the world, from old-country Slavic steps to ancient Chinese drumming traditions.

Folk motifs had an especially powerful resonance in the United States. The Big Four all seized on Americana, with its faded quilt of promises, as did Sokolow and Maslow, the latter giving new life to Depression-era square dances and banjo tunes. Meanwhile, Black dancers began to bring African American culture to the modern dance stage, from jazz music to plantation spirituals, buoyed by the fizzing energy of the Harlem Renaissance. Heritage, in its varied guises, became a rousing remedy for modern disaffection. Some dancers used it to ratify vibrant new visions of the future, others to evoke some distant 'before' and the perspective we've lost along the way.

There's a perception that modern dance in the interwar years was solemn and humourless, especially as dancers continued to spurn the enchanted landscapes of ballet, but alongside the era's earnest interrogations into love and marginalisation were vibrant displays of wit, comedy and satire. For many moderns, it was about intensity of feeling, whatever that feeling was – a shared commitment to expressing the thrust and vitality of the age. Together, they forged new possibilities for the dancing self, the female self in particular, recasting it as something that not only symbolised modernity but could also critique and shape it.

———

In 1926 Margaret H'Doubler, a dance instructor at the University of Wisconsin–Madison, coordinated the launch of America's first dance degree, with a focus on free forms and personal expression – a springing leap forward in the professionalisation of modern dance. Another key stride came in 1934, when Martha Hill and fellow denizens of Vermont's Bennington College established an annual summer dance intensive, recruiting the Big Four as faculty members.

Part artistic laboratory, part concert venue, Bennington became a cradle of modern dance innovation between 1934 and 1942, furnishing more than a thousand students with opportunities to study, create and perform with the movement's leading lights. The programme attracted a glinting starscape of collaborators in its heyday – including the sculptor Alexander Calder, poet William Carlos Williams and composer John Cage – and nurtured the creation of several pivotal works, from Martha Graham's *El Penitente* to José Limón's *Danzas Mexicanas*.

Dance education was evolving at the lower levels too. Aspiring dancers had new throughways into the field from a young age, especially in big cities around Germany and the United States, where social leagues and philanthropists created new ties between dance and social purpose. The settlement houses of New York City and Chicago – established to improve educational opportunities for working-class youths – brought affordable dance and theatre lessons to scores of emerging moderns in the interwar years, including Anna Sokolow, Sophie Maslow and Helen Tamiris.

Two key venues building out the pipeline in New York were the Neighborhood Playhouse, a conservatory with classes taught by Martha Graham and her musical director Louis Horst, and the Young Men's Hebrew Association on 92nd Street, a community centre that hosted some of the era's most lauded premieres. Founded as a working-class social hub, the 92nd Street Y was miles away from the high-society salons where Isadora Duncan and Maud Allan got their starts.

This suffusion of modern dance in local community exploded its visibility between the 1920s and 1940s. By the 1930s, performances weren't just taking place at opera houses and commercial theatres but also schools, town halls, community centres, festival tents, social clubs, even union halls. Modern dancers routinely crossed over with other stages during this period, from Broadway to Hollywood. Interestingly, the movement's elbow-length distance from ballet shortened as the classical sphere started to embrace some of the dissonance and serrated themes that fuelled modern dance. In 1930 Graham and Sokolow appeared in the first American production of *Rite of Spring*, a revival of Vaslav Nijinsky's seminal 1913 piece made for the Ballets Russes. Graham even started referring to her own works as 'ballets', despite the cavernous gap between her cutting steps and the velvety pointe work of the classical stage.

This boomerang of terminology echoed the growing grip and scale of modern dance creations. While some dancemakers kept their stage designs minimal, emphasising the emotive capacity of physical movement on its own, others supported their storytelling with theatrical configurations of music, lighting, text, costumes and props. Ensemble performances gained significant traction, including plot-driven productions that represented a new rejoinder to big-ticket narrative ballets like *Swan Lake*. Graham's company was one of several prominent all-female troupes to charge the stage in the interwar years. Where the first generation had channelled female agency with solo performances – individuals dancing their individuality – their successors hailed the clout of the collective.

The focused training regimes of the Big Four's companies and schools bolstered the scene's sway. By the late 1930s, modern dance had staked its claim as a distinguished, thriving genre of dance. True to its name, the movement continued to echo the pulse of the decade, even as its roots grew deeper and reached further. 'I remember sitting on the lawn with students at Bennington College in the thirties talking about the "dance of the future",' Sophie Maslow reflected in her later years. 'We could feel life changing around us and new things happening in the arts, and we wanted to be part of that future.'[2] She and her peers were plugged into the world around them, stirred to use their art to experience it, celebrate it, learn from it, question it. They had their eyes on change, from broadscale social reform to the transformative potential of self-empowerment.

———

As the ashes of the First World War settled, a new fire blazed around women's political enfranchisement. Between 1917 and the mid-1920s, most of the Western world granted voting rights to women, with many countries also opening the door to public office – landmark legislation that signalled a new era of female empowerment. Women's suffrage is sometimes framed as the end goal of the early feminist movement, when really it was a fulcrum in an ongoing push to secure better rights, visibility and welfare for women. 'We're sick of being specialized to sex!' a speaker exclaimed at a 1914 town hall at Cooper Union in New York City, where several hundred men and women had gathered to debate what the term 'feminism' meant to them. 'We intend simply to be ourselves, not just our little female selves, but our whole, big, human selves.' That same year, a prominent editorial called 'The Revolt of the Woman' declared that 'feminism will succeed; and, when it does come to pass, the human race will attain for the first time its full efficiency'.[3] Both remarks aligned women's self-actualisation with their ability to participate fully in society. They prefigured what would eventually distinguish this discourse from the dialogue around the New Woman: the demand to enshrine women's newly asserted freedoms in both the public consciousness and the law.

Second-gen modern dancers heeded the call for mindfulness that fired up the feminists of the era, foregrounding personal narratives and soul-searching in their art to create booming social and political reverberations. 'Out of emotion comes form,' declared Martha Graham,[4] voicing a mantra that many of her contemporaries shared. They used the motivation behind a feeling to steer its external expression, striving to embody awareness, honesty and intent in every movement. This, they felt, was key to bringing the secrets of the unconscious into focus, shedding light on the human experience. Some carried the idea of consciousness into the content of their dances too, including Graham, who dedicated much of her repertoire to interrogating the psyche of women, from mythic heroines to the contemporary everywoman, bringing new weight to the sincerity of emotion and the individual experience.

Their efforts coincided with a tidal shift in the public's understanding of feminism as an umbrella movement for widespread change – a fight for women's right to vote, yes, but also their rights to work, study, organise, own property and keep their last names. While feminist marches and lobbying efforts waned in the early 1920s – especially in the United States, where post-war anxieties created new tensions between patriotism and protest – the volume surged on conversations around gender equality. Women's role in the war effort had highlighted the importance of being an engaged, active citizen, galvanising them to fight for full entry into all arenas of society: political, economic and social.

Slowly but steadily, debate evolved into reform. New professions, from lawyer to military officer, were legalised for women. Major international women's sporting events came into view, starting with the 1921 Women's Olympiad in Monaco. Reproductive care – including access to contraception and even abortion in some countries – became increasingly available in the 1920s and 1930s. Working rights were fiercely petitioned, resulting in new laws protecting pay, pensions and employment rights. Advocates for these changes didn't always identify as feminists, but they shared a desire to even women's legal and social footing.

The high-octane events of the day – war, fascism, economic depression – provided raw fuel for dancers driven by emotive expressionism and consciousness-raising. Many responded directly to these issues onstage, positioning it as a site for critique and protest, like Dai Ailian, who choreographed for Chinese benefit concerts in the 1930s and 1940s, including a fundraiser for China's War of Resistance against Japan; and Margaret Barr, who created a range of dance commentaries on poverty and social degradation in 1930s Britain. Democracy, class and labour rights came under intense scrutiny. Graham preferred epic themes over current events, but she too had works that set hot-button issues in their sights, including a series of dances lamenting the atrocities of the Spanish Civil War – a conflict that also inspired impassioned creations from Sophia Delza, Jane Dudley, Lily Mehlman and Sophie Maslow.

Minority visibility became another important animating force in the American modern dance scene, especially for Black dancers like Edna Guy, Hemsley Winfield, Charles Williams and Allison Burroughs, who spearheaded the country's first all-Black modern dance recitals, readying the scene for the increasing participation by and appreciation of Black artists in the movement, including the emergence of all-Black companies. Maslow racially integrated her troupe around this time, another move against the marginalisation of Black dancers, whose increasing visibility on the concert stage teed up the searing protest dances against racism that would come into their own in the mid-century.

The moderns in this era sought to heighten awareness of injustice as a first step in combatting it, with a focus on the role of personal reflection in widespread social change – a tack strikingly paralleled with the convictions of suffragists like Marie Jenney Howe, who insisted that 'feminism means more than a changed world. It means a changed psychology'.[5] Hanya Holm, for example, famously advocated for intensity and rawness: 'A work must have blood.'[6] Her words connect the idea of progress to something visceral, a force that starts from within. At the same time that technical standards were rising in modern dance, so was attention to purpose and mindfulness, an acknowledgement that an understanding of self – our convictions and capabilities, in body and soul – is the lifeblood of cultural reform.

———

While the Big Four and their colleagues spent the 1930s creating new through lines between modern dance and political consciousness, there was a faction of moderns working on the fringes to push their dancing into the realm of political action. Radicals like Margaret Barr, Edith Lambert and Fanya Geltman took to the streets with a collectivist dance ideal that swirled together professional performance and recreational participation, using this to amplify the protest cultures around them, especially leftist causes seeking justice for the working classes. Again, New York City came to the forefront as a hub for revolution, with American moderns taking up the torch Isadora Duncan tried to light during her 1922 tour through works like *La Marseillaise*, animating the plight of the struggling masses. Many of these revolutionaries operated outside of establishment channels, but they gained widespread recognition thanks to magazines like *New Theatre* and *Dance Observer*, which became crucial arenas for debate about the place of political ideology in dance.

Some of the biggest names in this leftist movement found a home in the New Dance Group (NDG), a woman-led collective formed by a band of Hanya Holm's students in 1932. They devised an incendiary slogan – 'Dance is a weapon' – and dedicated themselves to socially conscious choreography, performance and teaching that battled against ills like poverty, hunger and oppression. One of the NDG's first public appearances was a mass dance demonstration at the funeral of a union organiser murdered by the police – 'a manifestation of our willingness to enter the ranks of the working class revolutionary movement', as affiliate Nell Anyon put it.[7] Within a year, the organisation had more than three hundred members – changemakers alive to the power of solidarity.

The dancemakers among the NDG's ranks were guided by two rules: choose a subject close to your heart, and make sure it's intelligible to your audience. For those drawn to militant stances, the aesthetics and precision of their choreography were secondary to its messaging; others, particularly those with professional training, worked to embed high technical standards. NDG dancers performed their works at street rallies, including the May Day parades of the 1930s, along with summer camps, union halls and recreational events sponsored by labour organisations.

The unions became a key site for education too, with NDG reps leading affordable dance classes for workers and their children, often interwoven with discussions of social issues. The aim wasn't simply to present dance to workers but to get them dancing themselves – exercise, recreation, learning and mobilisation all at once. The folk singer Woody Guthrie, who got a taste of this conscientious approach to cultural exchange when he performed with Sophie Maslow and other NDG dancers in the early 1940s, highlighted its value in an article for *Dance Observer*: 'Make your audience see the factory full of people, and make the factory know the audience, and you got the world by the tail on a downhill pull.'[8]

Maslow was part of a bold bloc of moderns who performed with the Big Four while also producing their own choreography via the NDG, presenting short dances inspired by the uprisings of the era, from war elegies to social satires. In 1934, the NDG joined the Workers Dance League, an umbrella organisation of socially conscious dance factions that also took in Anna Sokolow's Dance Unit. Soon after, Helen Tamiris helped launch the Federal Dance Project, a jobs-creation vehicle for out-of-work dancers, including moderns, with divisions across New York, Chicago, Los Angeles and elsewhere. A product of Franklin D. Roosevelt's Works Progress Administration, the FDP had the dual purpose of bringing culture to the American public, thickening the web between modern dance and the world of politics and governance. Its dancemakers, like those of the NDG and WDL, used their art to rouse and empower performers and their audiences.

By centring consciousness and social critique in their practice, the second-generation moderns gave new shape to the political, physical and spiritual semblances of freedom. They reimagined the relationship between dance and society, harnessing their bodies as powerful tools for progress, and steered thousands of women – creators, performers, workers – into the political fray, encouraging them to become agents of change for a fairer world. One where they weren't excluded or discriminated against, where they could be seen as part of humanity and not subservient to it – people with rich inner lives and endless potential. Whether they were agitating on the streets or sprinting across the concert stage, these moderns unified their dancing selves into a voluble, persuasive body politic.

ACT 2, SCENE 1

The last frontier

New York City, 1926. Jazz, modernism and a thriving post-war economy thump in zippy syncopation. Steamers skim the Ellis Island saltwash; poets contemplate the miles to go before we sleep. A thirty-two-year-old dancer named Martha Graham follows the urban symphony to Midtown, where she rents a studio in Carnegie Hall – a site for high, hollow contractions, a cadre of women striding in long wool skirts. Graham is their North Star, guiding them through each new terrain. Fast-forward to the 1960s: she's still performing, a thin, black-haired spitfire in her seventies. Skip ahead to today, where next-generation disciples take up the mantle at her prestigious dance school, the oldest in America.

The late, great Martha Graham is the subject of books, exhibitions, dissertations and documentaries, and even has a special archive in the New York Public Library. Dancers around the world study her technique and admire her shelf of superlatives: 'Icon of the Century', 'High Priestess of Modern Dance'. Graham was the first dancer to perform at the White House, one of the first to tour as an emissary for the US State Department, and the first in history to receive America's Presidential Medal of Freedom. While it's difficult to pin down her raw artistry in words, it's equally hard to overstate her footprint. She transformed the alchemy of modern dance and twentieth-century culture with it.

The first works to come out of Graham's studio were coloured in shades of Denishawn, where she trained and performed from 1916 to 1923, studying dance, set design, costume-making and more. In her later years with the institute, she instructed at the school and toured with its resident company, priming her professional profile with an electric turn in 1920's *Xochitl*, a feathered Aztec routine cast in Denishawn's signature exotic mould. A similar mysticism tinted Graham's first concert of original work, in 1926, an exhibit of gold kimonos and Indian flutes, but she started deepening her palette with inky new hues as she navigated into a creator role.

Heretic, which Graham premiered at New York's Booth Theatre in 1929, was her breakout work as a choreographer – a cutting group routine performed to a Breton folk song. Graham appeared in white, surrounded by a sweep of twelve women in black, their arms crossed, legs parted. She approached; they huddled closer. She pressed in; they rebuffed her. The movement quality was dramatic and angular, especially Graham's: recordings show her bowing her head, breathing deeply and drawing one elbow back like an archer gauging a mark. The piece is just a few minutes long, a glimpse of a loner pleading against a great grey world. 'I think no other dance quite represented her personal statement with such power,' Bessie Schonberg, one of her early dancers, remembered.[1]

With its undertone of dread, *Heretic* introduced the pensive expressiveness that would become Graham's calling card. It invoked a powerful leitmotif of her wider portfolio: deep dives into the psyche of women. You see it in *Frontier* (1935), a tender portrait of a fearless pioneer; in *Deep Song* (1937), where she raged against the ravages of war; in *Hérodiade* (1944), which tracks a woman in the grip of suicide; in *Seraphic Dialogue* (1955), a meditation on Joan of Arc's warring impulses. Graham found inspiration in a vivid range of sources: religion, mythology, revolution, Americana. But her works were powered by feelings, not plots or locales – penetrating sentiments that push beyond their settings. She saw the mind as the last frontier and used dance to explore its deepest recesses.

Some of Graham's most powerful works have no setting at all. *Lamentation* (1930) fathoms the visceral grasp of grief, using diagonal lines and the stretchy fabric of a tubular shroud to reflect a tense push and pull against the wrenching idea of forever. The lone dancer isn't a person but the personification of grief itself. Graham performed the work seated, in front of a black backdrop, giving the sense of something wonderfully, terrifyingly boundless, unconstrained by time and space. The vibrating choreography reminds me of e. e. cummings's poems from the 1930s, with their slants and startling disruptions. Towards the end of her life, Graham compared dance to 'the rawness of dramatic poetry . . . it can be like a terrible revelation of meaning. Because when you light on a word it strikes to your heart'.[2] *Lamentation* has this lightning quality; it synthesises pain, consciousness and expressionism, shocking a static word into something with a pulse. She didn't want us to witness grief; she wanted us to feel it ourselves.

'Martha warned us of the dangers of big, romantic passions,' Dorothy Bird, a Graham company member in the 1930s, would later reflect. 'Out went all the small, delicate, sentimental themes and the last ripples of the Delsarte System . . . Along with this went the stories that can be told in words.'[3] In her memoir, *Blood Memory*, Graham invokes an Icelandic term, 'doom eager',[4] to describe a stoic apprehension of psychology in her art. To her mind, the feelings that menace us are the ones worth living for, and she worked to create a vocabulary for caving these depths – sorrow, devotion, dislocation; 'the memories of things we dread to remember, things we wish to forget'.[5]

Graham's intense, almost psychoanalytic approach to the introspective – epitomised in *Night Journey*, her 1947 interpretation of the Oedipus myth, known for its iconic 'vaginal cry' gesture – reflected the reigning influences of Sigmund Freud and Carl Jung in the first half of the twentieth century, theorists with pungent ideas about our inner landscapes. A great swathe of Graham's portfolio squares with the existential yelps in the Book of Lamentations, a source of inspiration for *Lamentation*: 'Is it nothing to you, all ye that pass by?'[6] She shared the same burning questions around being and becoming that plagued the philosophers of her generation, from Martin Heidegger and Hannah Arendt to Jean-Paul Sartre and Simone de Beauvoir.

Graham created 181 works in her lifetime, conceiving each in its entirety – concept, choreography, costumes – and performing in most. She had a formidable ear for music, intensified by a long-running friendship with her musical director, the composer Louis Horst, and often worked with musicians to create original scores for her dances. Her collaborators would remember how she held fast to distinctions between different instruments and their corporeal reverb. 'Your body does not feel the same when you dance to strings as when you dance to woodwinds,' she once wrote, for example. 'It simply cannot . . . There is a different thing which hits against your body. The wall of sound holds you in a certain way. You rest on that tone.'[7]

It's easy to evidence Graham's influence in numbers and accolades, but the crux of it reveals itself in more essentialist terms. She pushed the paradigm of dance to ask grave new questions about vulnerability and resilience, keeping pain at the forefront of her practice – sometimes vivaciously, sometimes reproachfully. She presented women as envoys of humanity, not marginal figures in a world fuelled by men. Her interrogations charted new hinterlands of expression and power, giving form to the elusive wisps of the female unconscious.

Halfway through my university dance degree, I took a course taught by a former Graham company member. For a semester she instilled in us the uncompromising mechanics of Graham technique – the contractions, with their hissing exhalations; the taut pelvic swivels and spinal torsions; the crisp, sweeping strides performed with one arm raised and cocked at the elbow. Our teacher expected us to live in these movements, guided by the possibilities of our breath – an act of discovery, not practice. It squared with Graham's assertion, to an interviewer in 1985, that she never set out to create a formal technique, only 'to find myself, to find what the body could do'.[8]

We learned that for all its precision, Graham technique guides; it doesn't prescribe. Graham used this line of thinking to distinguish her approach from those of her contemporaries, including Doris Humphrey, who 'felt that everything could be taught according to rules and diagrams. I had always felt it was a far deeper, more visceral thing . . . To Doris [the centre of the stage] was a geographic place in the middle of things. When I saw it I thought, "But the center of the stage is where I am."'[9]

That same semester, I performed in a restaging of 'Steps in the Street' for a departmental dance concert. The piece is the middle section of *Chronicle* – Graham's 1936 production about the civil unrest of the era – and zeroes in on the wreckage of the Great Depression and the Spanish Civil War. It's a conceptual telling of hard-edged subjects: hunger, homelessness, exile. A dozen women wander the stage, their stomachs caved, necks craned. They stagger, assemble, disband, a geometry that contracts and expands like sparrows anticipating a squall. The choreography grabs hold of Wallingford Riegger's percussive score with thrusting fists and drumming bare feet. In signature Graham fashion, a single dancer resists the crowd, feet planted while others leap around her in a nervy, blue-black panic.

Outside of the studio, I learned about Graham's background and the mile-markers on her journey. How she grew up in Allegheny, Pennsylvania, in the 1890s, a mining town silted in the ashes of industry and Protestant reserve. How attending a performance by Ruth St Denis at fourteen, after her family moved to California, set her on a course for life. How she loved strongly and deeply, leading to dusky decrees: 'Never try to hold on to anything.'[10] She wrote this after her marriage to fellow dancer Erick Hawkins collapsed, twisting her heartbreak into a terse mantra. It syncs with a wider fatalism coursing across her biography. 'I have spent all my life with dance and being a dancer. It's permitting life to use you in a very intense way,' she said in a documentary shortly before she died.[11] 'Sometimes it is not pleasant. Sometimes it is fearful. But nevertheless it is inevitable.' I learned that she passed away in 1991, after sixty-five years of creating, her final years weighed down by alcoholism and the heft of everything she'd achieved.

Graham's life spanned the twentieth century from start to almost finish, a witness to the groundswells of change that shook the world in that time: industrialisation, migration, fascism, globalism, modernism, whole theories and hierarchies cresting into existence. You can see an almost ontological preoccupation with time in the early pages of her memoir: 'Even as I write, time has begun to make today yesterday – the past. The most brilliant scientific discoveries will in time change and perhaps grow obsolete as new scientific manifestations emerge. But art is eternal, for it reveals the inner landscape, which is the soul of man.'[12] Elsewhere she'd spoken about 'inner time' and the abiding feelings shared by people past and present.[13] That sense of eternality surges across her dance portfolio, even the pieces anchored to specific periods and places, buoying them like a foamy white surf.

Graham's passion for the revelatory quality of art – exemplified in her hope 'that every dance I do reveals something of myself or some wonderful thing a human can be'[14] – was a fog light for piloting the murky waters of modernity, especially in her work from the 1930s and 1940s, decades unsteadied by corkscrewing economics and the threat of totalitarianism. The lifeblood of these works is intimate, but you can see a political tinge too – dance as an insight into the weight of human behaviour. From her abstract solos to her booming narrative productions, interiority is a spark for burning appraisals of violence, mourning, hope and persever-ance, the significance of individual resistance and the power of collective will.

A lot of what I've learned about Graham has come from books, including *Blood Memory*, which unveils her thoughts, memories and creative philosophies with the same lucidity she brought to the stage. There's some wonderful academic analysis from Mark Franko, a documentarian of the political *esprit* that invigorated modern dance in the 1930s; and Agnes de Mille, her dear friend, offers warm personal insights in her biography of Graham, includ-ing a now famous piece of counsel from the dancer in 1943, after de Mille expressed doubt in her own creative faculties: 'There is a vitality, a life force, an energy, a quickening that is translated through you into action, and because there is only one of you in all of time, this expression is unique . . . No artist is pleased. [There is] no satisfaction whatever at any time. There is only a queer divine dissatisfaction, a blessed unrest that keeps us marching and makes us more alive than the others.'[15]

For all their illumination, though, it was physically inhabiting Graham's choreography myself that put me closest in touch with her piercing energy, helping me understand the role of scars and curiosity and bone-deep urges in her work. The weight of our skirts as we staggered stage right in 'Steps', down-and-outs on the breadline; the arc of our spines as we pitched forwards in cadaverous symmetry – every moment was a whisper intimating that bodies have the power to say anything, become anything. Dancing it awakened me to the gifts of mobility and bodily autonomy, to the bittersweet tang of an unknowable world. Vaulting in my long black skirt, hands cupped to my chest, I knew that my private experiences keyed into something bigger.

Graham productions are fiercely safeguarded, and only official regisseurs are allowed to restage them. I didn't appreciate at the time what a privilege it was to participate in one myself. Her technique challenges you to marry taut gestures – a striking arm, a tightened diaphragm – with real-world tensions, especially your own inner conflicts. Two years after my 'Steps' performance, when I tried to trace a symmetry between existentialism and Graham-era modern dance in a grad school essay, I called on those moments onstage, my pelvis tucked and lungs gusting, to help me consider the corralling force of dread. How it penetrates different eras and value systems, how it drives you to places you never thought you'd go. It was a tall order to transcribe on paper what my body knew to be true.

The title of Graham's memoir comes from an excerpt attempting to explain 'those instinctive gestures and thoughts that come to us, with little preparation or expectation' – intuitions that hold a particular significance for a dancer 'with his intensification of life and his body'. She presents, coolly and plaintively, the idea of a 'blood memory' that we can trace back to our parents and their parents before them, '[from] a time when the world was chaotic, when, as the Bible says, the world was nothing. And then, as if some door opened slightly, there was light. It revealed certain wonderful things. It revealed terrifying things. But it was light.'[16] I felt this whenever I put my body in motion that semester – the improbable swerve of psychology and theatre that lets us inhabit our own selves more fully by channelling an abstraction. The startling, superb whoosh of your shadow rising to meet you.

————

Without Denishawn, there would have been no Martha Graham Company, though Graham's writing reveals some tension in this fact. In her book she admires co-founders Ted Shawn and Ruth St Denis's artistic talents but highlights their lack of confidence in her as a performer. 'The critics [from a 1921 tour] spoke of me as the only one in [the] company to dance with passion and excitement. This, of course, did not sit too well with either Miss Ruth or Ted. To them I was still a nincompoop.'[17] Graham called on this liveliness when she struck out on her own, steering her movement language away from the ornamental inclinations of her teachers and towards a blazing, highly personalised form of expressionism. 'All of her movements were meaningful,' Sophie Maslow would later recall. 'Martha gave everything imagery or a meaning to guide the quality of the movement, or we found a meaning for ourselves in everything.'[18]

Graham left Denishawn in 1923 and – following a three-year interlude of performances with the Greenwich Village Follies and teaching posts at New York arts schools – set up her own studio, recruiting some of her students to join her in performing her new work. A review of their first concert, in spring 1926, hints at her early commitment to intensity: 'Martha Graham presents a series of pictures that fire the imagination and make a hundred stories for every gesture. Shall we say her dances are motion pictures for the sophisticated.'[19] The next few years were furiously prolific, resulting in dozens of short solos and small ensemble works, each with its own studied concepts for lighting and costuming.

Graham embraced a stark, minimalist visage in these early years, stripping away the fanciful patterns and Eastern imagery of her Denishawn days and dressing her dancers in dark wool dresses that coarsened the lines of her fleet-footed choreography. She organised principles of movement around elemental human motions: breathing, stepping, reaching, twisting. Her dancing had none of Isadora Duncan's silkiness, but you can see a parallel faith in the substance of nature and gravity. Solos like *Lamentation* (1930) and *Ekstasis* (1933), danced in long tubes of jersey, and 1931's *Primitive Mysteries*, a linear group piece inspired by Native American ceremonial dances, made her synonymous with the image of a solemn, sinewy woman grasping at something profound.

Early audiences admired the intensity of this aesthetic but sometimes questioned its hard-bodiedness. In 1934, Lincoln Kirstein, an impresario with a dream to Americanise ballet, criticised Graham's focus on 'the stark, earth-ridden, gaunt, inward-eyed woman. It is not feminine since it has neither amplitude or richness ... Her jumps are jolts; her walks, limps and staggers; her runs, blind impulsive gallops; her bends, sways.'[20] Michel Fokine of the Ballets Russes had made a similar appraisal a few years before: 'The girls were flying and walking on flat feet. The arms would either hang limply or be raised with elbows turned outward ... This seems to be a cult not only of sadness but of ill humor, crossness.'[21]

Their discomfort illustrates one of the major subversions of Graham's art: rejecting the assumption that feminine equals gentle and smiling. '[My earliest students] came to me with conventional notions of prettiness and graceful posturing,' Graham writes in her memoir. 'I wanted them to admire strength. If I could give them only one thing, that would be it. Ugliness, I told them, if given a powerful voice, can be beautiful.'[22] Her revision of beauty to emphasise effort rather than downplay it syncs with an ideal that stirred the first free dancers to break away from ballet. It also reflects a certain faith in the power of intent – that honest resolve is the path to authenticity, that 'movement never lies', as she was fond of saying.[23]

In *Blood Memory*, Graham takes a good-humoured view of her 'long woolen dances of revolt', like *Ekstasis*: 'looking back at them, they were pretty revolting. But I was really casting off Denishawn and its veils and exoticism with a vengeance, as most children do when they leave home.'[24] Despite her apparent disavowal, she kept many of these dances in her repertoire; they were as popular as they were challenging, prompting sold-out audiences throughout the 1930s and high praise from critics in thrall to her new direction of modern dance, especially the simmering tension she could build into a single action. To her amusement, Graham's studio took on a nickname in consonance with her weighty repute: 'House of the Pelvic Truth.'[25]

By the time her company turned ten, she'd created more than sixty dances that ranged from tragic to erotic to rosy. For his part, Kirstein soon became a fan, friend and mentor, thanks in part to their crossover at Bennington College throughout the 1930s, where Graham incubated some of her masterworks, including 1938's *American Document* – 'the most important extended dance creation by a living American', in Kirstein's estimation.[26]

Like many artists in the interwar years, including the modernists and the cubists, Graham embraced layered, unexpected forms and themes to explore the complexities of personhood in the modern age. 'Life today is nervous, sharp and zigzag,' she said in 1929. 'It often stops in mid-air. That is what I aim for in my dances.'[27] Her early company members hugely admired this discernment and the way she drafted the wider social mood – especially the anguish surrounding the Great Depression – into the very shapes and rhythms of her choreography.

In 1935, Graham debuted the first in a celebrated series of dances that harnessed Americana to pose questions around her nation's evolving identity. *Frontier* imagines a pioneer revelling in the magnitude of America's wilderness, an image inspired by the Graham family's move to the West Coast in her teens. 'Tracks in front of me, how they gleamed whether we went straight ahead or through a newly carved-out mountain,' Graham wrote of the train journey to California. 'Parallel lines whose meaning was inexhaustible, whose purpose was infinite.'[28]

She dressed herself in pink gingham, a ribbon tying back her hair, and swung her arms to a jubilant tailspin of drums and woodwinds. Beaming, she grasped onto a metal railing, part of a spare, spacious design by the sculptor Isamu Noguchi, who'd go on to create dozens of sets for the Graham company over the next fifty years. She pulsed her legs, hinging into the horizon. It was a sunlit collision of the intimate and the historical, the hope of one soul poised against a vast, rugged landscape – individualism as America loves to imagine it. When First Lady Eleanor Roosevelt invited Graham to dance at the White House in 1937, *Frontier* was one of four solos she performed.

In recordings of *Frontier*, you can see the capstone of Graham's technique at work: 'contraction and release', a stylised form of breathing that invokes principles of tension and relaxation. Picture a dancer inhaling, pulling in her spine, then releasing it to send a rhythmic flow of energy outwards. Graham called the spine the body's 'tree of life' – a wellspring for action and emotion, from ecstasy to agony. In *Frontier*, contractions are used to paint a portrait of joy and capability. In *Lamentation*, they arrest the body, a tension that never gets released.

Graham evolved her syllabus to include powerful jumps, strides and falls to the floor. Her classroom exercises often surged with contrast: sharpness paired with fluidity, a juxtaposition the photographer Barbara Morgan captured in a stunning 1940 action shot of Graham pitched forward, her left leg kicking her skirt into a lustrous crescent, her right wrist pressed to her forehead. It encapsulates in a single frame a former student's words about the burning quality of her technique: 'It wasn't cool, it was hot. And it was stripped of any ornamentation; it was like a knife cutting each time. It was stunning. It had an enormous use of space; just the body being flung into space.'[29]

Graham rarely allied herself with specific social orders or political factions, but she did use her work to contemplate power dynamics, including the plight of misunderstood women and the might of those who resist the masses. Her dances from the 1930s and 1940s – from the pelvic thrust of *Ekstasis* to the open-body contractions of *Night Journey* – were tied up in new articulations of anatomy, part of an ongoing discovery that 'each part [of the body] is in its own way dramatic'.[30] There's a tenor of progressivism to her confidence in the individual woman. Just as a single limb can redirect a story onstage, a single voice can champion change on the street, she felt.

This framing found an extra resonance against the rattle of women-led activism that unfolded during her career, especially in its first few decades. Graham became a dancemaker just a few years after American women secured the right to vote, and rose to national prominence right as they stepped into Washington for the first time. In New York City, labour organisers like Rose Schneiderman, Florence Kelley and Frances Perkins brought an unseen energy to the fight for workers' protections. By the 1930s, the social clubs founded by Eleanor Roosevelt's generation had evolved into something with a grittier purpose, leading the charge to improve social welfare for the downtrodden. Though she maintained that she was 'interested in human rights, not politics',[31] Graham was a resounding voice among a pioneering band of women imagining a fairer world in the interwar years.

She didn't take up arms in the workers' movement that gripped some of her fellow moderns in the 1930s, but in 1936 she publicly refused Joseph Goebbels's invitation to participate in the arts competition of the Berlin Olympics – a statement that would forever tie her to the protest scene. 'I would find it impossible to dance in Germany at the present time,' she stated, using her platform to denounce the Nazi regime and declare solidarity with Jewish people around the world, including her own Jewish company members. 'So many artists whom I respect and admire have been persecuted, have been deprived of the right to work for ridiculous and unsatisfactory reasons, that I should consider it impossible to identify myself, by accepting the invitation, with the regime that has made such things possible.' The following year she testified before the American Committee for Anti-Nazi Literature, urging artists to join her in resisting fascism. 'After the war . . . I was found on a list of those to be "taken care of" when Germany controlled the United States,' she noted in her memoir. 'I took it as a great compliment.'[32]

Graham premiered *Chronicle* a few months after her 1936 statement, an artistic comment on the totalitarianism that perturbed her. *American Document*, a patriotic tribute with a pro-democracy message, came in 1938, swirling folk songs, heritage imagery and excerpts from the *Declaration of Independence* and *Emancipation Proclamation* to celebrate the great American melting pot – a 'Joyceian [*sic*] manifestation of this land, this people whose history began, one stormy day with Plymouth Rock', as *Dance Observer* put it.[33]

While *American Document* takes a more political tone than *Frontier*, and is more world-facing with its pinwheels of red, white and blue satin, both epitomised a directive Graham would take up during the bracing years of the Second World War: the use of modern dance to 'bring forth an art as powerful as America itself'.[34] The latter was a staple of the US State Department tours

Graham made between the 1950s and 1980s, aimed at broadcasting American ideals of freedom and individualism abroad. Fittingly, it was part of the suite of works she showed when she did eventually visit a barbed-wired Berlin, in 1987, just a few months before President Ronald Reagan's 'Tear down this wall!' plea.

American Document's 1938 premiere marked the first appearance by a man in the Graham company. Erick Hawkins, whom Graham married in 1948, was number one in what would become a long line of distinguished male Graham dancers, including Merce Cunningham, Paul Taylor and Robert Cohan. Their incorporation led to stretched, fortified representations of sexual relationships across her growing repertoire, spurring works like *Every Soul is a Circus* (1939) and *Letter to the World* (1940), each of which features a romantic duet as part of a delve into the competing sides of one woman's personality. It also spurred her to expand her technical vocabulary to accommodate lifts and new conceptions of strength and speed. 'The arms came into greater play, and the movements had more flow,' company member Jean Erdman remembered in later years. 'But never, never, was that powerful center lost; that meaning of her vision. When [Martha] choreographed *Letter to the World*, what it meant to dance as a female came into the creating and performing of the work.'35

A growing political consciousness rippled through Graham's portfolio in the years after the Berlin Olympics. *Deep Song* (1937) joined *Chronicle* in lamenting the Spanish Civil War; *Immediate Tragedy* (1937) and *Errand into the Maze* (1947) probed the strength of the determined individual; *Appalachian Spring* (1944) celebrated the optimism of the American character. A vivid allegorical production danced to a Pulitzer-winning score by Aaron Copland, *Appalachian Spring* became one of Graham's best-loved works. Here she imagined herself as an eighteenth-century bride whose convictions are tested by the hardships of life in the Pennsylvania backwoods. Like *Frontier*, it had a fetching period setting that lent tenderness and verve to the idea of an unshakeable American spirit.

In keeping with her wider portfolio, ingenuity and intuition came into the characterisation of *Appalachian Spring*'s protagonist and her relationships with the figures around her. 'It wasn't a question of knowing her technique, but rather being able to sense what role of compassion I was to play based upon her role,' May O'Donnell, who danced the original Pioneer Woman opposite Graham's Bride, once said. 'Martha never explained things, you had to create from your own imagination . . . It was a psychological relationship.'[36] As Mark Ryder, a Graham dancer in the 1940s, put it: 'She not only used our bodies, she also used our inner lives, she co-opted our souls.'[37]

To me, this union of outer and inner landscape was Graham's biggest political flex, bigger than the pro-American ideals she disseminated with state support. In casting herself as women from fiction, history, religion, mythology, from her own mind and the minds of others – unnamed housewives and revolutionaries, Emily Dickinson, Joan of Arc, Clytemnestra, Jocasta, Medea, Emily Brontë – she expressed the private frictions and endeavours that keep the world turning. In *Appalachian Spring*, the struggle was uncharted territory; in *American Provincials* it was a strain between independence and puritanism, individuality and conformity. *Deaths and Entrances* (1943) considered impulses that defy tradition; *Cave of the Heart* (1946) confronted the vicious power of love. Women journeying to the ends of the earth for their passions, finding strength in dark corners, shaping their own providence.

Graham illuminated these power struggles in an age of changing political structures, shining light on the individuals at the crux of ideologies like democracy and freedom. She challenged the idea that women had to look, feel or act a certain way to make their stamp on the world. It was a call to arms in its very essence. As the critic John Martin described in a 1936 review: 'the vividness and intensity of her purpose are so potent that on the rise of the curtain they strike like a blow, and in that moment one must decide whether he is for or against her.'[38]

––––––

The web of celebrity Graham wove throughout her career was huge and intricate. She collaborated with artists, actors, fashion designers and composers, from Calvin Klein to Samuel Barber. For five years she worked with the photographer Soichi Sunami, and in the mid-1930s she struck up a long-running relationship with the artist Alexander Calder, who joined Isamu Noguchi in providing exquisite stage designs for her productions. Graham credited her collaborators with helping her get her art into the world, particularly Louis Horst. 'His sympathy and understanding, but primarily his faith, gave me a landscape to move in,' she said when he died in 1964. 'Without it, I should certainly have been lost.'[39]

As her prominence rose, she enticed a starry list of fellow performers into her sphere. Some of the twentieth century's famed classical dancers performed in Graham's work at one point or another – including Margot Fonteyn, Rudolf Nureyev and Mikhail Baryshnikov – while Hollywood icons like Bette Davis, Kirk Douglas and Gregory Peck headed to her studio for her commended lessons in movement and expression.

Some of Graham's most powerful relationships were with her students. Many of the dancers from her early fleet went on to evolve her principles into vibrant practices of their own, including Anna Sokolow, Bonnie Bird, Sophie Maslow, May O'Donnell, Jane Dudley and Pearl Lang. She also had an impact on leaders of other dance spheres in the mid-century, like Bethsabée de Rothschild, who founded Batsheva Dance Company in Israel in 1964, appointing

Graham as her artistic consultant; and Twyla Tharp, who studied with Graham in her twenties and went on to pioneer a salient crossover between ballet and modern dance.

Graham continued teaching throughout her career, at her own school and institutions like Bennington College and the Neighborhood Playhouse, showing hundreds of students the power of the pelvic tilt, coaching them for performances as well as dancemaking themselves − a legacy that revved along the modern dance scene and hugely progressed its institutional structures. Her early company was one of the world's first all-female troupes to grab the world's attention, and when she did welcome men, she used their presence to deepen rather than distract from her focus on female interiority.

Amid the gushing reviews and the many mentions of genius, as well as the establishment's conviction that Graham herself 'was modern dance', it's easy to forget that she wasn't immune to human folly or scrappiness. I love this anecdote from a performance with Ted Shawn in her final year at Denishawn:

> *At one point he grabbed me and dropped me on my head and I passed out for a few seconds. When I came to I bit him on his arm and drew blood. After I did that he ran from one side of the stage to the other, front and back, dripping blood. And it became a great scandal in the school. I suppose that is when my reputation for having a violent temper began.*
>
> *I was savage at that time. The critics said that onstage I blazed, and that is still my favorite review after all these years. I would do anything to be onstage . . . I was almost like an animal in my movements. I wanted to be a wild, beautiful creature, maybe of another world − but very, very wild.* [40]

The story illustrates Graham's heated artistry better than soubriquets like the 'Picasso of Dance' ever could. The same goes for the

parodies that followed her around, led by cartoonists and drag artists who exaggerated her into a gaunt, grim harpy, underscoring her
sway as a disruptor. In 1934, *Vanity Fair* published a caricature of
Graham next to the burlesque dancer Sally Rand, painting Graham
as a Munch-like ghoul lurking next to a resplendent, near-naked
vixen. A satirical script follows that imagines Graham 'haughtily'
telling Rand that she should cover up and learn to bare her soul
instead.[41] The message is clear: serious women are dreary and
unsexy. They should lighten up. Like Graham's Denishawn anecdote, it comes full circle to her own link between what threatens us
and what motivates us – the 'blessed unrest that . . . makes us more
alive than the others'.[42]

Despite, or maybe because of, these lampoons, Graham occasionally took aim at her own pedestal, showing an arch sense of
self-awareness. In 1932, she donned a long, striped dress for *Satyric
Festival Song*, a solo inspired by clowns who dare to mock the sacro-
sanct; and *Maple Leaf Rag*, a 1990 work set to a jaunty medley of
Scott Joplin's ragtime tunes, lovingly spoofed some of her signature
moves. *Maple Leaf Rag* was her final creation, completed at the age
of ninety-six, just a few months before she died – a joyous exclam-
ation point on a long, studious career.

In 1986, Andy Warhol produced a trio of technicolour screen
prints that vivified photos of Graham from *Lamentation*, *Satyric
Festival Song* and *Letter to the World*, affirming her status as an
American icon. Though she'd toured her work abroad widely, starting in Paris in the 1940s, and had experienced a mostly positive
reception to these international performances – including the
dozens she delivered during her US State Department tours, when
she performed for presidents in nearly thirty countries – her celebrity made its biggest splash on home soil. 'My interest was not in
Europe, and in some curious way, I feared it,' she later wrote of her

first tour, characterising her wariness as a portent to the early knee injury she suffered.[43] Fellow Americans Isadora Duncan and Loie Fuller had popularised modern dance on the Continent, and in fact had to go to Europe to have their work sanctioned as capital-A art, but Graham's reign shifted its nerve centre to the United States.

New York City, present day. Party girls hunt for the secret bars on St Mark's Place; dreamers still swim in visions of Broadway. Follow the city lights to the West Village, where a twenty-strong Graham company pairs back-catalogue classics with new commissions from external choreographers. Its résumé now includes appearances at iconic international venues: the Metropolitan Opera, the Acropolis, even the Egyptian pyramids. Past the mass of legacy, somewhere in its hollows, is a carmine flame rippling in the black.

'Where do I get my inspiration from?' Graham wrote in *Blood Memory*. 'Mostly from the excitement of living. I get it from the diversity of a tree or the ripple of the sea, a bit of poetry, the sighting of a dolphin breaking the still water and moving toward me . . . anything that quickens you to the instant . . . I love the idea of life pulsing through people – blood and movement.'[44] The company looks different today, more global, more athletic, but the psychological force of its founder carries on, the wild spirit of a woman running to greet the wind.

Isadora Duncan
in Edenic repose,
c.1917.

Studio portrait
of Duncan in her
London days,
c.1906–12.

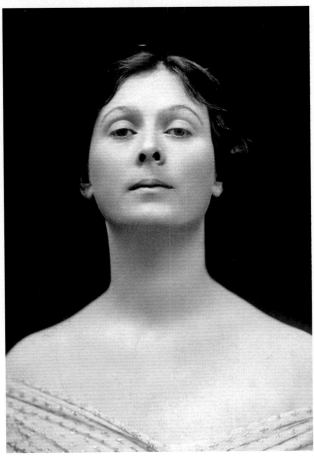

Loie Fuller conjuring a butterfly with a sweep of her wingspan, 1902.
Watercolour painting of Fuller in her 'Archangel' routine, 1902.

No. 518,347.   Patented Apr. 17, 1894.

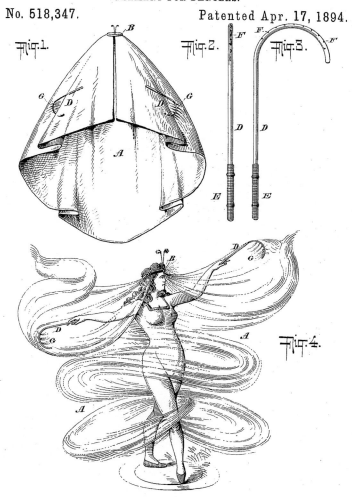

WITNESSES:

Gustave Dieterich.

H. B. Brownell.

INVENTOR

Marie Louise Fuller.

BY

R. C. Mitchell

ATTORNEY.

Patented design for a theatrical dancing garment by Fuller with
specifications for wands, a skirt and a crown, 1894.

Maud Allan as the sinuous Salome, *c.*1923.

Anna Sokolow instructing at a dance company in New South Wales, Australia, 1976.

Martha Graham in *Letter to the World*, dedicated to the poet Emily Dickinson, 1940.
Graham surrounded by her early company in her breakout work, *Heretic*, c.1929.

An ecstatic utterance from Pearl Lang, pictured at age 50, in 1971.

(*left*) Lang and Robert Cohan as the Couple in Red in
Martha Graham's *Diversion of Angels*, c.1954.

(*right*) Pearl Primus swinging low in *Hard Time Blues*, a critique
of sharecropping in the American South, 1943.

Primus striking one of her famous five-foot-high leaps for *Strange Fruit*, 1951.

Sultry cigarette smoke from Katherine Dunham in 'Le Jazz Hot', 1939.

An outflung Sophie Maslow in 'On Top of Old Smokey', from *Folksay*, 1942.

ACT 2, SCENE 2

The rebel with discipline

'I always danced from what I felt,' Anna Sokolow reflected during an interview that took place shortly before she died in 2000[1] – a simple distillation of a career defined by soulful plunges into justice, integrity and the merits of collectivism. Sokolow had form for humble reflections on her work, telling the press that dance was her preferred method of communication, not words. Her straight-shooting draws a neat line under the intimacy of her art, which traded in real-life concerns, not distant abstractions. Her choreography was emotionally driven and politically conscious, offering a humanist take on the conflicts in the world around her, from industrial exploitation to antisemitism. She blended poignant themes and simple everyday movements in her dancing to create a sturdy new idiom for challenging social inequality and drawing in marginalised voices.

America's union movement of the 1930s was a huge artistic stimulus in the early days of Sokolow's career, which geared up in New York City in 1929, when she started a nine-year stint as a dancer with Martha Graham's new company. Mass unemployment among industrial workers – an aftershock of the 1929 US stock market collapse – had American cities rumbling with appeals for labour reform, with hordes of artists joining the protest. Sokolow was stirred to join fellow fledgling moderns like Sophie Maslow and Helen Tamiris in a new kind of dancemaking that accentuated the issues of the picket line. She had an inside view of the union movement through her mother, Sarah, an organiser for the

International Ladies Garment Workers Union (ILGWU), one of America's first women-led unions. Sarah was the family's bread-winner, and in between factory shifts took her children to union strikes and Workmen's Circle dances, introducing them to a heady swirl of art and social activism.

Under the umbrella of the Workers Dance League (WDL), a leftist outfit formed in the early 1930s to promote dance as a force for social change, Sokolow started creating original solos that she performed at union meetings, animating the roots of her work-ing-class identity. The WDL, later renamed the New Dance League, sponsored concerts, demonstrations and debates, its members gal-vanised by the possibilities of dance as a megaphone for political expression. 'The unions were really my first audience,' as Sokolow put it, describing how 'poets or writers would read their work [while] singers and dancers would perform in their halls'.[2]

In 1933, she created her first group work, *Anti-War Trilogy*, which she and her colleagues performed at the First Anti-War Congress, an event sponsored by the American League Against War and Fascism. The production rallied motifs around unrest, diplomacy and protest, its dancers lunging and pivoting in taut assembly. It was a prototype of the allusive choreography that would come to typify Sokolow's career – winding, deeply felt compositions that didn't need linear narratives to ignite a story.

Anti-War Trilogy was the inaugural work of the Dance Unit, a small troupe Sokolow assembled to perform what she called 'revo-lutionary' dances[3] at labour unions and other sites of activism in the 1930s, including the historic Young Men's Hebrew Association at 92nd Street. She was just twenty-three – one of the youngest American choreographers to lead her own company – and doing all this in parallel to her Graham work, where she performed in early masterpieces like 1931's *Primitive Mysteries*. Many of her early company members were fellow working-class Jewish women pursuing a professional career in dance – a dynamic that distinguished the Dance Unit from the recreational troupes and agitprop collectives the WDL also marshalled.

Most of the early choreography Sokolow created with the Dance Unit critiqued pressing current events. There was *Strange American Funeral* (1935), which condemned the workplace safety standards responsible for killing scores of miners and steelworkers; *Inquisition '36* (1936) and *Slaughter of the Innocents* (1937), comments on the suffering caused by war; *The Exile* (1939), a dramatic censure of the terrors of Nazism. These weren't just artistic meditations but rallying cries for reform. By 1936 the Dance Unit was holding evening-long concerts of original work; the following year the company made its Broadway debut.

Sokolow's focus on social justice gripped audiences and her fellow modern dancers. She disseminated her messages on concert stages around New York City, along with festivals, meetings, rallies and fundraising concerts, steadily ascending to national, then international, prominence. Sokolow was the first American modern dancer to have her work presented on national television, and one of the first choreographers of any style, anywhere, to create a dance response to the Holocaust. She initiated modern dance scenes in Mexico and Israel, and became a fixture at the prestigious Juilliard School. She also brought jazz music to the modern dance stage, using it to reflect a new stratum of the American soul. Her output amounted to hundreds of dance works between the 1930s and 1990s – many dedicated to icons of progress like Anne Frank and Martin Luther King Jr – plus choreography for plays, operas and musicals.

The 1930s protest culture that ignited Sokolow's career continued to infuse it decades later. *Time+* (1966), for example, invoked camouflage and limbic staggering to denounce the Vietnam War.

Even her more lyrical, less hard-line works tapped into the counter-culture of their time. *Lyric Suite* (1953) had its stateside premiere in a concert by the New Dance Group (NDG), the left-wing faction dedicated to bringing politically charged dance to the masses. *Rooms*, Sokolow's 1955 meditation on urban loneliness, also had ties to the NDG: she cast it with nine affiliates of the group, eventually organising them into a new independent company.

Whether she was giving dance demos in union halls or producing rock ballets for the Joffrey, Sokolow's work was searing and sincere, wrestling towering ideologies into legible missives that invited audiences to stomp along with their thunder. The WDL infused dance with fiery purpose, but I think Sokolow sometimes treated it more like a balm, creating earnest, affecting works that moved beyond agitation into something inspired by reciprocity and acknowledgement. 'I felt a deep social sense about what I wanted to express, and the things that affected me deeply personally [are] what I did, and commented on,' as she explained it, underscoring the human perspective she brought to even her most polemic works.[4] She advocated for the individuals at the heart of the collective – the marginalised, the disaffected, the 'weak and hungry faces' the labour poet Ruth Lechner lamented in the 1930s, 'gaunt and streaked / With lines of rain'.[5] Her work was a powerful revolt against complacency, a witness to the rumbling turbulence of the time.

———

When Samuel Sokolowski left the stony streets of Pinsk, Belarus, for America in 1905, he stepped into a nation alight with the promise of investment and industry. His wife and young son emigrated shortly after, joining him in Hartford, Connecticut, where the Sokolowskis welcomed three additional children, including Anna in 1910. In 1912 the family relocated to Manhattan's Lower

East Side, a lodestone for Eastern European immigrants at the turn of the century. In a 1974 interview, Sokolow references Jacob Epstein's early 1900s drawings of the neighbourhood to explain its chaotic energy – mothers ushering unruly children, garment workers bent in concentration, pushcart vendors hawking merchandise past the Grand Street tenements.[6] Narrow streets tapering towards the broad yawn of the synagogue; ambition and opportunity and hardship jostling for position.

Sokolow's family settled in St Mark's Place, close to the charity hospital where her father was treated for Parkinson's disease and just a few blocks from the Yiddish theatre she attended every Sunday with her mother, the site of playlets dramatising the terrors of the pogrom. Around the corner was the Emanu-El Sisterhood of Personal Service, a local settlement house where a ten-year-old Sokolow went after school every day to take free classes in pottery, drama and movement.

She excelled in her dance classes, interpretive forays taught by Isadora Duncan enthusiasts, and left school at fifteen to join the Neighborhood Playhouse, an off-Broadway venue offering study under various emerging giants in New York's modern dance scene, including Blanche Talmud, Bird Larson and Martha Graham. The school – an offshoot of the bustling Henry Street Settlement – also offered lessons in composition, pantomime and the Delsarte movement system. Sokolow danced with the Playhouse's resident youth company while supporting herself with factory gigs and other odd jobs, including a part-time role assisting Louis Horst with dance composition classes.

Impressed by Sokolow's initiative, Martha Graham invited her to join her company in late 1929, just three years into its formation. For the next nine years, Sokolow was part of the vibrant fleet of dancers – which also included Sophie Maslow, Jane Dudley,

Bonnie Bird and May O'Donnell – that introduced the world to Graham's striking brand of modern dance. 'It was staggering,' Sokolow reflected in 1974. 'I just knew I was in the presence of something great.'[7] She originated roles in several key productions, including 1931's *Primitive Mysteries*, and reviews from her time with the company, especially when she became a soloist, highlight her technical proficiencies and compelling sense of drama.

A 'remarkable person with an amazing capacity for work', in the words of one of her early students,[8] Sokolow continued to take factory shifts between rehearsals, and began her own choreographic pursuits on the side, reworking elements of her Graham training into something chiselled and gracile. She even spent three months performing and lecturing in Moscow, where she sharpened her ideas around the possibilities of revolutionary dance. In 1937 she secured one of the first fellowships from the Bennington School of the Dance, where she continued to assist Louis Horst, learning how to set musical tones and rhythms against the themes and structures of dance choreography.

'I feel that Louis Horst is not mentioned frequently enough as an influence in modern dance choreography,' she'd later reflect, emphasising how the composer's mentorship enlightened her to her deep love of music and its pivotal role in her artistic ambitions: 'The great lesson from Louis was the search within oneself. Who am I and what do I want to do.'[9]

It's unclear whether Sokolow or Graham instigated her exit from the Graham company in 1938. As Sokolow described it to an interviewer: 'I was in her group until she decided that I wasn't "right". Then I left and went my own way.'[10] She'd later say that she didn't have 'the temperament of a disciple', suggesting some hesitation with Graham's style of leadership.[11] There's little on record from Graham on the subject, but an early passage in her memoir admires Sokolow as a 'remarkable' dancer, recalling how she 'was filled with the desire to dance, to move, to create, to enter new areas of life. Her mother did not approve. She wanted her to earn money, and dance kept her away from this, away from the sweatshop. But Anna kept doing both because she was filled with it . . . She danced with me at night, and worked in the sweatshop during the day.'[12]

In any case, Sokolow left the company with a solid body of training, a decent critical profile and a positive view of Graham's mentorship: 'Martha showed me the path I needed to follow. I was schooled and disciplined in her technique, but that was not my main interest, and, after that, although her influence will never leave me, I found my own way.'[13]

Thanks to all her extracurricular groundwork, Sokolow had a robust footing as an independent artist. The increasingly influential Popular Front, with its anti-war, anti-capitalist agenda, was fuelling new appetites for left-wing politics in the arts; the Dance Unit had, by this point, performed at an impressive range of venues, including Carnegie Hall. Sokolow participated in several political spectaculars the year she stepped away from the Graham company, including a dance pageant for the Communist Party's 1938 Lenin Memorial Meeting and a Negro Cultural Committee revue called *The Bourbons Got the Blues*. The dance sequences she choreographed for *Sing for Your Supper*, a 1939 government-sponsored variety show, received special acclaim for their anti-capitalist bite.

As a first-generation Graham dancer, Sokolow was attuned to the merits of a formal technique, but she declined to devise her own defined movement system as her profile expanded with new collaborations and dance studies. Instead, she called on the range of training she had and continued to undertake, from the Stanislavsky method of acting she'd learned in Moscow to her stints under Margaret Curtis at the Metropolitan Opera Ballet School and Muriel Stuart at the School of American Ballet, harnessing the individual aspects that stirred her. '[Sokolow] had a constant fund of concepts at her fingertips,' fellow Graham alumna Dorothy Bird remembered. 'Anna provided movements that were dissonant, strange, unbalanced, rhythmical, and spatially interesting.'[14]

In recordings of Sokolow's work, you can see a pedestrian simplicity to a lot of her gestures, but they're never mimetic, more like a dream version of something you might see in everyday life. She often used a single action – a hand reaching out to touch, a wriggling foot, a pensive, faraway gaze – as the starting point for a phrase, slowly intensifying it until it lapsed into something explosive. In 1969, she highlighted to an interviewer her 'particular sensitivity to the hands and neck', noting: 'The body has to have a central point that all organic movement comes out of . . . The nuances, the colors, the moods of the head are possible only if you are aware of the neck.'[15]

While her tack was more sociological than psychological, Sokolow shared Graham's fascination with motivation and the links between inner feeling and physical movement. She was renowned for stretching her 4-foot 11-inch frame into something towering, pushing past smoothness and precision into dicier, more poignant territory. 'No student could get away with decorativeness or the unpondered gesture,' Deborah Jowitt observed in her 2000 obituary for Sokolow in the *Village Voice*. 'Movement had to come from the gut. Audiences didn't leave her concerts smiling; they left stirred, altered, shaken awake.'[16] Sokolow carried this emotive focus throughout her career, even as mid-century innovators like Merce Cunningham brought cool, calculated abstractions into fashion. In 1976, she reiterated to the press her commitment to dance as 'a language to communicate feelings', emphasising, 'I never lie. It's my sense of justice.'[17]

Sokolow's innovations to modern dance didn't stop at form or content. She started the Dance Unit in sync with a wider movement to bring moving, high-quality performing arts to circles that were normally excluded from serious theatre. While other dancers in the union halls built new opportunities for grassroots participation among labourers, Sokolow carved out a space for professional dancers to bring their political passions to the stage – 'Entertainment as well as an attack on the ruling class,' as John Martin put it in 1934, referencing her 'devastating' wit in solos like *Histrionics* and *Romantic Dances*, which scorned the insincerity of the dance hall.[18]

A majority-female outfit for most of its duration, the Dance Unit showed the potential for bodies to transcend lines of class and gender in search of a higher humanitarian purpose – to dabble in spheres of debate that usually play out in wood-panelled rooms. There's a striking parallel here with Sokolow's own path as an artist, which rejected the usual arrangement of Eastern European Jewish families, in which women supported the family financially while the men pursued scholastics. Sokolow, aware (in her biographer Larry Warren's words) that 'the living sparks produced in the choreographer–dancer relationship may last the dancer for a lifetime'.[19] shaped her studio into a site of integrity and resolve, a catalyst for heightened awareness in both audiences and dancers themselves. She amplified crucial political issues in the themes of her productions while reworking traditional power structures in their very creation and presentation.

In 1939, the Guatemalan-born painter Carlos Mérida attended a Dance Unit concert in New York City and was moved to invite the company to Mexico City, where jolts of government funding were supercharging a radical arts scene in the wake of the Mexican Revolution. Mérida was the former director of the dance department at the Instituto Nacional de Bellas Artes (INBA) and saw potential for Sokolow's spirited dance to help spur on the cause. Sokolow headed to Mexico City with eleven of her dancers and her then partner Alex North, a composer who scored many of her works, and gave two dozen performances of repertory work at the Bellas Artes Opera House. It was the start of a long affiliation with Mexico that hugely propelled her soul-searching course of artistry. 'You can learn more about art there than here,' she'd later say. 'It's just in the air and in the people themselves.'[20]

For the next eight years, Sokolow spent several months of each year in Mexico, first creating dances for INBA's students and later working with the Mexican Ministry of Fine Arts to establish a state-sponsored modern dance company – a troupe that eventually evolved into the National Academy of Dance. Ever the workhorse, she also founded a local interdisciplinary outfit called La Paloma Azul (The Blue Dove), drawing together musicians, painters and dancers. 'For the first time in my life, I knew what it felt like to be an artist,'[21] she said, emphasising her kinship with the community that had produced giants like Diego Rivera and Frida Kahlo. Many of her pieces from this period looked to ethnic motifs to reflect changing ideas around Mexico's national identity: 1940's *The Wandering Frog*, for example, dug into indigenous folklore, while 1941's *Lament for the Death of a Bullfighter* considered colonial Spanish customs. 'The Mexicans, with whom I have worked for so many years, call me "the rebel with discipline",' she'd later state. 'I could not be more pleased with any description of myself than that.'[22]

Sokolow's residencies in Mexico prompted a deep probe of her own roots, spurring her to create a series of prominent dances about Judaism in the mid-1940s. A spectre of fear loomed over New York's Jewish community as news of Hitler's atrocities turned from speculation to fact. Hebrew schools fielded distressed families; European refugees were funnelled into makeshift yeshivas. Against this backdrop Sokolow found inspiration for dance about persecution and resilience, including 1943's *Songs of a Semite*, which relayed poems by Emma Lazarus, uniting the voices of Old Testament matriarchs with the contemporary Jewish woman. The work's final section showed a mass of Semite women marching together in defiant, powerful kinship.

Kaddish (1945) and *The Bride* (1946) also reflected on women's role within the faith. The latter was a group dance influenced by the gendered rituals of Orthodox wedding ceremonies, with Sokolow playing a young bride worried about her future. In *Kaddish*, named after the Jewish prayer for the dead, Sokolow dressed herself in a prayer garment conventionally worn by men, claiming its potency for herself as she delivered a slow, elastic dance of mourning. This focus on women struggling against patriarchal tradition revealed a new dimension of subversion to her portfolio, again underscoring her forte for redirecting an individual story into something that resonated on a political scale.

It would be another fifteen years before Sokolow's most pene-trating Jewish-themed work: *Dreams* (1961), her self-professed 'indictment of Nazi Germany'.[23] The brutality of the Holocaust shocked many Jewish artists into immediate activism in the years after the Second World War – including Sokolow, who furiously fundraised for organisations like Bonds for Israel throughout the 1950s – but processing its surfeit of tragedy was a raw, daunting task. Even art felt powerless in the face of horrors consistently described as 'unimaginable' – the death of God that Elie Wiesel documented in *Night*, the millions of bodies 'transformed into smoke under a silent sky'.[24]

This might explain the shifting thesis of *Dreams*, which Sokolow initially conceived as an allegory of powerlessness, humanity receding from the frame like a last dance between lovers. It was only later that she reworked it into an explicit comment on the Holocaust, incorporating new vignettes and imagery emphasis-ing the courage of its victims. 'When I started,' she explained,

'I had only the idea of dreams, but they became nightmares, and then I saw they were related to the concentration camps.'[25] The work came to include a procession of harrowing dances: a woman charging at guards, her face caught in a twisted scream; a group of bodies crumbling between the walls of a gas chamber. The score wove together words from Genesis, screaming horns and the furious chords of Bach. An onstage drummer swelled the volume. Sokolow continued to fine-tune the work throughout the 1960s, and at one point restaged it in Israel with a cast that included several Holocaust survivors.

Dreams hit a nerve with audiences all over the world, prompting the critic Clive Barnes to declare Sokolow 'the exponent of the theater of protest, that rare, rare thing, a choreographer with a social conscience'.[26] Like all of her work, it was a fist around the heart, calling on audiences to look inward and disavow the cruelty we know ourselves to be capable of.

———

Sokolow's work carries the idea that suffering lodges itself within us, becoming part of our physical fabric. You can feel this in *Dreams*, where the confiscation of dignity wears heavy on the characters, sending their bodies stumbling. 'Think higher, feel deeper,' Elie Wiesel famously urged us. Sokolow understood that the fight for justice isn't a dry manifesto to be analysed in a lecture hall; it's a wail from somewhere visceral and knowing. She gave corporeality to the idea of dispossession, asking her dancers to bear and synthesise the stress of it. 'She has the talent, the force, to leave marks – wrinkles on you,' the pantomime artist Juki Arkin once remarked of Sokolow. 'Sometimes I watch Anna teach and see a beautiful girl resisting what Anna is doing. I know this girl is going to stay pretty – no wrinkles, no scars, no understanding.'[27]

With her gritty refraction of emotion, especially in the early days of her career, Sokolow wandered the same social realist sands as many of America's interwar artists, creating blazing new links between the personal and the universal. Think of Dorothea Lange's photograph *Migrant Mother*, the anxiety of a generation etched into her forehead; or George Milton from *Of Mice and Men*, who epitomised a nation's displaced dreams. Sokolow took a similar tack in *Strange American Funeral* and *Case History No.–*, zeroing in on individuals – a deceased steelworker and an illusory vagrant youth, respectively – to highlight something systemic. She dug into the bone-chilling intimacies of their stories, magnifying them into something that could represent a whole community and even inspire action.

You can also read echoes of the narrative consciousness-raising efforts that fired up New York City's feminist circles in the early twentieth century, those progressivists who gathered to share personal confessionals under the mantra that to change institutions you first had to change hearts. Sokolow didn't view the individual in opposition to the ideals of collectivism, in the same way that she didn't see emotion as a preclusion to rationale. *Strange American Funeral* cheered on the labour reforms that came to roost in the 1930s, much like *The Exile* and *Kaddish* rallied Americans to the European Jewish struggle during the years of the Second World War. Change a mind, change a structure, change the world. The proof is in the uprising.

For all their galvanising, Sokolow didn't view these dances as propaganda. 'I never, for example, finished a dance with a fist up in the air, or took a red flag out and waved it,' she noted in 1975, distinguishing herself from some of the agitprop dancers working in her orbit. Instead, 'I tried to show people the truth, then let them make up their own minds.'[28] A particular strength of her choreography was using open-ended, non-linear storytelling that reflected the messy disarray of real life, where there are no tidy bows around oppression and disaster.

Another defining feature was her refusal to present solutions or happy endings. 'I never gave an answer to what I did,' she said. 'They used to say "you must finish it" and I would say "well, who knows what the finish is?" I still don't finish anything because I don't feel that anything ever ends.'[29] This focus on exposure rather than resolution prompted critics to brand Sokolow, not unkindly, a 'poet of chaos', 'prophet of doom'[30] and 'apostle of darkness'.[31] Clive Barnes summed up the pull of her merciless tack in a 1967 review: 'Miss Sokolow cares – if only to the extent of pointing out that the world is bleeding. I find hope in such pessimism.'[32]

A back injury forced Sokolow to stop performing in the 1950s, and she began reaching for more lyrical heights in her work, taking the questions that riled her and thinking beyond their real-world contours. *Lyric Suite* (1953) was a major current in this sea change, one of her first fully plotless works, twisting solos, duets and ensemble phrases into a plume of hesitation and surrender. It's set to a smouldering string quartet by Alban Berg, the dancers looping and twining across six movements. Frantic leaps follow thoughtful poses. One dancer spins with her head thrown back, withdrawing to the floor in a stiff plank; another breaks a moment of stillness by snapping his head to the side. It's a dance of impulse straining against reserve.

In 1955 she did something similar with *Rooms*, using a caustic jazz score to evoke the harshness of the city, where you can be surrounded by people and lonelier than ever. Here, the dancers rock and stretch on chairs, moving side by side but never together. The choreography is springy and abrupt, punctuating slow, supple sequences with body pops that pick up on the music's clanging curves.

Neither dance is aligned to a specific cause; they hinge on the politics of relationships and selfhood, invoking quiet moments you don't always see in Sokolow's earlier work, a search for the strength to confront a private battle. They don't look like Martha Graham's work, with its high kicks and dramatic releases, but they share her emotional immediacy, the focus on inner turmoil as a springboard for expression. You can see in these works that for Sokolow, lyricism wasn't sweet or easy; it was knotty, bristling, sometimes too intense to bear.

'I don't work in the abstract, and I don't work from the outside looking on,' Sokolow said of her approach. 'I get very involved in the thing. I'm not afraid to let an emotion take over completely.'[33] This is how you get into the bones of things, she felt – by exhuming and harnessing, by grabbing hold of your passions and guiding them to the surface no matter the cost.

———

Yellow is the first colour you see in *Anna*, an oil painting by Ignacio Aguirre, Sokolow's partner in her later years – a splash of it that spreads into a forehead and fish-hooks down to muster a nose. From here, brushstrokes of red take you to the trunk of a neck, roots spreading like the fibres in a muscular cross section. Greys, whites and a tiny fleck of blue organise themselves into the points and slants of a strong-jawed woman with wavy hair, a long neck and an off-frame gaze. It's a portrait of layers, thrumming with depth and diversity.

Sokolow struck a multiplicity of identities across her career: performer, creator, educator, activist. She toggled between styles and stages, choreographing on herself, her fellow company members and other outfits too, from Berlin Ballet to Nederlands Dans Theater. She assembled several companies of her own and collaborated with many others, sweeping a constellation of musicians, campaigners, playwrights, actors and students into her cosmos. Like the moderns before and after her, she broke away from existing forms and discovered new ones.

The singularity of Sokolow's work didn't pigeonhole her to a single audience; her compelling, accessible compositions chimed with a wide spectrum of people, from union members and other leftists to balletomanes and patrons of the opera. In a 1937 review, a critic writing for a local paper in Massachusetts highlighted the strength of Sokolow's professional training as an elevating factor in her practice, praising her for 'bending the dance technic [sic] she learned under Graham ... to the service of social art', noting that this 'wedding of form and social theme' offered people a 'reality they had not found elsewhere in the dance'.[34] Sokolow received favour from both fringe and establishment outlets, including the *Daily Worker*, which deemed her 'a revolutionary dancer of the first rank',[35] and the *New York Times*, which was taken with her 'admirable courage in directing her dance into other and more fruitful channels'.[36] She bridged a gap between different audiences and sites of discovery, stepping between classes and tastes with artful dexterity.

Strange American Funeral, Sokolow's 1935 indictment of precarious industrial conditions, was an early illustration of her wide appeal. The year it debuted, it was shown at a WDL festival, the 92nd Street Y and Carnegie Hall – the latter as part of a shared concert with Martha Graham, Doris Humphrey and Charles Weidman, signifying her ascent into the big leagues of modern dance. The choreography was set to a musical rendition of a 1924 poem about the real-life death of an Eastern European steelworker who fell into a vat of molten metal in a Pennsylvania mill, and drew a powerful analogy between the mechanised toil of the trade and the physical metallisation of its victim, 'whose flesh and blood turned to steel'.[37] Sokolow received almost unanimous praise for its intense, principled stand against inhumane factory conditions. There are no recordings of the work, but reviews hint at vigorous, angular formations, the dancers assembling and disbanding with the spiky rhythms of its score, evoking the doggedness of a worker's rally.

Case History No.–, a solo Sokolow debuted at the 92nd Street Y in 1937, had a similar effect. Here she gave voice to the disaffected urban youth, tracing a through line between poverty, petty crime and tumbledown futures. Again, she combined polished dance forms with sober subject matter, this time using a sudden 'neurotic bravado', in the words of one critic, to depict the misplaced aggression of alienation.[38] Another reviewer praised Sokolow for depicting 'the lifetime of thousands of youths who roam this country as vagrants and petty criminals . . . their willfulness, frustration, desperation, the hunted suspect, the third degree, the cringing crying boy killers, the last mile.'[39] The dance epitomised her kinship with the working classes – 'the urban people', as an ally at the *New Masses* magazine put it in 1937, 'their "walks" in life, the simplicity of their gestures, the honesty of their emotions and action. These people are her material, the source and substance of her dancing.'[40]

Sokolow's appetite for new audiences and new springs of inspiration never slowed. In 1953 she joined the dancer and choreographer Jerome Robbins – one of her prodigious convoy of students, which also included Pina Bausch and Martha Clarke – in taking up a sponsorship offer from the America-Israel Cultural Foundation to help give wings to Israel's fledgling modern dance scene. She started out working with a Yemenite troupe called Inbal to evolve Yemeni folk dances for the concert stage, and in 1962 she established the Lyric Theatre, Israel's first repertory dance company.

For two years, Lyric dancers restaged works like *Dreams*, *Rooms* and *Lyric Suite* for audiences around Israel. 'We danced in places where no group would appear today,' one of them recounted.

'We danced on tables tied together with rope, on concrete, on the floor, on stacks of hay. Of course we danced in Tel Aviv, Jerusalem, Haifa, Nathanya, but also in the settlements of Kidron, Ein Hon, Tivon, Lahav . . .'[41] The company didn't have the durability of Bethsabée de Rothschild's Batsheva, which eventually absorbed most of the Lyric's dancers, but it was a stepping stone to a new local dance scene where artists could support themselves on a consistent wage and weren't tied to a single creator.

The diversity of Sokolow's career continued to multiply in her later years: she added plays, operas, musicals and dance theatre productions to her portfolio, inspiring a reputation as 'the Solzhenitsyn of twentieth-century dance'. She was still forming new companies in her sixties and staging large-scale productions in her eighties, guided by an indefatigable energy to look within and draw out her deepest aches. 'Remember!' Sokolow urged choreographers in a 1980 interview. 'You are dancing about people, about humanity. Who or what is humanity? You!'[42] Her ideals of innovation and progress offered a new take on the American Dream, not rooted in distant frontiers but the in-your-face, heart-thumping concerns of the urban underclass. She was a roaring bullhorn, a racing pulse. She trekked the dark to find the light.

ACT 2, SCENE 3

You and me and all others

Two years before Martha Graham's *Appalachian Spring* captured hearts around the United States, one of her dancers released her own shimmering take on the American spirit. Sophie Maslow's 1942 production *Folksay* quilted together folk ballads from Woody Guthrie (America's beloved 'Dust Bowl Troubadour') and verse from Carl Sandburg (the 'poet of the Prairies'), using heartland imagery to depict magnificence in everyday happenings: romance, friendship, neighbourly exchange. The women of the cast swished their petticoats in square dances and stepping jigs. The men wore plaid and barrel-leaped from the wings. Melancholy melodies cried out, a dull ache in the heartstrings of Guthrie's lyrics, which cut a backcloth of rivers, peaks, prairies and wheat fields.

Guthrie accompanied Maslow's troupe onstage for *Folksay*'s early performances, brightening the blues of ballads like 'I Ride an Old Paint' and 'On Top of Old Smokey' with homespun banter between songs. Maslow's sprightly modern dance and Guthrie's down-home lyricism made soulful bedfellows for Sandburg's poetry, a straight-talking salute to the everyday folks working the nation's lands: 'The people is Everyman, everybody / Everybody is you and me and all others'.

While it wasn't a political critique, *Folksay* debuted at a high-strung moment in American history, just three months after Japan's surprise attack on Pearl Harbor, the catalyst for the United States' participation in the Second World War. Anxiety about the future of democracy thickened the air. An early advertisement for *Folksay* trumpeted its 'win-the-war spirit and theme', and Guthrie added another pro-justice dimension by fixing a sticker to his guitar that said: 'This machine kills fascists.'

The work itself, however, made no mention of soldiers or battle or foreign threats; instead, it visualised harmony and high spirits, linking the American ethos to an amity sown on home soil, reaped sea to shining sea. Maslow wove together rural imagery and urbane theatre, celebrating the power of cultural diversity at a vulnerable time. She looked to reassure, not provoke, finding strength and confidence in goodwill.

Look beyond this swinging timbre and you can see an accordance with some of the social protest dances coming out of New York City, Maslow's homestead, in the 1940s, many of which paid the same earnest attention to the working class and the heights of human persistence. Like Anna Sokolow and other allies of the leftist dance movement, Maslow addressed a national identity in flux, declaring that the American story belonged to everyone, no matter where they came from or how recently they'd arrived. She showed, in an age of political instability, an unshakeable faith in the nation's prospects. Crucially, she embraced heritage as a springboard for progress, accenting age-old values that still resounded in the national psyche: resilience, liberty and self-determination.

One of Maslow's gifts to modern dance was bringing it an uplifting, honeyed warmth, revealing a new dimension of its expressive potential. She was an intuitive mover, drawn to swinging displays that take your eyes on a darting journey. Pictures of her dancing in the 1940s often show a knee-length circle skirt arcing in a half-moon as she sweeps a leg upwards or leaps up high. There's a brilliant photo from her *Folksay* days that captures her suspended mid-air in a long, lithe diagonal, her upper body twisting left while her legs pull the opposite way, the back one cocked. She's beaming, her hands clasped on the small of her back like someone with a happy secret. You can sense her affection for dance, and the way she radiated it outwards, levelling the expanse between herself and her audience. She had a songful approach to performance and believed strongly in the power of legible choreography: 'Because I want to have an audience feel the way I do about what interests me or what moves me I try to make my dances as clear as possible.'[1]

Reflecting on his years working with Maslow, Guthrie wrote that she was 'an awful good person – you know – one of the kind that works hard and likes everybody she sees'. He recalled her stage presence as sweeping and splendid: 'She danced and brushed and scraped around so much that she really did cover the whole place.'[2] The critic Margaret Lloyd, a prominent voice in the 1940s, admired a similar charm in Maslow's choreography, *Folksay* in particular, which she found 'simple and heart-warming and endearing', its dancing 'radiantly outflung, joyous and free'.[3]

Folksay is one of many works in Maslow's portfolio that uses the genial quality of folk culture to reframe modern dance as an art that can reach all classes and creeds. Her portfolio – bursting with scores of choreography by the end of her fifty-year career – wandered California deserts and Bayou swamps, Slavic and Sioux traditions, stories from the Russian shtetl, stoking warm-hearted ideas of home, wherever it is. Like Graham, an early mentor, Maslow was fond of Americana, though she tended to focus on contemporary rural scenes rather than the ventures of pioneers past – Okie grangers surveying the farmstead, schoolgirls on a stroll past the general store. Dreams, bravery, heartache, humour and patriotism were recurring themes.

'This type of material has an appeal to audiences because they can respond to it and they feel themselves part of it all,' Maslow said shortly after she created *Folksay*.[4] Across her catalogue you can see a steady conviction to draw her art and her audiences into the same plane of understanding – to make herself, as she once put it to Lloyd, 'part of and not apart from the common man'.[5] In a 1946 interview with *Dance Magazine*, Maslow spoke about the philosophy of the Dudley-Maslow-Bales Trio, her troupe at the time:

> *We're popular, if by 'popular' you mean 'of the people.' But this is the Age of the Common Man and it is the common people who are the backbone and the strength and hope of our civilization and our culture. We as artists, and above all as thinking people, are touched by problems of our fellow man because they are our problems . . . In our dancing we try to express a common emotional experience. If we succeed, then we have helped make the modern dance healthier and more vital as an art form.*[6]

A New York City native born in 1911, Maslow had a parallel trajectory to Sokolow, her lifelong friend and colleague. The two were just a year apart in age; both had Russian Jewish roots and cut their choreographic teeth in the justice-conscious blocs of the Workers Dance League, inspired by its mission to lend modern dance a blue-collar resonance. Like Sokolow, Maslow studied at the Neighborhood Playhouse as a teenager, spent around a decade as a member of Martha Graham's company, and became a prolific choreographer in her own right, bringing her work to all kinds of stages, from union halls to off-Broadway theatres to the New York City Opera. Their shared sense of progressivism sent them both to a crucible facing many modern dancers in the 1930s and 1940s: how to wrangle the groundwork of their forebears into something that satisfied their own creative ambitions.

For Maslow, moving forward meant looking back – to folklore and vintage musical traditions, to heirloom customs and legacy rites, to vernaculars of the old country, where antique patter captured the holler of voices on the margins. She took a pickaxe to the American mythos, which promised success to anybody willing to work hard enough, digging into her homeland's histories to find the grains of enduring questions around opportunity and autonomy. She plucked the colloquial from the fringe and placed it centre stage, making modern dance accessible and communicative in a barnstorming new way.

———

The 1930s were a banner decade for youth activism in the United States. The Great Depression blew in a nationwide dust cloud of poverty and unemployment; fascism knuckled Europe in a vice grip; racial segregation was an under-acknowledged tarnish. New emblems of deprivation came into play: breadlines, flophouses, relief offices, shanty towns. Worried for their future, young people rallied for jobs and better working conditions, fighting against discrimination and isolationism. Factory workers went on strike; college students marched in the streets; African Americans assembled youth coalitions. New York City, benefited by its profusion of universities and national loudhailer, was an especially generative ground for agitation – a vociferous ferment of boycotts, mass meetings and debates.

Over on the Lower East Side, the radical artists of the New Dance Group were busy organising concerts and assemblies that used modern dance to lift the voices of the working class. Maslow joined the NDG's ranks in 1934, teaching classes at the group's integrated school and giving dance demos to members of the International Ladies Garment Workers Union, taking up the mantle on a key NDG tenet: to engage ordinary people in the modern dance sphere as more than just viewers. 'Movement [is] not a privileged activity,'[7] Maslow felt, highlighting an accessibility issue that persists in dance even today – the sense that it's not possible or worthwhile to take it up as a layperson, that you can't start dancing if you haven't always been dancing.

These early days of teaching form a brief but impactful bullet point on her CV. It wasn't about uplifting the underclasses into some higher sphere of culture but reimagining the fabric of modern dance to introduce its joy and empowerment on a recreational basis. Academics of this slice of dance history have observed an exciting feminist undertone to the NDG's application of dance as an act of expression and self-discovery, especially considering the group's appeal to Jewish women from immigrant families, whose roots reflected knotty views around female decorum and body image.* For me, Maslow's work on this front also strikes a chord with her radical vision for patriotism in works like *Folksay* – the sense that true exceptionalism isn't about rejection but inclusivity.

Like many other descendants of Eastern European Jews finding their way in early-twentieth-century New York, Maslow had the seeds of revolution in her bloodline. Her father was a Russian socialist whose politics led to a brief stint in a Moscow prison as a young adult. His early days in New York took him to Brooklyn, a cradle of Yiddish culture at the turn of the century. Maslow grew up under this vibrant umbrella of art and theatre, spending her summers at Camp Kinderland, an upstate arts retreat run by the Workmen's Circle, a Jewish socialist outfit. In her teens she studied under Irene Lewisohn at the Neighborhood Playhouse and graduated from the institution's arts programme, which involved several years of training with Martha Graham. In 1931 she joined Graham's company, the start of a twelve-year affiliation

---

* Judith Brin Ingber in particular, an Israeli choreographer and scholar who writes delicately about the relationship between Judaism and the body in the introduction to *Seeing Israeli and Jewish Dance*.

that included original roles in influential productions like *American Document* (1938) and *Deaths and Entrances* (1943), where Maslow joined Graham and Jane Dudley in dramatising the Brontë sisters' tussle against convention.

The socio-political tint of Maslow's youth deepened during her tenure with the Graham company, the colourways between dance and activism continuing to merge: 'First we went to the socialist bookstore, then to classes with Martha Graham,' as she described it.[8] In 1934, she began creating and performing her own compositions for NDG and WDL concerts, starting with *Themes from a Slavic People* (1934), a lyrical solo she danced to Hungarian folk music. A string of ripped-from-the-headlines motifs followed: *Two Songs about Lenin* (1935), where Maslow clenched and twisted to a Soviet folk song; *May Day March* (1936), a dance response to the pro-labour May Day marches; and *Women of Spain* (1938), a contemplation of class tensions that she co-created with Dudley, a collaborator on the WDL scene.

These forays were more about evoking a feeling than banging a drum, but a sensitivity to injustice nipped at their heels. Maslow's strong Graham foundation lent a gravitational vigour to her compositions, especially as she started incorporating folk motifs and experimental movement styles. Edna Ocko, a founder of the NDG, praised Maslow in a *Daily Worker* write-up for having 'quiet strength and power [that] grows more effective with each successive appearance'.[9] She'd struck on a cogent métier: using cultural touchstones, not polemic, to imagine a better future.

Maslow's bond with Dudley deepened in 1942, when the two teamed up with Humphrey-Weidman dancer William Bales to form a trio dedicated to dances 'for and about the people', infusing their performances with a lively jamboree spirit. They toured the States for twelve years, serving helpings of humour, sorrow and whimsy to colleges, theatres and other small venues around the East Coast and Midwest. A programme from a 1944 performance at Bennington College shows the gamut they could run in a single show: a 'colonial charade' involving Benjamin Franklin; a romantic daydream of a sailor away at sea; and meditations on grief and courage during the Franco regime in Spain.

Margaret Lloyd was an early fan: '[They] made modern dance unformidable, friendly, a language that could speak of contemporary and colloquial subjects without determined Americana or social-consciousness fisticuffs,' she remembered. 'It spoke of patriotism and love, grief, anger, courage, laughter, and other common things, so that all could understand.'[10] The trio often drafted in props, instruments and other trimmings to heighten their theatricality. A duet called *Inheritance*, for example, saw Bales read aloud a letter written by an ailing insurgent to his unborn child while Maslow danced the role of the soldier's anguished wife.

Maslow's time with the Dudley-Maslow-Bales Trio was a trial run for what eventually became a signature treatment of folk traditions in her work. She dusted off rustic ballads and texts, peppered her choreography with the hotfooting steps of a barn dance: clogging, with its thumping downbeats; hoedowns and snaking grapevines too. Her allusions criss-crossed regions and time frames; she didn't replicate folk cultures so much as evoke their essence – the warm glow of a hearth, the flush of a community with a shared cause. She arranged her steps within taut frameworks, giving them a robust structuring force that complemented her hearty emotional twang, creating something that was homey and high culture at once – scenes audiences might even imagine themselves joining in on. She'd do something similar with jazz in her later years, channelling the rhythms of Duke Ellington and Lawrence Ferlinghetti into a stylish beatnik caprice called *Poem*.

Dust Bowl Ballads, a pair of solos Maslow danced to songs from Woody Guthrie's like-titled 1940 record, exemplifies her cosmopolitan talents. Guthrie wrote the album to laud the grit of the Okie farm families turfed from the Southwestern Plains in the 1930s, when an unholy trinity of droughts, dust storms and debts sent them westward in a bid for survival. Maslow – wearing an apron and a wide-brimmed hat – strode, skipped and ambled across the stage in 'Ain't Got No Home' and 'Dusty Old Dust', stepping heel-toe with one bare foot as she swung the other into a cocked extension. She rolled on the floor, waved her hat in the air, slapped dust from her knees, stretched out her thumb like a hitch-hiker.

The mood was contemplative but never sombre – a lighter take than John Steinbeck's *Grapes of Wrath*, for example, though inspired by the same westbound wanderers. Reconstructions of Maslow's solos show a tender, affable quality that lopes in step with Guthrie's amiable storytelling, where sweethearts take comfort in wry repartee:

They sighed and cried, hugged and kissed
Instead of marriage they talked like this
Honey, so long, it's been good to know ya.[11]

Maslow would later tell an interviewer that she was drawn to Guthrie's music for its 'special way of looking at a tragic situation in a humorous way that made it livable . . . That seemed to me peculiarly American.'[12]

In restagings of her *Dust Bowl Ballads* solos, you can see how Maslow's choreography buttressed folksy antics with her expert technical training, the dancer's spine unlocking like a spring as she rebounds from a forward pitch, stretching herself upright. A promotional photo from the 1940s shows Maslow standing with her hands in her pockets, lips parted, peering at some faraway horizon.

She's swaying to one side, like a tree bowed by the wind, her toes raised but her feet planted in stark fortitude. Guthrie admired her sense of control, recalling: 'Sophie's body looked so healthy and so active ... like it would do almost anything she told it to do. All she had to do was notify it.'[13]

Maslow premiered *Dust Bowl Ballads* in 1941 as part of an NDG programme that also included performances by the American Square Dance Group and the Lindy Hoppers. A reviewer at the time highlighted how her performance was 'infused by deep feeling, tenderness and humor by turns', and praised the lucidity of her phrasing: 'Simple and crystal clear in pattern, never too sophisticated in movement or "technique," for the style of music to which [it is] set.'[14] It was organic, discernible and resonant – clear in intent as a Carolina sky.

———

Maslow's relationship with Woody Guthrie is a charming footnote of her legacy. She'd performed *Dust Bowl Ballads* to recordings but was determined to get the singer to perform live with her for the premiere of her follow-up piece, *Folksay*, choreographed to tracks from the same record. Guthrie's daughter Nora would later recount a difficult start to the collaboration: 'The first rehearsal was a complete disaster, as Woody could/would not play the song the same way as he recorded it. Nor could he even play it through the same way twice. Rushing to get to their places, dancers were bumping into each other, falling all over each other, and being thrown up in the air with no one there to catch them on the way down.'[15]

'My jig was up,' is how Guthrie described it. In 1942 he published an article describing his early days working with Maslow and her dancers, crediting them with important lessons in cooperation. 'I fell in love with two of the dancing girls just by the horse sense they talked in explaining to me the business of organization. One girl told me the theatre was like a factory. The people are like the wheels. If they don't all turn the same way at the same time they'll tear each other up.'[16] He later married one of these dancers, Marjorie Mazia, with Maslow as their witness – a twist with the charm of a Guthrie ballad itself.

Folksay debuted at the Humphrey-Weidman Studio Theatre in March 1942, with dancers from the NDG joining Maslow, Jane Dudley and William Bales in what the critic John Martin felt 'must be one of the most beautiful and genuine works in the whole range of contemporary dance'.[17] Guthrie thumbed his guitar through a string of songs, while fellow folk singer Earl Robinson chimed in with verse from *The People, Yes*, preaching the virtues of vitality and scrappiness in Carl Sandburg's poem, a plain-speaking churn of lore and reality.

It was Maslow's biggest work to date: nine dances with ten dancers between them, arranged across ensemble phrases, small group dances and a solo for Maslow, which she danced to 'On Top of Old Smokey'. The troupe wore denim and gingham; they sauntered, scrapped, flirted, called out to each other, trotted in single-file lines and ballooned into a circle. 'Aw, Nuts' sent two men squaring off in a skirt-chasing rivalry; 'I Ride an Old Paint' saw the cast take up reins and mimic a horseback ride. Maslow and Bales played lovers in Guthrie's goofy rendition of 'Sweet Betsy from Pike', bouncing in spirited synchronisation. She perched on his shoulder, hand to her forehead like a voyager on the lookout, then dropped to the floor in a plank, spurring him to yank her upright. ('Get up, Betsy, you'll get sand in your eyes!') *Folksay* ended with the ensemble striding across the stage in a heart-swelling trek of kinship and fortitude. 'Unless you are pretty insensitive to the people that are America it is guaranteed to leave you with a lump in your throat,' Martin reiterated in a later review.[18]

After *Folksay* debuted, the *Daily Worker* declared a schism in New York's leftist dance movement, drawing a contrast between Maslow's uplifting brand of socially conscious dance and the biting diatribes of the era's fist-pumping agitprop performers: 'The day of gloomy grotesquery, when modern dancers drove their points home with hammer blows . . . is gone.'[19] For me, putting these factions in opposition creates an unnecessary hierarchy, when really each had its own strengths and tenacities, especially in terms of highlighting the humanity of the underclass. Maslow's strength was delivering her message of togetherness in a polished, sunny-side-up tone. She showed that progressivism doesn't have to be blood-boiling; equally, that a woman who taught classes wearing lipstick and a red, fringed bolero could tackle serious topics. ('I didn't know it was okay for modern dancers to be glamorous,' one of her students would later recall.[20]) Maslow didn't divide the movement but rather diversified it, in sync with her broad-minded vision of the American character.

Folksay's casting added an important political dimension to its message of inclusion. Around half of Maslow's troupe were Jews from immigrant families, and the Black modern dancer Pearl Primus also performed in early versions, including a 1944 television broadcast, making it one of the first high-profile interracial productions in modern dance history. Later that decade Maslow would cast Donald McKayle and Ronne Aul as well, two up-and-coming Black moderns. By incorporating these minorities, Maslow laid claim to a heartland traditionally associated with white Christian values, showing that the American story belonged to everyone. She worked on the social margins, using the very principles that make folk culture itself a radical art.

Throughout her career, Maslow strode in step with the leftist factions in her orbit, including the NDG, which championed the power of the group in art, politics and everyday life. According to

Guthrie, her sum-is-greater-than-its-parts mantra influenced him from day one: 'I saw why socialism is the only hope for any of us, because I was singing under the old rules of "every man for his self" and the dancers was [*sic*] working according to a plan and a hope.'²¹ Her collectivist vision, while world-facing, also tapped into an impactful philosophy within her own profession: that modern dance can be for and by everyone.

———

Oral traditions have always played a big role in the American tale. Cowboy plots, campfire songs, murmurs from the old country, all yellowed with time and excursion. We tell and retell our legacies to keep them alive, blurring their ridges into something we can bear – our very own origin myths, etched into family trees, with emerald wings and shoulder blades of bark.

After the decimations of the Second World War, oral testimonies were some of the only chronicles left for many Jewish communities. In the United States, musicians, writers and performers scrambled to record these narratives in art, giving them life beyond the mouths that kindled them. Their hunt often sent them towards stories of pre-war Russian Jewish village life, especially those by Sholem Aleichem, a turn-of-the-century Yiddish immigrant whose tales of exiled families were immortalised in Joseph Stein's 1964 musical *Fiddler on the Roof*.

In 1950, Maslow put her own spin on Aleichem's browbeaten villagers with *The Village I Knew*, a collection of character studies that celebrates the customs and foibles of the shtetl: the candlelit Shabbat dinners, the raucous fraternising after prayers ended. 'This horrible experience [of the Holocaust] made me realize that as much [as] I thought I was American, I was just as much Jewish,' she said of its conception. 'I then wanted very much to do something Jewish.'²²

Told over seven episodes, the production transferred many of Maslow's usual beats – folk songs, swinging line dances, tender portraits of the everyday – to a vibrant Eastern European setting. Recordings show clusters of men and women divided by gender, each group swaying in pious orthodoxy; later everyone links arms and jigs across the stage, tradition thrown to the wind, skirts and headscarves flying. Most of the scenes brought Maslow's signature wit, including a festive, springy parade, the women hoisted onto the men's shoulders; the final one, however, called 'Exodus', was an about-face into the pain of expulsion, the group fleeing towards an uncertain future. Once again, Maslow used an interracial cast, affirming her message that dance can transcend race and religion in addition to borders and centuries.

She debuted *The Village I Knew* with the New Dance Group at the 1950 American Dance Festival (ADF), a venture she'd recently helped establish, and restaged it many times in the coming decades, including with Batsheva in Israel, where Zionist optimism brought out a new dimension of its pluralist thesis. The production's success spurred her to follow up with a series of Jewish-themed works, including *Anniversary* (1956), which commemorated the 1943 Warsaw Ghetto uprising, and *Ladino Suite* (1969), based on a medley of Judaeo-Spanish folk songs.

Maslow also created choreography for a string of Israeli fundraising concerts throughout the 1950s and 1960s, including an ANTA Playhouse spectacular called *Israel Through the Ages* and more than a dozen of the Madison Square Garden Chanukah Festivals, continuing to cast Jewish, Black and gentile dancers alike. The dance writer Deborah Jowitt, who performed in *Anniversary*, admired Maslow's organic approach to dancemaking in her 2006 obituary: 'She didn't come to the studio with everything planned; often, we sat around while she wrung the choreography out of herself. But I remember running home and describing to my room-mates how amazingly, how powerfully she had turned the fact of dancers simply bouncing in a lunge, without traveling an inch, into the exodus of Jews from the Warszaw ghetto.'[23]

These works, while focused in their themes, didn't narrow Maslow's view. Throughout the 1950s, she choreographed new works for ADF, including 1953's *Manhattan Transfer*, plus dance scenes for operas, plays and musicals. She continued making sunny compositions, like *Decathlon Etudes* (1976) and *Voices* (1980), both with lush symphonic scores; and politically conscious ones too, like *Visions of Black Elk* (1978), based on the massacre at Wounded Knee. In the 1970s she returned to a Sholem Aleichem text to choreograph for a musical called *The Big Winner*, and in 1980 she turned to the songs of Woody Guthrie once again for *Woody Sez*, a comedic reprisal of Dust Bowl themes.

Maslow stepped between various leadership positions at the NDG and, as the years ticked by, leaned more intensely into her convictions around the merits of a rigorous modern dance education like her own Graham training. 'It's harder now to teach a simple, straight, graceful smooth walk than it used to be,' she commented in the 1990s. 'Some of these things are done today with too much lightness. Dancers have spectacular technique and can do just about anything, but it seems to be less meaningful because they employ no weight in the movement. They are not interesting movements when they are just tossed off.'[24] Her commitment to sincere storytelling and working-class representation never flagged; even in her eighties she could be found staging performances in synagogues and com-munity centres, giving fresh life to the cornerstones of her practice.

With her amiable, beaming visage, Maslow was an unlikely ambassador for the splinters of anti-elitism. But her life-affirming tack was groundbreaking – an important complement to the highly personalised excavations we associate with Martha Graham and the justice-seeking activism that fired up the NDG. Maslow was an influential advocate for representation, using her art to engage her audiences in a wider understanding of heritage and self-actualisation – where we come from and where we're headed. Her dancing was lyrical and lovely, but she never saw it as a decorative activity. Like the feminist consciousness-raisers of her generation, she harnessed private intimacies – the tender happenings of the everyday – and used her platform to ripple these outwards, basking in their bright humanist sheen.

ACT 3, CURTAIN
Rewriting the self

Cast

KATHERINE DUNHAM
PEARL PRIMUS   PEARL LANG

with

VALERIE BETTIS
JULIA LEVIEN
MAY O'DONNELL
BERYL MCBURNIE
HADASSAH SPIRA EPSTEIN

and

DANCE COMPANY

In some ways, the moderns who found their feet in the 1940s and 1950s occupied a star-bright spot of modern dance history. The scrappy establishing years were over; training, funding and creative production flourished around the globe, fostering opportunities for international exchange and recognition. At the same time, the tempest of a war-torn world squalled on, rattling the arts with two decades of conflict and racial tension. Dance became an assertion of fortitude in an age marked by intolerance and dehumanisation. The late-stage moderns tapped into the cultures around them with more might than ever, seizing on the rebellious spirit of their art to contend with the aftershocks of a whole world once again drawn to arms.

While Doris Humphrey, Charles Weidman and Hanya Holm disbanded their performing companies in the 1940s, the temple of modern dance education they'd built with Martha Graham stood tall, bathing scores of young artists in its light. Together the Big Four continued to prop up the next generation by instructing at two vital new endeavours: Jacob's Pillow, a project that evolved out of Ted Shawn's artistic commune in the Berkshires in Massachusetts, and the American Dance Festival, which Bennington originator Martha Hill founded at Connecticut College in 1948. Both programmes facilitated premieres by leading and emerging choreographers, including prominent third-wavers Pearl Primus and Pearl Lang.

By the 1940s, many of the Big Four's early company members were deep into their own ventures, like Valerie Bettis, a Holm protégée and choreographer of *The Desperate Heart* (1943) – a tense, poetic showing that Louis Horst judged 'the finest solo work in the entire modern dance repertory of this decade'.[1] American modern dance grew beyond their influence too, thanks to Julia Levien and Hortense Kooluris, who gave new resonance to Isadora Duncan's school of thought, and Katherine Dunham, who trained scores of up-and-comers in her bespoke new fusion style.

Outside of the United States, Anna Sokolow continued her work with Mexico City-based dancers throughout the 1940s, while Beryl McBurnie, having dazzled Manhattan with a series of calypsonian 'coffee concerts', returned to her native Trinidad to launch the influential Little Carib Theatre in Port of Spain. The following decade, Helen Lewis, a Czech Holocaust survivor who'd taught dance to children during her internment at Terezin, moved to Belfast and pioneered a vibrant new scene in Northern Ireland.

Germany's once towering expressionist dance scene lost its shine around this time, the Third Reich having co-opted 'free' dancing as propaganda for its abhorrent ideologies, but a handful of standard-bearers kept the expressionist flame alive as internationally touring soloists. In the meantime, a fire was sparked in the newly declared State of Israel, where culture-friendly *kibbutzim* (communal villages) intensified interest in the performing arts, modern dance included. Some Israeli moderns took their moves on the road in the late 1940s; others performed at home under the direction of local spearheads like Yardena Cohen. The following decade saw significant cross-pollination between American moderns and their Israeli counterparts, including Sokolow's partnership with Sara Levi-Tanai, founder of Inbal Dance Theater; and Pearl Lang's with Ahuva Anbary, a future Batsheva dancer.

The pacesetters of this era were responsible for some major new techniques. José Limón developed a sweeping style that used visceral twists of the body to strike an emotional high note, while Dunham merged modern, African and Caribbean moves to showcase the beauty of Black dance traditions. Both found vital inspiration in their ethnic heritage and their international travels. Limón, in the mould of his mentor Charles Weidman, was on the front lines of a legion of male moderns who marched to prominence in the 1940s and 1950s, including Erick Hawkins, Martha Graham's erstwhile partner and another instigator of a gripping new technique. The draft took Limón, Hawkins and several of their peers out of the frame in the war years, but they returned to civilian life with a new vigour for the stage. Hawkins – like Paul Taylor, Merce Cunningham and Alvin Ailey – launched a company in the 1950s that's still in operation today.

As forms diversified during this third wave, so did content, especially with the growing embrace of personal history as choreographic material. Graham had shown the possibilities of hot-blooded introspection, dance as 'a kind of fever chart',[2] and her successors dialled up the temperature, especially Pearl Lang and May O'Donnell. A highlight of the latter's portfolio was *Suspension* (1943), a solo that invoked T. S. Eliot's poetry to meditate on a tender personal memory: 'At the still point of the turning world . . . there the dance is.'[3] Pain and angst were common themes in this age of self-reflection, but so were expressions of lightness and joy that defied the gravity often associated with modern dance in its previous era.

Some third-wavers relished lush theatre and vivid displays of drama; others opted for minimalism and cool irony, a taste of the postmodern iconoclasm to come in the 1960s. Aesthetics aside, both camps carried the torch of experimentation forward, lighting the way for pulsing new examinations of identity.

———

The moderns championing individuality in the mid-century did so in tandem with shifting values around the significance of self-representation. While the term 'identity politics' wouldn't come into play until the 1970s, the years of and following the Second World War hummed with a buzzing new discourse around racial and ethnic marginalisation, especially in America. The ideals of equality propping up the Western Front strained against the day-to-day discrimination many citizens faced on home soil. Identity became a major concern for Black and Jewish dancers in particular, who began foregrounding their heritage and lived experiences in their art to challenge oppressive stereotypes. Together their efforts hugely diversified the movement's corps and its body of themes, giving it a dynamic new stature.

With racist attitudes mostly excluding them from ballet, a vibrant contingent of Black artists made their home in modern dance. Katherine Dunham toured America with one of the world's first all-Black modern dance troupes in the 1940s, paving the way for younger associates like Talley Beatty and Alvin Ailey to take their own companies forward, while Pearl Primus became an overnight sensation in New York City, briefly teaming up with fellow Trinidadian Beryl McBurnie, another prominent face on the Manhattan scene.

The New Dance Group (NDG), an early proponent of racial integration, created new opportunities for Black dancers like Primus to learn, teach and produce throughout the 1940s and 1950s, as did the 92nd Street Y, which continued to boom as a site for socially conscious performance in the mid-century, including fierce stands against racism. As prolific creators and leading educators, Primus and Dunham had a game-changing influence on the racial diversity of modern dance. Like the actors of Harlem's Little Theatre Movement before them, who carved out dramatic roles for and about Black Americans in the interwar years, they asserted a crucial new visibility in an arena with a high artistic cachet.

The war years also piloted in a prominent fleet of Jewish American moderns conscious of their ethnic roots. Thanks to the bountiful school-to-stage grapevine seeded by philanthropists like Irene Lewisohn, and the Big Four's embrace of Jewish newcomers, the barriers of the Denishawn years, when many companies excluded or set quotas on Jewish recruits, had mostly fallen by the 1940s. Between them, Sophie Maslow, Anna Sokolow and other Jewish front-runners on the Big Four circuit used their platforms to open doors for newcomers, welcoming next-gens like Pearl Lang into the fold. Again, the 92nd Street Y played a key role, with its annual competition series giving several breakout Jewish dancers a leg up, including Noami Leaf Halpern, a Palestinian immigrant who went on to found Boston's Festival Dance Company.

The Y, Jacob's Pillow and the NDG studios were critical junctures for Black and Jewish moderns to intersect and collaborate in the 1940s and 1950s. There was also some overlap across the major American troupes, and in Israel too, which Primus, Beatty and Lang all toured in the 1950s. Like her student Donald McKayle, a fellow Black modern, Primus danced under Maslow before branching out into her own choreography. McKayle later appeared with Martha Graham's dancers for a season around the same time that Matt Turney and Mary Hinkson – two of the first Black women to graduate from the University of Wisconsin–Madison dance programme – commenced long-term stints as Graham company members. Hinkson went on to portray the Hebraic warrior Yael in Lang's *Song of Deborah*, while Turney danced the Pioneer Woman in Graham's *Appalachian Spring* – both high-profile instances of transracial casting in the mid-century. In the meantime, Alvin Ailey joined Lester Horton's racially integrated company before starting his own in 1958.

This collision of backgrounds and experiences sparked a rich new gamut of ethnic-inspired modern dance styles, all more authentically conceived than the exotica of the Denishawn studio. Lang brought unseen Jewish traditions to the American stage in the mid-century, while Dunham and Primus worked in striking Black vernaculars, from West Indian drumming to plantation dances of the rural South. In the early 1940s Primus teamed up with Hadassah Spira Epstein and Jean Erdman to lead the Ethnic Dance Division at the NDG school, offering classes in African, Caribbean, Jewish, Hindu and Hawaiian dance. In weaving these styles into the modern dance web, they created powerful new outlets for exploring the role of heritage in our private and public lives.

———

In 1942, Redd Evans and John Jacob Loeb hit America's airwaves with a banjo-strumming song about a riveter named Rosie working her tail off for the war effort. The next year, Norman Rockwell visualised Rosie as a strapping redhead in a denim jumpsuit, and J. Howard Miller branded her with a confident slogan: 'We Can Do It!' This punchy image of womanly moxie lodged itself in the American psyche like an axe in a log, immortalising a poster girl for the millions of women who rose up when their country needed them most.

Rosie endures today as a symbol of the seismic shift the Second World War had on women's self-conception – the new futures they dared to imagine after proving they had the strength and nous to keep a war-jostled country on course. Some had taken over operations on the home front; others had joined their brothers, husbands and sons in uniform. They'd swapped skirts for trousers, solo housewifery for long hours working hand in hand with different races and creeds. They'd helmed munitions plants, built B-17s, even piloted planes. It was the first paying job for many, and the wages were far higher than domestic positions like maid or nanny. Things would – could – never go back.

In 1946, Eleanor Roosevelt read an open letter to the women of the world, urging them to seize on this newfound energy to real-ise their political potential. Delivered at the launch of the UN's Commission on the Status of Women, the first intergovernmental body dedicated to gender equality, her speech exemplified a wider ongoing crusade to increase women's participation in world affairs.

That women had been begged into the factories under the guise of national duty hugely complicated ideas of patriotism in the years after the war. During the war years, America's Rosies were applauded as true patriots and indispensable public servants, but once the Axis fell, they were told the best way they could serve their country was to hand their jobs over to returning GIs. Motivational posters glamorising war work fell out of favour in the late 1940s, replaced by mass media that beckoned women back into the home, from sitcoms about smiling suburban families to ads for gleaming new kitchen appliances. For all their hard work, they were cast as the supporting characters in the national narrative, not the protagonists – the 'second sex', as Simone de Beauvoir put it.

Behind the apple-pie facade came a rumble of discontent. Why were gender roles flexible at times and fixed at others? Shouldn't the women of the nation get to decide for themselves what is and isn't 'the American way'? Some of the era's breakout modern dancers waded into the conversation, including Pearl Primus and Katherine Dunham, who – building on their forerunners' weapon-isation of dance against oppression – used their work to pose pertinent new questions about the freedom and representation of minority women like themselves. Acutely conscious of the sting of modern-day bigotry, from the sickening legacy of Jim Crow to the recent depravities of Nazism, they joined Pearl Lang and others in challenging the modern dance sphere to include more voices and stories. How could it claim to be the face of American dance when their own histories were still on the margins?

Dunham and Primus's interrogations came on the cusp of America's civil rights movement, which found a powerful foothold in the post-war years thanks to a compelling 'Double V' campaign that linked the fight for democracy abroad to the fight for racial equality at home. They were two key players in a drive to reimagine African dance legacies for the stage, from ancient indigenous rituals to the colourful customs that sprang into life in colonial settings. Carnival dances, slave spirituals and even dance hall jigs like the jitterbug came into play, as did emphatic motifs and thematic frameworks, including testimony from the cotton fields. Their efforts shone new light on the depth of Black heritage, and underscored the pain of life in a country that still segregated its water fountains by colour.

Their Jewish contemporaries also pondered crucial questions of identity after the war, united in dismay at the atrocities of the Holocaust. Lang and Noami Leaf Halpern built vibrant stage careers dramatising Jewish subjects and stories, from Yiddish fables to the matriarchs of the Old Testament, while Hadassah Spira Epstein, Dvora Lapson and Fred Berk worked to integrate historic Jewish practices into the modern dance curriculum, including Israeli folk dances and the rituals of prayer. Like Dunham and Primus, and like Isadora Duncan, Martha Graham and Sophie Maslow before them, these dancers sensed the power of the past as a prism for contemporary concern.

By the mid-1940s, modern dance had moved beyond the working-class focus that had fired up its revolutionaries in the previous decade, though ties to the left wing remained strong. The NDG continued encouraging dancers to seize on the headline issues of the day, an approach that moved Primus to set racism in her sights with works like *Strange Fruit* (1943), sharpening its protest edge by performing it at race rallies and clubs aimed at servicemen. Meanwhile, Lang showed her stripes by choreographing for Jewish festivals and Zionist fundraisers. In 1940, Dunham appeared on the cover of a National Association for the Advancement of Colored People (NAACP) circular, drawing a powerful correlation between modern dance and the fight for social justice. The following decade would see her national loyalties – like those of Primus – called into question as Cold War politicking began to frame social critique as anti-American.

Whether they were squaring off against prejudice or emphasising the beauty of diasporic traditions, the mid-century moderns made huge strides in crystallising positive images of their personal heritage. They swirled the arcane and the present-day, elevating long-ago histories into something tangible and relevant, from burning critiques of inequality to uplifting portraits of resilience. They championed a world view where diversity wasn't just *a* but *the* way forward for society – a pluralistic stance that brought back into view Duncan's assertion that the dancer of the future 'will not belong to a nation but to all humanity'.[4]

———

In the late 1930s, a young Katherine Dunham gave an interview about her *raison d'être* as an artist: 'to take [Black] dance out of the burlesque – to make of it a more dignified art'.[5] She was responding to a critical subtext that would incense and motivate her for the next sixty years: the insinuation that Black dance traditions weren't technically or artistically rigorous. That Black bodies moved differently to white ones. That 'ethnic' dance belonged in a distinct (read: inferior) category from mainstream modern dance.

Dunham, along with Primus and Lang, was a headliner in a battle for legitimacy that thrust intersectional tensions onto the modern dance stage in the 1940s and 1950s, including gendered stereotypes of minority women. For Jewish moderns, the antisemitic 'exotic Jewess' motif loomed large, an oversexed caricature exemplified in paintings like Henri Regnault's smouldering *Salomé*. Discrimination also lurked within their own communities, where conservative beliefs around modesty made the very act of a Jewish woman dancing onstage a subversive one. Hadassah Spira Epstein made waves with her 1947 solo *Shuvi Nafshi*, showing that piety was not incompatible with public performance, while Lang joined Anna Sokolow in highlighting the sidelining of women within the faith by wrapping her arm in a prayer garment reserved for men. Lang also staged the stories of biblical heroines like Esther and Deborah, fearless leaders who marched their people towards a better future. These dancers emphasised the Jewish woman as an agent of strength, liberation and progress – an exciting precursor to the debates that would grip Jewish feminists like Trude Weiss-Rosmarin and Rachel Adler in the 1970s.

For Dunham and Primus, charges of hypersexualisation and primitivism posed a threat as they laced African and Caribbean-inspired dances into their craft – outgrowths of deeply racist thinking around the proclivities and capabilities of Black women. The narrow-minded ethnic/modern hierarchy plagued them both, even after they became lodestars in their field. The article accompanying Dunham's 1940 NAACP magazine cover, for example, called her 'the leading colored dance artist in this country'[6] – one of many instances where a critic praised her talent while parsing it in terms of race. Like Primus, she responded with deep, considered examinations of indigenous dance customs that honoured their origins while adding a dash of modern artistry.

Both dancers were especially academic in their approach, under-taking anthropological fieldwork in countries like Haiti, Senegal and Nigeria to ensure their grasp was authentic.

Together with Lang and other peers, they danced the dynamism of the diaspora, salvaging deep-rooted traditions and reworking them into vibrant new ones. They were exceptional among their generation for amplifying minority voices and giving insightful rep-resentation to marginalised communities. Thanks to their labours, modern dance matured into something richly multicultural – a vehicle for diversity, cultural awareness and vital new negotiations of self.

ACT 3, SCENE 1

A handful of dream-dust

Long before Beyoncé broke the internet with 'Formation' and its gothic whispers from the bayou; before Childish Gambino laid a trap beat against the Gwara Gwara; back even before Alvin Ailey baptised the world in the hymnal waters of *Revelations*,* there was another African American artist bringing indigenous Black dances to the global stage: Katherine Dunham, the 'Matriarch of Black Dance', who expanded the lexis with pulsing new idioms, from Brazilian majumbas and Creole mazurkas to American jazz beats and the percussive rituals of Haitian vodou.

Between the 1930s and 1960s, Dunham danced these patters in Broadway theatres and Hollywood films, nightclubs and community halls, plus major stages across six continents. She clocked the power of Black dance traditions, the heart-thumping artistry that turns a vulnerable body into an almighty talisman, and she made the world see it too.

Dunham was a woman of many firsts: the first modern dancer to bring African and Caribbean themes to the mainstream, the founder of America's first self-supporting Black dance company, and the first African American asked to choreograph for New York's Metropolitan Opera. She was part of the first generation of Black women in America to attain university degrees, and went on

---

* The most widely seen work of modern dance to date, performed for an estimated 25 million people since its creation in 1960.

to become one of the world's first dance anthropologists, a spear-head of anti-colonial discourse in the field. She broke new technical ground with a unique movement system that fused established principles of ballet and modern dance with the rippling gaits of the African diaspora, including Caribbean, African and American traditions – the first formal technique to unite these styles.

Dancer, choreographer, anthropologist, author, activist – Dunham straddled all these vocations in parallel, making her the first, possibly only, modern dancer to have an offstage body of work as textured and full-bodied as her dance catalogue. Her writing portfolio – which encompasses ethnographic studies, scholarly articles, a children's tale and an achingly raw memoir – is a hefty legacy in its own right, and speaks to a mind brimming with ambition. After her thirty-year stage career wound down, Dunham spent another four decades progressing the possibilities of modern dance through education and public service, earning a Kennedy Center Honor, a National Medal of Arts and a Distinguished Service Award from the American Anthropological Association for her work.

Dunham's early dance training took place in and around Chicago in the 1920s and 1930s, a choppy era for the Windy City, especially the South Side, where she lived with her aunt Lulu for two years after her mother died. Fleeing the tyranny of Jim Crow, waves of Black Southern migrants had begun re-ridging the city's topography, diversifying neighbourhoods previously defined by Irish industrial stock. With new competition for work and housing, the city became a pressure cooker for racial friction.

The strife was double-edged – a spark for violence, including a lethal race riot in 1919, but also a renaissance of Black art and culture. Poets and playwrights mused on new attitudes around African American identity, representation and consciousness. Bold words from civil rights activists Margaret Walker, Dorothy West and Richard Wright thickened the air across Chicago – 'that city so deadly dramatic and stimulating', as the latter would write, '[where] we caught whispers of the meanings that life could have'.[1]

Born in 1909, the daughter of an African American father and a mixed-race French Canadian mother, Dunham was alive to the complications of race – the contrasting styles of worship between a Black church and a white one, for example, and the social currency of a mother who could pass as white. In her memoir she recounts hearing music coming from the doorways of Deep South migrants during a childhood trip to St Louis: '[the music that had] struck so far down into a substance that had never stirred or made itself known before that now, at this moment, began a possession by the blues, a total immersion in the baptismal font of the Race . . . Deeper than prayer and closer to the meaning of life than anything else'. She admired their quiet perseverance with the same reverence she'd later bestow on traditions she encountered in the Caribbean: 'They turned inward, way, way, inward, deep into something people are supposed to know about and don't look at, or knew a long time ago and lost touch with.'[2]

Dunham took her first dance classes in a high-school Terpsichore club, modernesque forays into Dalcrozean and Laban-inspired movement, and branched out into ballet when she enrolled at the University of Chicago in 1928, where she completed an anthropology degree and studied dance on the side with figures from the Civic Opera and Chicago Opera, including ballet, modern dance, Spanish, Balinese and other ethnic styles. Ludmila Speranzeva, a Russian dancer who'd previously trained with Mary Wigman, was an especially big influence, introducing her to the evocative properties of expressionist and interpretive dance.

Dunham's college years stepped in time to the last blasts of the Jazz Age and the oomph of the New Negro discourse, which envisioned a radical, egalitarian future for African Americans. She was a fixture at the newly formed Cube Theater, and later the Dill Pickle Club, mingling with bohemians, scholars and writers, including a young Langston Hughes. She impressed her anthropology professors with questions about the emerging field of ethnochoreology. She performed in Cube productions, attended shows by Isadora Duncan's legacy company, took masterclasses with luminaries like Léonide Massine and started to offer dance lessons herself. In 1931 she formed an all-Black student troupe called Ballet Nègre.

The group disbanded after just one performance, a small balletic showing at Chicago's Beaux Arts Ball called *Negro Rhapsody* – a reflection of Dunham's growing interest in her racial identity, especially her African roots. Encouraged by a mentor to focus on modern dance, she started feeling out eclectic, edgier movement qualities. She assembled the Negro Dance Group in 1933, again enlisting fellow Black dancers, and managed to secure the troupe a prominent engagement with the Chicago Opera: a restaging of Ruth Page's *La Guiablesse*, based on a Martinique folk tale about a sumptuous she-devil, with Dunham dancing the lead. The electric production seeded her fascination with dance customs from the Caribbean – traditions that had endured the slave trade and taken on a life of their own.

While Dunham surrounded herself with an eager cohort of Black dancers, the wider world of modern dance in the 1930s was a mostly white crowd congregated in New York City. Edna Guy, Hemsley Winfield and Asadata Dafora were making important inroads in bringing Black dancers and themes to studios and stages, but none had the profile or resources to run companies on a par with giants like the Big Four. When Dunham hit it big at the end of the decade, earning enough acclaim to support her own all-Black touring troupe, she was a rarity.

This acclaim sprouted from her theatrical approach to modern dance, with its innovative blend of established and untapped styles. She plaited together classical lines and archetypal frameworks with supple moves from ancestral shores: undulating spines, start-stop isolations, rhythms that accented the torso and sinuous curves of the wrist. She drafted in folk drumming percussions and pulsing jazz tempos, and cast herself in racy, mysterious roles, presenting lushly costumed creations with names that trumpeted their colourful rhythms: *Choros*, *Rites de Passage*, *Tropics* and *Le Jazz Hot*.

These weren't the knee-slapping antics of the vaudeville Chitlin' Circuit, one of the primary dance spheres available to Black performers in the years of segregation; they didn't have the colonialist tinge of Josephine Baker's much-loved 'Banana Dance', either. Dunham's works were their own distinct synthesis of sparkle and shadow, art and enquiry, tapping into something vivid and deep-rooted – the 'dream-dust'[3] of Langston Hughes's early poetry, maybe, with its primordial rivers, 'ancient as the world and older than the flow of human blood in human veins'.[4] Her productions were hugely popular between the 1930s and 1960s, and created a luminous showcase for what Alvin Ailey – one of her best-known protégés – hailed as 'a unified Afro-American dance'.[5] Her unique technique is still taught today, including at the Ailey School.

A key fulcrum in Dunham's career was the travel fellowship she won in 1935 to study the African origins of local dance cultures in the Caribbean. She spent close to two years conducting ethnographic fieldwork in Jamaica, Martinique, Trinidad and Haiti, investigating Coromantee war dances, the hip-swivelling shay-shay, raucous Carnival customs and rituals of the African deity Shango, hopping into the dance circles herself to learn these moves with her own body. She spent the longest part of her trip in Haiti, enthralled with the African ancestry of the vodou religion, observations that she eventually shaped into a master's thesis. As part of her research, she even became initiated as a mambo, the religion's highest honour available to a woman.

Film footage from 1962 shows Dunham at her house in Port-au-Prince – which she bought in 1949 and lived in for long periods of her later life – demonstrating the dances that started it all: cool spins and hinges, a bobbing to-and-fro, barefoot shuffles to a foot-jangling drumbeat, the percussion finding outlets in her chest, her elbows, her chin.[6] She's smiling, eyes cast downward with the same graciousness that carries her writing in her 1969 anthropological text, *Island Possessed*, where she recounts the spell Haiti cast on her during her first visit, with its mango trees and tangles of bougain-villea, chauffeurs in starchy white suits: the 'faded aristocracy . . . forced to earn a living, yet still remaining genteel, [reminded] me of relatives I felt myself to have outgrown'.[7]

When Dunham returned from her fellowship in 1936, she brought back crucial insights into the beauty of Black heritage. Despite receiving further funding for academic fieldwork, she opt-ed to turn her professional attention to dance, with the reasoning that bringing these customs to the concert stage would reach more people than a scholarly post. She began wrangling her new and exist-ing dance studies into a vocabulary that could capture their cultural spellwork, reassembling her dance troupe and travelling to New York to test it out. Using funding from the Federal Theatre Project, she choreographed, staged and starred in *L'Ag'Ya* in 1938, one of the first in a parade of high-profile, highly praised productions.

Set in an eighteenth-century fishing village and inspired by a Martinique fighting ritual, *L'Ag'Ya* presents a love triangle that ends in tragedy. Dunham played Loulouse, a woman subjected to a dangerous love spell, *cambois* magic procured from a jungle cleric. She crowned the composition with a shimmying charm dance.

Performance footage from 1947 shows her dressed in frothy petti-coats, like fistfuls of sea foam, gliding past crouching drummers, swaying villagers and the suitor ready to seize what he can't seduce. She cranes her neck, unfurls her arms, pumps her chest. Off comes a layer of her dress to reveal bare shoulders and a tumble of ruffles. She hinges forward, her skirt whooshing, her feet skittering in a brisk promenade. Another layer off. Like much of Dunham's port-folio, *L'Ag'Ya* is remembered for its shimmering theatricality and creative spotlight on unseen cultures. It visualised the body as an archive for the throb and bloom of long-forgotten histories.

When she developed the Dunham technique, she yoked it to the idea that dance is something we inhabit, not just practise. She called her technique 'a way of life',[8] aligning body and mind in mystic sym-metry. 'You make this field around you, and you're the centre of it, and that's all you're interested in,' you can hear her tell a student in film footage from the 1980s.[9] The dancer is practising the 'Rocking Horse', an up-and-down move that relies on an open, hinging hip. As she ripples through the exercise, you can see wisps of principles that Martha Graham popularised in the 1930s, including a keen awareness of breath, tension and gravity.

You can also see the fluent body articulation that defines certain African styles, especially West African dance. The dancer's torso is active, eloquent – heaving and isolating in suave equilibrium. Dunham often choreographed to polyrhythms, asking her dancers to listen for contrasting metres and move different body parts to different rhythms at the same time. She saw this as an expression of spirituality – a way to hug the music and channel its radiance.

Dunham's highly methodical, highly musical technique was a powerful disruptor to a mid-century dance establishment blinkered by racist assumptions, including the widespread belief that Black dance traditions were undemanding and that Black bodies were naturally predisposed to certain types of movement (making jazz dance, for example, easy to master and classical ballet impossible). Dunham prided herself on the strength and rigour required to perform her choreography, and once told an interviewer that *Rites de Passage*, her 1941 work inspired by ancient puberty, fertility and funeral rituals, 'was my big answer to people who felt that primitive things were always just without form and without discipline'.[10]

By crafting her innovations into a specialised rubric, Dunham challenged a flawed taxonomy, diversifying it with new ideas, vernaculars, bodies and identities. The critic Robert Sylvester applauded the 'speed and physical precision' of her technique in his 1946 review of *Bal Nègre*, a three-act Broadway revue that toured the United States for nine months, declaring: 'If things were run properly in this town, every quote American unquote ballet company would be forced to go up to [the] Dunham school for biweekly lessons.'[11]

At the time of their release, Dunham's productions offered important comments on the contemporary Black experience. *L'Ag'Ya* brought a full cast of Black dancers to audiences who'd never seen this outside of vaudeville. *Rites de Passage* confronted the idea of sexual impulse as immoral, and faced censorship because of it. *Bal Nègre* drew together Carnival merengues, island fighting dances and ragtime medleys, celebrating each as an exquisite legacy art form. *Southland* (1951) dramatised an antebellum lynching with gut-twisting candour, a political critique that cost Dunham crucial US State Department funding. She didn't weigh these refrains down with esoteric thought; she cracked them open with soaring, soulful dance. The locales and rituals she animated – from plantation songs and tribal initiations to Florida swamp shimmies – conjured something both fresh and deep-rooted at once, finding an authenticity not through imitation or realism but enthusiasm and respect.

Conscious that her scenarios often abstracted certain practices or swirled together different cultures, Dunham called on programme notes to highlight her creative licence. A 1955 playbill for *Rites de Passage*, for example, stated: 'The rites herein represented do not refer to any one particular society, neither do they pretend to represent the enaction of a realistic ceremony. They have been created in an effort to present, at least partially, the deep emotional interest which every primitive community feels in the individual and to expose the intense personal experience which accompanies every profound change.'[12] She had a similar note for *Southland* when it premiered: 'This is the story of no actual lynching in the Southern states of America, and still it is the story of every one of them.'[13]

In recordings of Dunham's work, you can feel her passion for the customs they showcase, an energetic admiration for their unique evocations of life and community, even the ones with bleak origins. I have a star-bright sense memory of practising some of the styles from *Tropics and Le Jazz Hot* in a vintage jazz course at university: the cakewalk, the juba, rollicking social dances that originated in slave circles as expressions of kinship. We strutted, strolled, patted our thighs. We laughed when we were told to romp faster, louder. There's a puzzle to be solved in these dances, a skirmish inside your own skin to knit a dance born of bondage into something zipping and free. Sometimes the contrast lands uneasily, like an unconscious smirk in the face of bad news. But when you figure out how to reconcile it, you can feel its energy in your guts, issuing fire as you lark along.

———

1940 was the year Katherine Dunham went from luminary to lodestar. In the four years since her Caribbean research trip, she'd built up a robust portfolio of solo and ensemble dances, securing engagements across the stages of Chicago and the occasional New York

City gig too, including a choreography credit in a musical revue called *Pins and Needles*. In February 1940 she performed in a one-off concert that would end up igniting her star. *Tropics and Le Jazz Hot* was her company's first Broadway appearance, booked to fill an empty Sunday slot at the Windsor Theater, and made such a splash that the venue rebooked it for another three months.

The 'Tropics' portion of the show strung together Caribbean and Latin-themed numbers, including the elegant 'Rara Tonga', a solo based on Melanesian folklore, while the 'Jazz' part thrived on bluesy Americana tributes. The show introduced 'Batucada', inspired by the Bahia region of Brazil – a flirty, hip-swaying solo that sent Dunham twirling in a foot-tall turban and a floor-length frock, beaming as a fisherman wound her up in his rope. It was one of the show's best-loved moments and became a signature Dunham routine.

Tropics and Le Jazz Hot drew sold-out crowds and rave reviews across its extended run, spurring George Balanchine – in his heyday as the architect of neoclassical ballet – to cast Dunham and her company in his choreography for a new Broadway musical *Cabin in the Sky*. Swiftly dubbed 'the hottest thing on Broadway',[14] the show ran for five months in New York and another few along the West Coast, opening the door for several Hollywood films that put Dunham on the national radar, starting with *Carnival of Rhythm*, a 1941 Warner Bros. picture that cast her opposite Archie Savage and Talley Beatty. Her next stage spectacular, *Tropical Revue*, propelled her to international fame.

Despite its name-boosting, Hollywood had strained Dunham's finances and well-being. 'I have lost many opportunities and much income by refusing to play the role of a maid,' she lamented in a 1942 letter to her stepmother, disheartened by the racial discrimination that plagued the industry.[15] That same year, after turning down a studio contract that insisted she replace her darkest-skinned dancers, Dunham left Los Angeles and hired the impresario Sol Hurok. He'd previously managed tours for Isadora Duncan and the Ballet Russe de Monte-Carlo, and helped Dunham refocus on staging her own productions, a step change that led to the creation of *Tropical Revue* in 1943.

Devised as a three-act extravaganza, *Tropical Revue* reprised some of Dunham's existing choreography, including routines from *Tropics and Le Jazz Hot*, and worked in new dances too, spicing up the *mise en scène* with a jangling orchestra and procession of onstage musicians. Dunham populated the first and final acts with colourful numbers like 'Rara Tonga', and sandwiched *Rites de Passage* in between as a pensive centrepiece. Her husband John Pratt, who began creating stage designs for Dunham in the late 1930s, designed dazzling costumes and sets, while Hurok placed ads billing the show in jazzy terms: 'a musical heatwave . . . Boogie! Shimmy! jazz and jive!'[16]

For many critics, *Tropical Revue* was a bold, cultured showing – 'projected with a finesse and adroitness based on discipline, control and intelligence', in the words of a Cleveland writer, who deemed Dunham 'a show woman of great deftness, both as a director and as a performer'.[17] For others, the hip-grinding and belly-baring – especially in *Rites de Passage* – weakened her claim to high culture. One New York critic referred to Dunham's performance as 'revealing, tempestuous and torrid',[18] while a public official in Boston banned the inclusion of *Rites de Passage* on the grounds that it was 'suggestive and offensive'.[19] You can read the racism in their consternation – a discomfort with Black bodies defying their long history of commodification and hypersexuality. Dan Burley, a Black critic, took a more nuanced view, declaring that 'Katherine Dunham is today to dancing what Duke Ellington has been to swing music'.[20]

The criticism facing Dunham echoed the hand-wringing over Maud Allan's *Vision of Salome* four decades earlier – the implication that female sexuality is vulgar, that embracing it means you can't possibly expect to be taken seriously. One of Dunham's most radical acts as an artist was confronting the smart/sexy dichotomy and insisting that she could be both. The opening scene of *Veracruzana*, an ensemble number she created in Mexico around 1947, squared this in witty form: she lounged on a hammock thumbing through a copy of *Madame Bovary* while her lover rustled beneath her skirt. Eight years later, a photograph of Marilyn Monroe reading *Ulysses* in a swimsuit would explode this conceit on the world stage.

Audiences, for their part, had little issue with Dunham's voluptuous aesthetic. Like *Tropics and Le Jazz Hot*, *Tropical Revue* shattered its initial engagement, evolving into a three-month Broadway run followed by a year-plus national tour and an engagement in Canada. The final number, 'Cakewalk', saw Dunham reappear in a succession of different costumes to jubilant applause. The show stabilised her finances enough for her to continue choreographing new pieces in New York, including 1945's *Shango*, inspired by the African god of thunder.

In 1947, Dunham took her company to Mexico – the start of a twenty-year period of round-the-world tours that introduced her extravaganzas to Europe, North Africa, East Asia, South America and beyond. She found an especially appreciative audience in England in 1948, where her show *Caribbean Rhapsody* took hold, steaming in the same year that the HMT *Empire Windrush* brought a generation of West Indians to British shores. Her Continental reception in the late 1940s was also red-hot, particularly in Paris. 'La Dunham is sweeping Europe in a way that tops even Isadora Duncan,' proclaimed one 1949 dispatch.[21]

While not without their snags, these early years on the road were a welcome retreat from the fractious racial landscape of mid-century America. Despite steely efforts from the National Association for the Advancement of Colored People and other organisations aligned against racial discrimination, the legacy of 'separate but equal' dogged the United States in the 1940s and 1950s. Thousands of neighbourhoods, schools, lunch counters and restrooms, even parks and cemeteries, remained segregated by race, especially in the South, where Jim Crow statutes still held a vicious grip.

Throughout the *Tropical Revue* tour, Dunham's troupe was asked to graciously receive applause in states where Black residents' taxes routinely went to white-only services. On several occasions they had trouble finding hotels that accepted Black guests, and Dunham's interracial marriage regularly drew hostile comments.

In 1944, the same year that the word 'racism' appeared for the first time in a US Supreme Court judgement, Dunham used her curtain call to inform an all-white audience at the Memorial Auditorium in Louisville, Kentucky, that despite their standing ovation, her company would be ending its engagement early because 'I have discovered that your management will not allow people like you to sit next to people like us.' She went on to reference the ongoing Second World War, and her hope that the fight 'for tolerance and democracy' overseas would prompt a much-needed self-reckoning at home.[22]

The incident was the start of an increasingly public stand against racism. In 1950, during a tour of South America, Dunham filed a lawsuit against the Esplanada Hotel in São Paulo for its refusal to accept guests of colour, a move that sparked political protests and the introduction of a new law banning racial discrimination in Brazil. That same year, she worked with the National Symphony Orchestra of Chile to create *Southland*, a rebuke of America's antebellum past, and her most political work to date.

Told over two scenes, *Southland* depicted a wealthy white woman's false rape accusation against a Black field hand. The first, set on the grounds of a lush plantation, climaxed with a mob hanging the field hand from a magnolia tree; the second saw the Black community mourn his death in a conceptual fever dream that played out in a steamy club setting. The work sported Dunham's characteristic insertion of ethnic styles – including folksy plantation dances and a breakneck Cuban habanera – but its sobering narrative and graphic themes extinguished any glint of festivity. Its introduction in a communist country, in the middle of the Cold War, when Americans' right to criticise their country came at the risk of being labelled a traitor, imbued it with an extra layer of dissent.

Heedful of such tensions, the US Embassy in Chile halted *Southland* after just one performance, pressuring Dunham into cutting short its debut run in Santiago. She remounted it in Paris in 1953, but this second showing was its last. Still, the chorus for civil rights chanted on. The 1950s brought a pumping fist of bus boycotts and lunch-counter sit-ins. Rosa Parks refused to give up her seat, and fifty thousand people filed past the lynched teenager Emmett Till's open casket. *Brown v. the Board of Education*, the 1954 Supreme Court case that ruled racial segregation in schools unconstitutional, burst open the dam of segregation. It was the era of Ralph Ellison's *Invisible Man* and James Baldwin's musings on the journey to freedom, 'uphill all the way'.[23] Dunham, like her peers, would not go gentle into that good night.

———

When Dunham joined the University of Chicago's anthropology department in 1929, she was moved by a lecture from one of her professors, Robert Redfield, on the African origins of popular African American dances. He later became her adviser, steering her towards ethnographic studies of dance that considered its social power within a changing society. This was an emerging area of anthropology, and Dunham's fieldwork in the Caribbean drove it forward with an innovative research approach that prioritised on-the-ground participation over neutral observation. She learned the dances that she witnessed during her trip, experiencing their sensations, the way a single tilt of the head or curl of the finger can change their whole message.

Turning her attention to dance became a way for Dunham to remain an 'intelligent investigator', as she put it, while continuing to pursue her 'strong drive for motion – rhythmic motion'.[24] You can see 'artist' and 'scholar' interlaced across her biography: in the rich sensory language of her academic writing, in the meticulousness of her technique, and the craft that went into her productions. When Dunham opened her famous dance school in 1944, in Manhattan, she swiftly expanded it into an interdisciplinary institute offering courses in anthropology, psychology and logic alongside dance, music, drama and Caribbean studies.

Her school swelled in size and prestige over the next decade, becoming an influential hub for dance and movement studies. Gregory Peck, Sidney Poitier, James Dean, Marlon Brando and Shirley MacLaine all moved through Dunham's studios at one point. Syvilla Fort, one of her early company members, played a key role in the school's management, teaching Dunham technique and ballet, and José Limón and Archie Savage also ran courses in the early years. A scholarship programme brought numerous up-and-coming Black performers through the doors, including Eartha Kitt, who joined the school in the 1940s and later danced and sang with Dunham's company.

Despite their glowing reputations, Dunham's troupe and her school both suffered from precarious finances. In the mid-1950s she closed the latter and secured a handful of international film appearances for her company to keep it afloat between stage shows; the following decade, she shuttered that too. Dunham's last Broadway appearance was in 1962, in a Haitian-themed revue called *Bamboche!*; three years later, her company sang its swansong with *L'Ag'Ya*. In between, she set a series of evocative dances for the New York Metropolitan Opera's new version of *Aida*, and made trips to Senegal, Nigeria and Morocco, where she established several important ambassadorial connections.

These visits to Africa opened the door to a new avenue in her career that reimagined dance not just as performance but as a social act – a powerful methodology in the early years of the Black Power movement, with its focus on embedding racial pride across the cultural and political spheres. Harnessing both her anthropology and dance expertise, Dunham returned to Senegal in 1966 as a US State Department cultural adviser for the inaugural World Festival of Negro Arts, serving as President Léopold Senghor's artistic and technical director, and spent almost two years in Dakar helping train the country's National Ballet. Back on American soil, she took up an artist-in-residence post at Southern Illinois University, working with writers, performers and anthropologists to establish a new curriculum embedding dance within the wider discipline of anthropology.

Illinois soon became the site of another Dunham legacy: the Performing Arts Training Center (PATC), in East St Louis, which she established in a vacant high school as an antidote to the city's mounting gang problem. Dunham assembled a team of teachers from former company members and local residents, and together they led free classes in Dunham technique, percussion, music evaluation and more, all aimed at underserved youths. She swiftly confirmed her street cred by getting arrested at a Black Power meeting, garnering attention from the national press and significant new interest in her initiative.

The assassination of Martin Luther King in April 1968, around ten months after the PATC opened, was a litmus test for Dunham's community vision. East St Louis erupted in riots, and Dunham begged the city's gang members to come to her centre to release their frustration in a cathartic drum circle. As the dust settled, her outfit continued to grow, expanding into an accredited institute that offered classes for college credit and to the wider community. Dunham added theatre design, karate and other eclectic courses to the curriculum, and even organised a small resident company to give recitals to the public. In time she began running master's seminars that attracted dancers from around the world – a programme she continued to run every summer until her death in 2006.

Her activism reached new heights in 1992, when Dunham, aged eighty-three, went on a forty-seven-day hunger strike to protest the US discriminatory deportation of Haitian refugees fleeing political persecution. It was a deafening howl from a woman who'd spent sixty years raising her voice against misapprehensions of Black bodies.

Dunham spent her life bestriding different identities: glamorous and intellectual, theatrical and serious, cosmopolitan artist and public servant. While these parallel tracks sometimes made it difficult for critics to place her work – as one reviewer said of *Tropical Revue* in 1944: 'Broadway calls it sex, critics call it art, science calls it anthropology, but whatever it is, it's worth your money'[25] – they created a new paradigm for cross-cultural celebration. Dunham transformed perceptions about the seriousness and importance of Black dance traditions, her solo roles in particular, which presented a woman of poise and complexity, in touch with the heritage rhythms that shaped her unique self. She paved the way for Black performers to rejig the hierarchy of modern dance as well as their own sparkling self-conception.

ACT 3, SCENE 2

Blood at the root

When Abel Meeropol wrote 'Strange Fruit' in 1937, he apprehended in verse the lawless brutality of lynching, a horrifyingly persistent practice in America's Jim Crow years: 'Southern trees bear strange fruit / Blood on the leaves and blood at the root'.[1] Meeropol wrote the poem as an elegy for Thomas Shipp and Abram Smith, Black teenagers hanged by a lynch mob in Indiana in 1930, their murder documented in a grisly photograph by Lawrence Beitler. It contrasts the fragrance of poplars and magnolias with the stench of death, casting Black bodies as 'fruit for the crows to pluck' – a dehumanisation that underscores the bitterness of grief.

Billie Holiday brought a new tenor of contempt when she sang Meeropol's words at New York's Café Society in 1939, winding her vocals into something curled and baleful, an eerie echo of 'the bulging eyes and the twisted mouth'. And when Pearl Primus danced to them four years later, aged twenty-four, she transformed them into a full-body lament, holding their anguish in her shaking hands. Primus opened her dance with a collapse, slumping face down; she crawled on the floor, shrugged her back and scampered her feet, beat the ground with her hands, 'gathering the consciousness of mankind to this act of cruelty and injustice', as she put it.[2] She thudded in place, slashed across the diagonal. You could hear her body as it slapped the floor, heavy with suffering. She ended with a blunt, thrusting fist in the air.

Fellow dancers would marvel at her fierce new renderings of modern dance, the thumping falls and miraculous rises, while reviewers praised Primus's somatic turmoil, a compelling framework for fathoming the unfathomable. Like Holiday, Primus was Black, and she bore out her inner angst in her art. 'Dance is the fist with which I fight the sickening ignorance of prejudice,' she stated in 1968. 'It is the veiled contempt I feel for those who patronize with false smiles, handouts, empty promises, insincere compliments. Instead of growing twisted like a gnarled tree inside myself, I am able to dance out my anger and my tears.'[3] She was a true radical, raising her fist two decades before the Black Power movement clenched the gesture for its logo.

For close to fifty years, Primus created dances that protested racism, from solos condemning the ills of chain gangs to group works broadcasting the richness of African heritage. She also spent decades teaching native Black dances to performers around the world, elevating the profile and cultural worth of unsung traditions. She used her body to contemplate, to contend, to refute, to bear witness; 'to go around, scale, bore through, batter down or ignore visible and invisible social and economic walls',[4] in her words. Her contemporaries described her as a powerful mover with the thighs of a sprinter, a short woman who could jump five feet high, propelled by the force of righteous indignation. Martha Graham said Primus moved like a panther – another link to the Black pride she presaged.

Primus often framed her mission in corporeal terms, a physical destiny: 'It was like a mandate,' she reflected in 1994, the year she died. 'It was something I had to do . . . I was given a body strong enough.'[5] Her dedication to her cause was intense, particularly in the 1940s and 1950s, when her outspokenness triggered scrutiny from the FBI. Like the revolutionary Black artists in her ambit, Primus was unwilling to ignore racial discrimination. She countered it with anger and perseverance, using her body as a dais to promote a dignified Black identity.

An interesting twist to Primus's rendition of *Strange Fruit* is that she didn't cast herself as a Black mourner but as a white lynch mob member remorseful of her complicity. 'The dance begins as the last person begins to leave the lynching ground and the horror of what she has seen grips her, and she has to do a smooth, fast roll away from that burning flesh,' as she described it.[6] This perspective brought a taut psychological complexity to the subject, posing new questions about inaction and regret. It was a subversion of minstrelsy at a time when blackface was still common on the American stage, a counter to the idea that a black-and-white lens could be applied to a social ill as dense as racism. Later she'd reprise *Strange Fruit* at Café Society, the very nightclub where Holiday immortalised the poem in song, immersing herself in the political cabaret scene that fostered Meeropol's verse to begin with.

Primus was an artist of many layers – a creator, performer, researcher and educator who built a physical scaffold for things you can't touch: bigotry, indignity, pride. When she began adding more African-themed dances to her repertoire in the 1950s, joining her critiques of racial inequality in the United States, she introduced a rich pan-African vision that showed how Black people everywhere could lay claim to their heritage and promote social change through dance. Whether she was confronting racism or celebrating diversity, she brought complex topics to the stage and challenged us to stay silent. She laid the possibilities for progress bare and made them impossible to ignore.

Primus premiered *Strange Fruit* (at that point titled *A Man Has Just Been Lynched*) at New York City's 92nd Street Y in February 1943, in a concert that featured four other emerging moderns, including Julia Levien, a performer trained by one of Isadora Duncan's dancers. According to the critic John Martin, an early advocate, Primus's performance brought the audience to their feet, where they 'literally yelled for more of her'. Deeply impressed by her energy and technical proficiency, he named her 'Dance Debutante Number One' in his review for the *New York Times*, remarking that she deserved her own company.[7]

Primus's performance that night – which also included a dance rebuke of sharecropping, plus a tribute to Harlem swing traditions – resounded at a time of growing resistance to the segregation laws that had blighted the United States for more than half a century. Emboldened by the nation's stand against fascism in the Second World War, Black Americans were pushing for justice at home. In 1944, the same year that Katherine Dunham made her defiant Kentucky curtain call, Primus broadcast a robust opinion in the *Daily Worker*: 'In America's bosom we have the roots of Democracy, but the roots do not mean there are leaves. The tree could easily grow bare. We will never relax our war effort abroad but we must fight at home with equal fierceness. This is an all out war; we will not stop fighting until everyone is free from inequality.'[8] Again, trees and their knotted boughs become an allegory for Black bodily freedoms.

From her first years as a dancer in the early 1940s, Primus used her art for both social protest and self-discovery. *African Ceremonial*, one of the dances she debuted in her breakout concert at the Y, was the first in a long line of works exploring her bloodlines. She choreographed to African American spirituals, like *Motherless Child* (1947), contemplating the horrors of slavery; brought the legacy of Jim Crow centre stage in *Slave Market* (1944) and *Steal Away to Freedom* (1952); and animated the ache of several poems by Langston Hughes, including *To One Dead* (1946). Primus was one of the first dancemakers to bring these thorny ideas to the stage, dancing a campaign for deliverance at a time when Black bodies were routinely criminalised. She danced the convolutions of bondage and freedom, tapping into a vibrant diasporic cultural continuum and giving airtime to the defining social issue of her time.

Like Katherine Dunham, Primus took a scholarly approach to her examination of Black themes, undertaking extensive research into African, Caribbean and African American cultures, even before enrolling in an anthropology graduate programme in 1945. She completed academic fieldwork across the Southern United States, Africa and the Caribbean, and eventually gained a doctorate in African and Caribbean studies, along with the Distinguished Service Award from the Association of American Anthropologists in 1985 and several major awards of state, including a National Medal of Arts and the Liberian government's honoured Star of Africa. She travelled widely to explore and share her passions, showing a similar fascination in the junction of dance and culture that inspired Dunham, especially the conviction that dance is a key part of the life of the people. The two never worked together, but their combined efforts opened the stage to Black dancers, allowing them to recover traditions degraded by slavery and diluted on the vaudeville stage.

Unlike Dunham, however, Primus eschewed pizzazz and showmanship. 'You could see her connection to the earth,' Billie Allen, a fellow performer in the 1950s, recalled. 'She wasn't interested in being glamorous or pretty.'[9] Primus danced to simple settings, letting her body tell the story of the cultures she observed, and favoured moves that were visceral and not theatricalised. She had a few forays into Broadway, including a Caribbean revue featuring some Dunham dancers, but mainly avoided venues associated with popular entertainment. 'This is the work I was meant to do: to show the dignity, beauty and strength in the heritage of peoples of African ancestry,' she remarked in the last year of her life.[10] Her body was her theatre – a site to reflect, react and build power.

The year 1943 was a boon for Primus. After wowing at the Y in her first solo performance, she booked a short gig at Café Society in Greenwich Village, one of New York City's first racially integrated mainstream cabarets. Launched in the late 1930s to showcase Black talent, the club was a hot spring for artistic premieres and political debate, helping raise the profile of emerging voices like Lena Horne and Hazel Scott.

In a small slice of floor space normally reserved for singers or speakers, Primus danced in fifteen-minute intervals, introducing the downtown crowd to her floor-beating art. Jacqueline Hairston, a dancer who later toured with Primus, recalled the electricity she brought to these evenings: 'The atmosphere was open and alive . . . we were enthralled, ecstatic, unbelieving. It was all part of Black people being welcomed.'[11] Primus's performances were so popular that the venue extended her gig into a ten-month engagement. In between shows she continued to create, producing a dozen dances in a year.

Throughout 1943, John Martin continued to praise Primus's 'superb elevation, her speed, her dramatic power' in the *New York Times*, saying that 'no other Negro dancer has in any comparable degree touched on an art so aware of its racial strength and so true to it'.[12] Bridling his praise within the purview of 'Black dance', and not the wider modern dance scene, was an act of critical segregation that would affect Primus throughout her career. Martin's reviews lacked the exoticism many dance critics furnished as her profile grew – the characterisations as a 'dusky little dancer',[13] racism that hit a fever pitch when she travelled in Europe – but his racialised distinctions reinforced the wedge between modern dance and 'Black' modern dance, implying they had different faculties and should be appraised separately.

He qualified it a few months later, when the *New York Times* ran side-by-side ads of Primus's Café Society show and Katherine Dunham's brand-new *Tropical Revue*, with corresponding pull-quotes from Martin to advertise both. Primus was deemed 'the most gifted artist-dancer of her race . . . for by any standard of comparison she is an outstanding dancer without regard for race'. For Dunham, he wrote: 'Sex in the Caribbean is doing all right.'[14] It was the start of a critical gulf between the two moderns that often pitted them against each other. Even writers who praised Primus unequivocally often did so at Dunham's expense. It was unfathomable that their approaches could contrast and still have their own merits.

Primus's profile got a national boost when she performed at the first Negro Freedom Rally, in the summer of 1943, appearing alongside Duke Ellington and Paul Robeson before a twenty-thousand-strong crowd at Madison Square Garden. She presented two solos: *Hard Time Blues* and *Jim Crow Train*, each a critique of Black oppression in the rural South. Langston Hughes, who'd directed the pageant, commemorated her performance in poetic fashion in a Chicago paper: 'The way she jumped was the same as a shout in church . . . It was like a work-weary sister suddenly shouting out loud on a Sunday morning when the minister starts singing, JESUS KNOWS JUST HOW MUCH I CAN BEAR.'[15]

As with Katherine Dunham's Kentucky curtain call, Primus used her platform at the rally to align the fight for civil rights with the war abroad, a comparison that was noted in her FBI file. 'I know we must all do our part in this war to beat Fascism and I consider the battle against Jim Crow in America part of that fight which is taking part on the battlefronts of the world,' she proclaimed from the dais. 'Each one of us can field a weapon against Jim Crow and Fascism and my special one is dancing. I shall continue to protest

Jim Crow through my dancing until Victory is won.'[16] Later that year she had an audience with Eleanor Roosevelt and the civil rights activist Mary McLeod Bethune as part of Asadata Dafora's African Dance Festival at Carnegie Hall. By the end of 1943, Primus had formed her own small company, reworking her solo choreography to magnify its power across a group.

It was a meteoric climb for someone who'd only begun dancing a few years earlier. Born in Trinidad in 1919, Primus and her family immigrated to Manhattan when she was a toddler, joining a wave of working-class West Indians ablaze with 'little pockets of tropical dreams in alien tongues', as Hughes once put it.[17] Family lore rooted her birthplace in the mountains of Port of Spain, a shotgun shack atop a viper pit; her ancestral tree, however, had roots in faraway places: the Grenadines, the Ashanti tribe of Ghana, the Ibo of eastern Nigeria, even Germany, the birthplace of her paternal Jewish grandfather. Discussions of the family's African heritage were everyday features of Primus's home life. As a teenager she took occasional dance classes at small studios and Works Progress Administration sites, though her main focus was track and field, where she excelled as a sprinter and set school records in the high jump.

Primus was a serious reader and one of few Black students to attend the selective Hunter College in the late 1930s, where she studied biology and premedical sciences. While she used her free time to start an after-school dance club during her undergraduate years, she had her professional heart set on a career as a doctor. Unable to find work as a lab technician, though, due to racial discrimination in the medical field, she took a series of odd jobs after graduating, including a role as a wardrobe assistant for the National Youth Administration's (NYA) dance company. In 1939, when a dancer dropped out, Primus was hired as an understudy, and she found a new focus for her energy.

After a year dancing with the NYA, she auditioned for the New Dance Group (NDG), becoming its first Black scholarship student in 1941, and began a stint of furious study under the biggest names in American modern dance: Martha Graham, Doris Humphrey, Charles Weidman, Sophie Maslow, Anna Sokolow, William Bales, Jane Dudley and Helen Tamiris. She learned the principles of choreography and music, including how to navigate themes, variations and the slews of a composition. She got the chance to perform with Maslow and Dudley, play around with her own choreography, and eventually teach classes, where she led students in modern, African, jazz and blues styles.

Primus's athletic training was a bonus, giving her a speed and brawn that far outstripped that of her peers. Her movement quality was dynamic and explosive; she became known for sky-high leaps and classroom exercises that required immense endurance. In her study of mid-century modern dance, the critic Margaret Lloyd took note of the awe-inspiring aerials of *Hard Time Blues*, one of Primus's early solos: 'Pearl takes a running jump, lands in an upper corner and sits there, unconcernedly paddling the air with her legs. She does it repeatedly, from one side of the stage, then the other, apparently unaware of the involuntary gasps from the audience.'[18] Maya Angelou, who studied with Primus during her brief dance career in the 1950s, said she cried the first time she saw her perform: 'I'd never seen such strength and grace at the same time.'[19]

By the 1940s, the NDG had moved beyond the militancy that energised members in the previous decade, but its ethos still revolved around social democracy and politically motivated dance. Primus's time with the group helped her identify the discrimination that had shut her out of the medical profession and investigate the potentials of artistic activism. She played around with established modern dance principles, adding in rhythmic variations and bent-kneed pelvic rolls.

She prioritised intensity, physically and emotionally, and forged visceral blows of movement that left the floor vibrating in her wake.

A conscientious learner, she put months of research in the first works she created under the NDG, including 1943's *African Ceremonial*, a solo inspired by a Congolese fertility legend.* She went to the New York Public Library to read about regional dances and social customs, interrogated her family on the Ashanti practices of her grandfather, a Trinidadian religious leader, and studied the gracile curves of African sculptures and artefacts. Her interest in African traditions had a strong social purpose of cultural retrieval:

> *I see Africa as the continent of strength; it is a place with ancient civilizations, civilizations wrecked and destroyed by the slave-seekers. I know an Africa that gave the world the iron on which now it moves, an Africa of nations, dynasties, cultures, languages, great migrations, powerful movements, slavery . . . all that makes life itself . . . And when I think of my people here in America too, I see something that they have to see clearer, that whites have to know about. I see the long road we have trod, the movements for freedom we have been in, from the slave revolts that dot our early history, up to our participation in the Revolutionary War.*[20]

Primus saw cultural study as key to the fight against racism. 'Our culture is equal to the culture of any other race, but we must take the time to study it and recognize it. It will help us in our battle for freedom.'[21] Her convictions were deep enough that she paused her performing career just a year after it started in favour

---

* Primus debuted the routine at the 92nd Street Y, alongside *Strange Fruit*, and later expanded it to include fourteen dancers and a group of live drummers, dancing her own vibrant solo section on top of an altar.

of an extended research trip to the American South. Her aim? To 'know my own people where they are suffering most'.[22] She spent six months of 1944 in rural Alabama, Georgia and South Carolina, where she posed as a migrant farm worker, picking cotton and fruit and attending worship services and community socials, observing her workmates as they stooped, chatted, endured and extolled.

'The Jim-Crowism I encountered affected me like the shock of a fist hitting me full force in the face,' she'd later reflect. 'The discrimination is so vicious that it hangs like a blanket of darkness over all the colored people all the time.'[23] The experience motivated her to rework some of the dances she'd created with the NDG, and to create new ones, when she returned to New York in autumn 1944, working in the hallelujahs she'd witnessed in the fields and the pews.

Hard Time Blues, for example, with its spotlight on sharecropping, took on a new air of resistance as 'a protest against the system which robs the people of the fruits of their labour'.[24] Primus performed the dance to a live folk song, embodying its deep-bellied cries: 'Give me food, give me shelter, give me something.'[25] She swung low to the ground, pushing away invisible walls; tucked her knees up high and leaped upwards in defiance. She gathered her anger in her hands and let it rip in a gruff, thigh-beating finale.

Dances like *Hard Time Blues* made a splash when Primus performed them at labour organisations and rallies throughout the 1940s, including events organised by American Youth for Democracy. In 1946, she formed a company with a small band of musicians and the dancers Joe Nash and Jacqueline Hairston, and toured the East Coast and Midwest college circuit with a programme combining Deep South-themed dances, jazz and blues numbers and a series of African-inspired works, including *Dance of Beauty*, inspired by the Watusis of Rwanda. A Boston reviewer praised Nash and Hairston's harmonising presence, calling them 'dancers of grace, style and variety, able, like Miss Primus, to go from capricious foolery to impressive symbolism'.[26]

Offstage, the racism that inspired Primus's work hounded her troupe: restaurants that refused them entry, guest houses that forced them to leave before other guests got up in the morning, even the odd picket sign outside venues where they were due to appear. Several performances with *Strange Fruit* on the bill were cancelled at the last minute with no explanation; and at various points across the tour Primus was trailed by government informants employed to monitor potential ties to the Communist Party – a probe that would last years and prompt the creation of a Security Index Card in the dancer's name.

She was never charged with anything, but she was deposed on several occasions and had her passport temporarily confiscated in the 1950s as part of the FBI's investigations. The incident echoed the 'unconscious protest' of possessing a Black body that Richard Wright lamented in 1940's *Native Son*: 'Every desire, every dream, no matter how intimate or personal, is a plot or a conspiracy. Every hope is a plan for insurrection. Every glance of the eye is a threat. [Your] very existence is a crime against the state!'[27] By simply existing as a Black artist, Primus challenged the American status quo. The State Department's consternation underlined the very necessity of her art.

Her Southern expedition in 1944 was the first of several key research trips that shaped her career. In 1948, after a performance in Nashville caught the attention of a member of the Rosenwald Foundation board, the body that funded Katherine Dunham's Caribbean fieldwork in the 1930s, Primus won a $4,000 grant for a study tour of West Africa. She spent eighteen months learning dances from dozens of tribal groups across Angola, Cameroon, Nigeria, Liberia, Senegal, Belgian Congo and the Gold Coast – the 'strange but hypnotic marriage between life and dance' that inspired ceremonials and fertility rites, court dances and social initiations, spiritual invocations, war dances, fire dances, celebrations of birth and death.[28] Some of these were recreational customs danced by villagers; others were concert dances by professionally trained performers.

Primus learned new articulations of the head, torso and feet, how to isolate different parts of the body at the same time, ways to navigate counter rhythms and move between different social classes and contexts. She became deeply involved in the communities she visited, and left with several affectionate nicknames, including 'Omowale' (Yoruba for 'child who has returned home') and Adora (Ibo for 'daughter of all').

Peggy and Murray Schwartz, dear friends Primus made when she started teaching at the State University of New York at Buffalo in the 1980s, would remember her 'as much a woman of words as she was of movement'[29] – a reference to the extensive written output of her travels, which included letters, essays, magazine articles and lectures, plus a diary with detailed notes, impressions and poetry. She wrote about local geography, food, customs, political organisations, work, languages and scenery, all part of her attempt 'to learn from [the peoples of Africa] the basic truths of dance and life'.[30] A Caribbean immigrant with relatives in Africa and an American upbringing, Primus was living proof of the diaspora. Dance was at the centre of her search for identity as well as her overarching world view.

A dispatch from her travels, published in an American newspaper in late 1949, told of the personal transformation she underwent as she learned from cultures that cherished dance as an everyday, deeply personal practice. Writing 'by the light of a tiny lantern and a sputtering twig dipped in palm oil' from the village of Kahnplay, Liberia, Primus reported on 'devil dancers' who rushed out of the bush to greet her with drums, summoning the whole village to dance for days in her honour. 'So it is everywhere in Liberia.

The people run down to the rivers to sing you across – and when you join in their dance you are lifted in their arms.'[31]

She didn't just keep notes on the dances she encountered on her trip; she developed a technical system for codifying them, giving them a home and a life beyond their origins – a precious treasure trove for future generations. When she returned to the United States in 1950, she started wearing African clothing, a vibrant shopfront for her new sense of self. She later established a school in New Rochelle, New York, and set to sharing what she'd learned – the 'Bakuba' warrior dance of Zaire, the engagement dance of Sierra Leone, the dances of Nigeria's Fanti fishermen and the upper classes of Benin. Her dance classes evolved to include lectures on the cultures at hand, and the use of props such as scarves and maracas. She continued touring, introducing the steps of Africa to new audiences across the nation.

'Fanga', a Liberian dance of welcome, became a staple of Primus's practice in the 1950s and is now taught across the world because of her influence. It's a choreography of chants, racing rhythms and small jumps that become wider and broader, moving in time with intricate shoulder vibrations and flat-footed strides in a circle. Where she kept the throbs of solos like *Hard Time Blues* for herself, refusing to reconstruct them on others, *Fanga* became a building block of her school and her performances – a dance for everyone, and an emblem of how she'd left home to find home. 'I welcome you,' she wrote in the programme notes of a 1951 performance. 'I stretch my arms to the earth and to the sky for I alone am not strong enough to greet you.'[32]

———

The American civil rights movement was something of a semi-conscious cause in the 1940s, not fully awake to the fury that would crack open the culture in the decades to come. The language of imagination and reverie gripped the Black artists of the day. Langston Hughes urged his countrymen to hold fast to their dreams; later would come the Harlem fantasies of the painter Jacob Lawrence and the exhortations of Martin Luther King, with his bold dream for the nation. Dancers brought their aspirations to the stage as illusions and trances, even nightmares, using the body to connect these to reality.

When Primus danced to *The Negro Speaks of Rivers*, Hughes's 1921 meditation on Black ancestry, she used his pensive language to highlight the concrete pain of inequality, zeroing in on the plight of African Americans in chain gangs and cotton fields. The choreography included spins and pivots, her body pitched in a long, pressing slant, fingers spread wide. *Jim Crow Train*, also inspired by a Hughes poem, gave a similar treatment to segregation, making its menace known.

Dancing these charged works during the 1940s brought Primus acclaim as well as spite. Some reviewers held that her dancing was undisciplined, formless; that her rejection of lyricism was not a choice but a shortcoming of her race. The same administration that subsidised her start in the dance world surveilled her when she wandered too far into the realms of creative expression. A bystander spat on Primus before a 1944 performance in Virginia, a state papered in antebellum vestige. Nevertheless, she kept creating, highlighting the brilliance of Black culture with sorrow songs and empowering rites. Her persistence took her to Broadway, Jacob's Pillow, the West Coast; onwards to England, where she performed for King George VI; then France, Italy, Finland and Israel, the latter tour making stops at settlements and army camps.

The 1950s opened the door to several more influential field trips, including a homecoming to Trinidad, where Primus reconnected with Beryl McBurnie, an artist she'd briefly performed with in the early days of her career. The visit also introduced her to Percival Borde, a dancer and drummer with McBurnie's Little Carib Theatre, and Primus's eventual life partner. When she became pregnant with their son in 1954, she continued performing late into the pregnancy and resumed shortly after his birth, proudly bringing the image of motherhood centre stage like Isadora Duncan before her. Primus's reflections in her later years on the gravity of her art also bore a manifest resemblance to Duncan's: 'I didn't choose to dance about a flower or a running brook or something. I chose to answer the ills of society with the language of dance.'[33]

Primus saw out the decade with a two-year sojourn in Liberia, one of the major players in the mid-century Pan-African movement, a global, cross-cultural strive for unity among people of African ancestry. She'd just received a master's degree in education, and together with Borde helped found and direct a performing arts centre in Monrovia, Liberia, bringing the region's indigenous dances to a theatrical setting. It was the first of several major cultural projects she'd conduct in the coming decades, working with bodies like the Ford Foundation and the US Office of Education. The Primus-Borde School of Primal Dance, which they set up in New York City in 1963, was instrumental to her doctoral studies – the basis for a series of cross-cultural teaching methods that she tested across dozens of local elementary schools in the 1960s and an endeavour that earned a commendation from the White House Conference on Children and Youth.

Starting in the 1970s, Primus took up teaching stints at several US universities, including New York University and Hunter College, her alma maters, and in 1979 she and Borde founded another institute, this time in Upstate New York, along with an associated company called Earth Theater, synthesising Primus's research into classes that blended African, Caribbean, African American and modern dance styles. It was the culmination of nearly forty years of promoting African dance as an art form worthy of study and performance. While her focus was now on directing rather than performing, her passion for social critique hadn't changed. The same year she founded her new institute, she choreographed *Michael, Row Your Boat Ashore*, a biting response to the racially motivated Alabama Baptist Church bombings of 1963. Her last known appearance onstage came in 1981, at the Theatre of the Riverside Church in Manhattan.

As a teacher, Primus artfully combined her studies in dance, anthropology and education. Hours were long, and exercises were tough, taught without mirrors and occasionally accompanied by harsh words. 'Your thighs burned so much, you couldn't walk down the stairs,' one student remembered. 'We would leave there at 1 a.m. We used to dance down the street and sing on the subway. We actually got to the point where we lived and breathed dance. She was more than our teacher. We put her on a pedestal, she was like a goddess to us.'[34]

This warm-blooded insertion of self was the backbone of Primus's career. She bridged the distance between conceptual subjects and the sensations we feel with our own skin, delivering a dance that hinged on acknowledgement and connection. She harnessed her body as a channel for fury, pride and authenticity, marrying art, politics and anthropology in a visceral new way – dance as a scream, dance as a head bowed in worship. She empowered herself when no one else would, rising up on the winds of her own culture and others, towards vital new reflections on racial identity.

ACT 3, SCENE 3

Between two worlds

There are three sets of vibrations in Pearl Lang's 1960 production *Shirah*, inspired by a Hasidic parable about a mountain spring
flowing towards the heart of the world. The first is found in Alan
Hovhaness's melancholy score, which sounds the same trembling
notes as the legend at hand, a story of yearning, limitation and
rebirth. The second comes when the dancers unfurl shimmering
white cords across the length of the stage, weaving them into a taut
lattice and plucking them like harp strings. And finally, there's the
hum of the dancing itself – hypnotic, sinuous spirals brought to a
quiver with thrumming heels and thumping fists.

Lang danced a sonorous central solo when *Shirah* premiered, arms
flying upwards in radiant bliss. The critic Doris Hering remembered
the work as an 'ecstatic utterance',[1] like the Book of Daniel's Song
of Creation, a joyous coupling of physical prayer and the holy life
force behind it. Lang's associate Ze'eva Cohen also recalled it in
spiritual terms: 'It felt like the inner soul has just been struck.'[2]

Devotional imagery frequently featured in Lang's repertoire,
which included nearly three dozen dance works inspired by Jewish
culture, from ethereal abstractions to swishing narratives, many
created between the 1950s and 1970s. A Chicago native and
second-generation Russian Jewish immigrant, Lang was captivated
by the Hasidic tradition of 'ecstatic dance', a sacrament purport-
ed to lift people to heavenly heights. She filled her choreography
with rapturous displays of feeling, channelling her conviction that

passion can elevate dance into something transcendental, not just for performers but audiences too. Her emotive style was strongly influenced by Martha Graham, her long-term mentor, and held fast to the alliance of inner sentiment and physical movement – a distinguishing tack at a time when colleagues like Merce Cunningham were starting to explore the disaffection and asceticism associated with postmodernism. Unswayed by a critical establishment increasingly inclined to find Graham-era dance 'a little too obvious in its pulse',[3] Lang embraced introspection and poetic expressionism in her art for more than fifty years, celebrating her Jewish heritage with unabashed lyricism.

Yiddish literature and music were some of Lang's favourite sources, stemming from her childhood immersion in Chicago's Yiddish arts scene in the 1920s and 1930s, skippered by Ashkenazi immigrants who used theatre to recreate the familiar beats of the shtetl. Lang's first language was Yiddish, and she regularly sprinkled its argot into rehearsals and interviews. She set several dances to verse by balladeers like Itzik Manger and gave impassioned readings of Yiddish poetry with her husband, Joseph Wiseman, an actor she met in the 1960s while directing a theatre production of Shalom Ansky's *The Dybbuk*. In 1975 she brought Ansky's Yiddish classic to the dance stage with a brooding production that intensified its mystical underbelly.

Like Pearl Primus and Katherine Dunham, and like many of her Jewish contemporaries, including Hadassah Spira Epstein and Pauline Koner, Lang found huge artistic inspiration in her ethnic roots and used her art to explore diasporic customs, often modernising them with a feminist spin. While these dancers applied a revivalist lens, incorporating indigenous and folk dance idioms into their practice, Lang focused her innovations on content, not form. She embraced the stories, songs and tribulations that fortify the Jewish chronicle – Old Testament heroines, prophetic writings, Hebraic traditions, even the devastation of pogroms, ghettos and concentration camps – and vivified them with a modified version of Graham technique, offering a modern lens for consideration.

Lang's cosmopolitan self-image further distinguished her from Epstein and Koner, soloists who infused their visage of Jewry with bejewelled headdresses, dark make-up and glimmering, midriff-baring costumes. Lang, by contrast, favoured simple, streamlined silhouettes, again using modern sensibilities to ignite her historical themes. She also worked with some of the great Jewish composers of the twentieth century – including Steve Reich, Aaron Copland, Zalmen Mlotek, Sergiu Natra, Jan Radzynski and Mordecai Seter – to connect her themes to new contexts and give them contemporary resonance.

Lang's devotion to Jewish material made her exceptional in the mid-century modern dance sphere, even alongside Anna Sokolow and Sophie Maslow, senior counterparts who frequented many of the same circuits as Lang between the 1940s and 1960s, from the Graham studio and Jacob's Pillow to the Chanukah Festivals at Madison Square Garden. The Jewish-themed dances Sokolow and Maslow created in the post-war years represented a small fraction of their overall portfolios, whereas Judaism informed more than half of the sixty-plus dances Lang created in her career, starting with *Song of Deborah*, her first major piece of choreography.

Based on the victory hymn of Deborah, the prophetess who led the Israelites in battle against Sisera, *Song of Deborah* is one of several Lang works that reconsiders the identity of Jewish women. Lang originally conceived it in 1949 as a duet for the new dance department at the Juilliard School of Music, dancing the role of Deborah opposite the warrior Yael. Over the next two decades, she reworked the piece several times, expanding the cast and changing the music for different settings, including a 1970 restaging for the Jewish Theological Seminary of America. A rotating cast of principals brought new interpretations of Yael over the years, from Ze'eva Cohen, a Yemenite dancer from Tel Aviv, to Mary Hinkson, an African American Graham alumna.

The production's scale and impact grew with every revision. By the time *Song of Deborah* aired on a television broadcast in 1970, it had a full company of male dancers to summon Sisera's fearsome brigade of Canaanites. There were boots, helmets and rocky plains, blasts of music overlaid with a voice reciting the almighty incantations of Deborah, the Bible's only female judge, who stepped up to battle and 'arose a mother in Israel'.[4] The embellished *mise en scène* enhanced Deborah's depth rather than overshadowing it. She was fierce and fearless, swelling in strength as her enemy encircled her.

Lang danced the same vigorous choreography she'd devised twenty years earlier: clenched fists, pumping arms and deep lunges that slashed like a sword. She added an extra dimension of womanpower by winding a strip of metal around her arm, a nod to the tefillin, the Jewish garment reserved for men at morning prayers. Like Anna Sokolow in *Kaddish*, this was a silent challenge to the exclusion of women from certain parts of the faith, aligning the reverence surrounding the garment with a strong female leader.

Lang's Deborah was robust and dedicated, pious but not passive. She stood in stark opposition to the 'belle juive' stereotype popularised by nineteenth-century European artists, who often depicted the Jewish women of history as perilously sexy beauties from the East – Salome chief among them, particularly as imagined by Oscar Wilde and Maud Allan. Deborah's heroism also defied what Jean-Paul Sartre identified as 'an aura of rape and massacre'[5] associated with this exoticised motif. Lang debuted her vision just a few years after the Silverman siddur (a well-known Conservative prayer book) changed its wording to stop thanking God 'for not making me a woman' and instead give praise for 'making me a free person'* – a progressive stride Lang channelled in her portrait of female leadership.

Svelte, lissom and remarkably fleet-footed, Lang was a charismatic performer, often diverting eyes away from her fellow dancers and onto herself. Even when they were unconvinced by certain compositions, critics tended to single out her luminous stage presence. As one noted wryly in 1972, 'almost everything Pearl Lang choreographs is a solo – whether it is for one person or twenty.'[6] Known for her lyrical intensity and clean, fluid geometry, she imbued her dancing and her choreography with a swishing combination of speed, elegance and drama.

Lang cast her dances with top performers from a range of fields, including theatre and ballet, and pushed them to move with the same passion she did, articulating their drama through atmosphere and a concentrated, precise passage through space. 'Don't tell us you're angry,' an interviewer observed her telling a student in 2002. 'Dance the anger!'[7] Movement wasn't just a demonstration of feeling to Lang; it was a summoning of inner strength, an act of self-empowerment. Like Deborah, Miriam and the other heroines of the Old Testament – the 'first women's libbers', by her reckoning[8] – she positioned herself as a torchbearer for her people, dancing their resilience in her own commanding way.

* Debra Newman Kamin and Alisa Pomerantz-Boro, presidents of the Rabbinical Assembly, discuss the details of this change in a *Jewish Telegraphic Agency* article from 6 July 2018, noting that 'Women clergy still have a long way to go in the Conservative movement . . . And there are the typical challenges that far too many working women confront everywhere: pay gaps, questions about how we will care for our children, comments about our clothing and appearance, worries that we are shortchanging our children and spouses, and symptoms of superwoman syndrome because we want to do it all.' ('Conservative movement is closing its gender gap, but there is still work to be done')

Along with her own concerts, Lang's career included performances in several Broadway musicals, a two-decade stretch on the
Juilliard School faculty and a thirty-five-year association with
Martha Graham's company, which she joined as a twenty-year-
old, swiftly gaining Graham's favour and eventually inheriting her
original roles – the first dancer to do so. In 1952 she established
the Pearl Lang Dance Theater, the font of more than sixty original
dance works. In their early days, Lang and her dancers could often
be found trying out new numbers at the 92nd Street Y, where young
moderns flocked to Fred Berk's Wednesday night Israeli folk dancing classes; two decades later they joined forces with Alvin Ailey's
troupe to spearhead the new American Dance Center. Lang's
artistry earned her two Guggenheim fellowships, an honorary
doctorate and scores of awards for services to Jewish culture.

For half a century, she straddled different spheres of identity
and interest. She was both a Graham acolyte and an independent
artist, a fixture of the establishment and its fringes. She combined the urbanity of modern dance with the old-country charm
of Yiddishkeit, leading her to new threads between history and
modernity, and to pluralistic incarnations of 'home' – America,
Russia, Israel and beyond. She used her work to delineate and
reconcile these dualities, marrying her own singularity with the
universals of the human experience.

———

Freida Lack gave birth to her daughter, Pearl, in 1921, the same
year Isadora Duncan moved to Moscow to cheer on the Russian
Revolution. Duncan's star was starting to cause more drama than
favour in the United States, but Freida was a steadfast fan. 'My mother
saw every concert Isadora gave when she came to Chicago,' Lang said
in a 1989 interview, highlighting it as a formative influence on her

own dance journey. 'I grew up with pictures of Isadora in the house, the whole romantic legend.'[9] Lang never saw Duncan perform – she gave her last performances in the US the year after Lang was born – but when she was three or four, her mother took her to a performance by the Duncan Dancers at Chicago's Orchestra Hall, where she watched these protégées skip to a buoyant Russian score, channelling their predecessor's glowing, independent spirit. Soon afterwards, Freida enrolled Lang in a dance school that promised Greek tunics and a free-form approach to ballet – not exactly Duncanesque but reasonably close.

Dance, music and theatre were the essentials of Lang's upbringing. Her parents – immigrants with family ties to Pinsk and Vilnius – were avid patrons of the Chicago arts sphere, frequenting its many institutions, from the Chicago Symphony to their local Yiddish theatres. They played piano, wrote poetry and took Lang and her brother to concerts, operas and dance productions, introducing them to beloved expressionist performers like Harald Kreutzberg. After school, Lang took drama, dance and music lessons at the Albany Park Workmen's Circle before accompanying her mother to night school to learn English.

'I am a product of Yiddish education, which, as I look back, was a gift,' she reflected in 1986. 'When I look around me and see how other people grew up, I realize I was absolutely blessed by what I learned.'[10] While she would end up swapping 'Lack' for 'Lang' early on in her career, under the advice that it was a more stage-friendly name, Lang never stopped foregrounding the heritage that moulded her.

As a teenager Lang studied modern dance with Frances Allis, founder of the New World Dancers, and performed publicly for the first time in 1937, enlisting her fellow students to join her in a self-choreographed work to Mozart's *Eine kleine Nachtmusik* at the Chicago Opera House. She also appeared in a Works Progress Administration-associated solo created by the ballet director Ruth Page around this time, and participated in a series of masterclasses by Martha Graham, Doris Humphrey, Charles Weidman and Hanya Holm when they visited Northwestern University.

It was her first encounter with the New York City modern dance establishment, and her lucid, animated dancing impressed Graham and Humphrey enough that each invited Lang to New York for further training. Intrigued by Graham's 'mysterious' elan, Lang accepted her invitation and landed a coveted spot in her company after just a few months of Graham study – a ladder-climb that ruffled some feathers in her Chicago neighbourhood. 'It was a big *skandal* at home,' she reflected in her later years. 'I used to choreograph for the *shuln*, the Workmen's Circle schools ... Then I danced with the Martha Graham Company.'[11]

While Lang's working-class Russian Jewish background put her in tune with many of the dancers who found homes in the Graham and Humphrey-Weidman studios in the 1930s and 1940s, the cultural aspirations of the Lack household gave her an advantage over those counterparts who left school early and joined their families in the factories. Lang's parents cheered her on as she tried her hand at theatre, dressmaking and choreography. The granddaughter of a rabbi, she was encouraged to take her academics seriously and supplement them with a scholastic grasp on the history of Judaism, a dynamic that enriched her thinking and ideals as an artist. Before devoting herself to dance full-time, she attended a three-year programme for gifted students at the University of Chicago.

Lang's biblical studies uncovered some inspiring instances of dance and movement across the early scriptures: David leaping before the Ark, Miriam's drumming Song of the Sea, the Israelites' dance around the Golden Calf. 'All my bones utter thy praise,' she told an interviewer in the 1980s, paraphrasing David in Psalm 22 – the passage that inspired her interest in ecstatic dance. 'You have the whole body dedicated to the moment . . . that's dancing to me.' Lang credited this euphoric expressionism with drawing her to Martha Graham as a fledgling dancer. 'Because it's not an outer design; it's not the arms and the legs making designs. It's the inner person crying in that movement.'[12] She excelled at Graham technique and swiftly established herself as a masterful exponent in the 1940s. When she started her own company the following decade, she favoured dancers with Graham training and liberally applied its principles to her own choreography, including contraction and release, which she called 'Martha's great gift to dance'.[13]

Partial to the intensities of theatre, Lang combined her rapturous choreography with vivid lighting, music, projections and chants to illuminate the drama of Sephardi canticles and divinations from the Kabbalah. In 1951, she created a duet that would lay the groundwork for one of her best-loved productions. *Legend* isolated the climax of *The Dybbuk*, when Sholom Ansky's protagonist, Leah, becomes possessed by her dead lover's spirit. Lang danced Leah's anguish with consummate lyricism. She wasn't the only dancemaker inspired by the 1914 play: Anna Sokolow debuted her own take in 1951, and versions from Sophie Maslow and Jerome Robbins followed in the 1960s and 1970s. But when Lang reworked her duet into a two-hour production in 1975, renamed *The Possessed*, it surged into position as one of the century's most celebrated dance interpretations of *The Dybbuk*, conjuring its ethereality without lapsing into spectacle.

Ansky's narrative is set in an eighteenth-century Hasidic shtetl in Eastern Europe. Over three acts it charts the tragedy of Leah and Channon, lovers wrenched apart when Leah's father forces her into an arranged marriage with the heir of a wealthy family. Channon dies after immersing himself too deeply in dangerous secret scriptures, and the fateful dybbuk – an incubus of his wronged soul – possesses Leah. A violent exorcism leads to her death, and her spirit journeys to meet Channon's in the afterlife.

The original title of the play translated as 'Between Two Worlds', a reference to its dichotomous motifs of life and death, and a fitting corollary for Lang's fascination with the liminal essence of ecstatic dance. She preserved Ansky's narrative structure and matched its juxtapositions with her own: folk imagery sharpened with lashings of modern dance, scenes of beauty and horror, anguish and desire. Meyer Kupferman and Joel Spiegelman's score – a blend of Hasidic chants, bells and murmurs – brought another layer of drama. 'Rarely has a choreographer exhibited such feeling for her material,' the *New York Times* declared when Lang premiered her full-length retelling in January 1975.[14]

Lang made her conceit of contrasts known in the opening act, where Leah appears before Channon in a silvery dress, a lustrous apparition gliding in the shadows of the dim synagogue. The *Village Voice* applauded the stirring collision of Leah's 'rippling, sweetly sinuous' dancing against the shuddering movements of the rabbinical students, who 'clutch themselves, hunch forward, and twist their torsos from side to side in short jerks [expressing] the doggedness, the blinders-on view of life, the frustrations of the Talmudic scholars'.[15]

Another vivid scene comes in the second-act Beggars' Dance, based on a Hasidic wedding tradition that invites the impoverished to dance with the bride. Lang's interpretation, a 'fierce and violent and wild dance', in her words,[16] imagines a legion of indigents grabbing at Leah as she droops her head in defeat. The pinnacle of the production, Leah's solo of possession, saw Lang pulse her frame in a trembling show of fragility and grit.

The Possessed is a keystone work in a colourful portfolio that mingles historical, fabled and contemporary facets of the Jewish story.

Works like *The Encounter* join *Song of Deborah* in celebrating the triumphs of Lang's people, while *Two Poems of the Holocaust* and *Cantigas Ladino* lament their persecution. *I Never Saw Another Butterfly* (1977) is a searing epitome of this latter faction – a requiem based on diaries recovered from Theresienstadt, the Nazi camp that claimed the lives of thirty-three thousand European Jews between 1941 and 1945, nearly half of them children. Lang set scenes of suffering against fleeting moments of joy, including a passage that describes a child smiling by mistake, a moment she illustrated with a burst of exuberant leaps.

This poetic grasp of paradox was the crux of Lang's boldness as a dancemaker. She gave vital new shape and appraisal to the contradictions of humanity – our debates over this world versus the next, our twin capacity for greatness and cruelty. To me, the most inspired tightrope Lang walked was her subtle subversion of the heritage she commemorated. The composition of her works – women and men dancing together onstage – defied the Orthodox Halacha that prohibits the sexes mixing in dance, while her subjects often called into question the role of ancient tenets in the modern world. These are the same sparks that ignited the Jewish feminism movement of the 1970s, when women in the United States and Israel banded together to push back against marginalising precepts within the Jewish faith, including the glorification of modesty and the exclusion of women from the *minyan*, a pillar of communal worship. A keen critical thinker, Lang used ecstatic dance to contemplate the vigour of its genesis as well as the shortcomings.

Lang's breakout years as a choreographer unfolded in the 1950s, but her professional career started a decade earlier, when she moved to New York for a summer intensive at Martha Graham's dance school. Graham had instructed Louis Horst to seek Lang out during his 1941 tour to Chicago with Agnes de Mille and pass on her invitation to the programme in person, which Lang accepted without pause. Lang's start wasn't so seamless – she twisted her knee an hour into her first class and had to sit out the next two weeks – but she quickly rose to the top of her class with her virtuoso grip on Graham's sharp angles and emotive intensity. She joined the company as a soloist a few months later, aged twenty, making her debut in a performance of *Letter to the World*, Graham's acclaimed dedication to Emily Dickinson.

Many of Graham's earliest dancers had moved on to their own ventures at this point, including Anna Sokolow, Sophie Maslow and Dorothy Bird; Lang was part of a robust next-generation troupe that included Erick Hawkins, Merce Cunningham and Jean Erdman. Between 1941 and 1952, she originated principal roles in a string of key repertory works, including *Deaths and Entrances*, *Appalachian Spring*, *Dark Meadow* and *Night Journey*. You can sense her commanding stage presence in photographs from this time, which show her neck stretched in regal aplomb, her lips parted as she gasps in air for a high contraction, skirt whirling behind her. *Diversion of Angels* (1948), inspired by Wassily Kandinsky's bold use of colour on the canvas, introduced one of Lang's best-loved Graham roles, the Woman in Red – an embodiment of romantic love that sent her slicing downstage in a slash of crimson.

During her early years in New York, Lang supported herself with complementary engagements, including a jigging ensemble role in the 1942 premiere of Maslow's *Folksay* and an appearance in a 1951 revival of Henrik Ibsen's *Peer Gynt*. She briefly worked as an assistant to de Mille, dancing in three of her Broadway musicals in the 1940s, and also appeared in *Touch and Go*, a 1949 musical by Helen Tamiris.

In 1946 Lang made modern dance history by becoming the first dancer to take over one of Graham's own roles: Mary in *El Penitente*, a protagonist that coalesced Mary the Virgin, Mary Magdalene and the grieving Madonna. Graham was famously reluctant to watch others perform the work she'd so painstakingly crafted – she once called the experience 'a circle of hell Dante omitted'[17] – and she relied heavily on Lang when she started her retreat from the stage.

Lang, who recalled the responsibility as 'frightening', used it as an opportunity to channel the personalised approach to expression she prized in Graham's work: 'I thought, "Well since she's chosen me to do it, I cannot say no, and I'm not gonna dance it exactly the way she did it. I have to find my way with it."'[18] For the rest of her time as a soloist with the company, and in later decades, when she returned for guest appearances, Lang took over Graham's leading roles in *Primitive Mysteries*, *Hérodiade* and *Appalachian Spring* among many others, enthralling audiences with her own take on these dramatic meditations on psyche.

The experience built her name as a great interpreter of Graham's work, and she continued to guest with the company into the late 1970s, when she reprised the title role in 1958's *Clytemnestra*, Graham's take on the murderous queen of Mycenae. Lang also taught technique and composition at the Graham school for many years, and oversaw revivals of masterworks like *Hérodiade* as late as the 1990s. She was notoriously difficult to impress in the classroom, and it became an unspoken understanding that dancers looking to join the Graham company had to first pass muster with her.

When it came to showing her own work, Lang's mastery of Graham's technique was something of a double-edged sword, drawing critical praise but also directing attention away from the themes she animated. Critics reviewing Lang's productions often focused on the Graham-inspired aesthetic and her stylised variations of it, the way she 'made perfect organic use of the Graham technique to express something from her own heart', as the *New York Times* put it in 1977.[19] You rarely read about her striking meditations on

Jewishness, though, or the significance of bringing its songs and figures to the stage. In the modern dance canon, Lang's remit is usually filed under the same umbrella as Graham's interest in religion and mythology, ignoring the distinction that Lang's innovations were tied to the very act of exploring her own ethnic heritage. Works like *Shirah* and *Song of Deborah* epitomise the signature use of personal emotion that made her dancing exultant and irresistible. To overlook this is to overlook her resonant, uniquely feminist synthesis of historical themes and contemporary womanhood.

———

When the State of Israel was formalised in 1948, the principles of early Zionists like the nineteenth-century poet Emma Lazarus, who likened 'the re-establishment of our physical strength' with 'the reconstruction of our national organism',[20] graduated from idea to reality. In the 1950s, heartened by their country's role in the fall of Nazi Germany, American Jews gave a new boost to the Zionist cause, fastening a thread between the democratic ideals of a re-established Jewish homeland and the ethos that won the Allies' fight against totalitarianism.

Philanthropy in support of Israel flourished, thanks in large part to the Women's Zionist Organization of America, which shored up pro-Israel education and activism projects, and the Israel bonds effort, aimed at investors looking to support the emerging Israeli economy. New York's Madison Square Garden became the site of one of the biggest fundraising endeavours of the era: the Chanukah Festival for Israel, an extravagant annual event that promised concertgoers a sparkling spectacle of Jewish-themed music and dance in return for the purchase of Israel bonds.

For moderns like Lang, Anna Sokolow and Sophie Maslow, each of whom staged choreography for the Chanukah Festivals in the

1950s, the event was a chance to step outside the usual critical arena and present their art in a more festive setting. Lang performed in at least five festivals, including the 1956 event, where she restaged *Song of Deborah* to live music from the New York Philharmonic. In 1967, she took the piece to Israel itself, arriving on one of the first commercial flights after the Six Day War to reset her choreography on the Batsheva Dance Company, adding new scenes, new music and a set commissioned by a local artist. *Song of Deborah* was now *Tongues of Fire* – a blazing statement of resilience at a testing time for the nation.

In Israel, as with her tours across the US, Italy, Denmark, the Netherlands and Canada, Lang's ruminations gripped audiences with their verve and forward-looking slant. When she died in 2009, the Jewish dance historian Judith Brin Ingber commemorated 'the positive forces of her energy, artistry and imagination. Her dance beautified moments, it beautified our literature, and she made us see the power in our identity and culture.'[21]

While Lang herself steadily gained momentum between the 1950s and 1970s, securing commissions to choreograph for major outfits like the Dutch National Ballet, Boston Ballet and the Yale Repertory Theatre, her company structure was fitful, contracting and expanding to fit around her other engagements, including guest teacher gigs in Switzerland, Sweden and Israel. She joined the faculty of Juilliard's new dance division in 1951, where she taught for eighteen years, and was part of the first European-American course in contemporary dance at Kurt Jooss's Folkwang School in Essen, Germany, in 1959. Lang also taught at Jacob's Pillow, the Neighborhood Playhouse, Connecticut College and Yale's School of Drama, and in the 1970s set up shop in a renovated Manhattan church to co-direct the American Dance Center with Alvin Ailey.

Lang's students came to know her as a rigorous teacher who refused to compromise on her standards and routinely raised her voice to get more passion out of them. She assigned laughter and anger studies, had her dancers break down choreographic phrases into painstakingly detailed steps and practise them until they'd perfected the sequence. In her Graham classes, she rearranged her warm-ups to start with contractions rather than the traditional bounces, concerned her dancers weren't giving them the attention and priority they deserve. 'Somehow, I don't think Martha would have minded my changing the order.'[22]

She demanded perfect attendance and lamented the underwhelming effort she sometimes encountered in the classroom: 'Coming from a shule . . . we had idealism. You worked for something, and it was a work ethic. If you didn't work, you were a good-for-nothing, a *leydik-geyer*.'[23] Pina Bausch, a supernova of modern dance theatre, studied with Lang early on in her career, and a nineteen-year-old Madonna did too.

A tireless artist, Lang continued performing until 1989, when she was sixty-seven years old, and kept on creating as the twenty-first century swooped into view. She was still teaching classes at the Graham school just weeks before her death in 2009. At her funeral, a representative of the Congress for Jewish Culture gave a tribute in Yiddish, while Lang's husband, Joseph, recited the Kaddish, the prayer of mourning that Lang herself danced in 1977.

'[Dancers] have to have life in them,' she commented in her later years. 'It can't just be steps and technique.'[24] Her impassioned outlook marshalled her audiences to new grasps of the depth and force of women, both within a Jewish setting and the world beyond. A prodigious exponent of Martha Graham's bodywork, Lang defined her own practice not by form but by filter, embracing rhapsodic subjects and guiding them into new realms of expression. She walked the line between pride and humility, spirituality and the virtue of material acts; the kind of artist who downplayed her prolific career ('*s'hot zikh aleyn gemakht*' – 'it just happened'[25]) while insisting that 'every class is a prayer'.[26] As one critic reflected in 1977: 'Grace and strength are united in her natural dynamic – she gives femininity a good name.'[27]

CODA

A blessed unrest

The curtain began to descend on modern dance in the 1960s, when its inheritors spooled the movement's innovations into a web so multifaceted that it no longer had a discernible centre. Philosophies expanded; styles diversified; new technologies, media and fusions came into play. Satellite projects like Israel's Batsheva Dance Company, once moulded by Martha Graham, took on a life of their own. Threads of artistry became so varied and intertwined that a new catch-all term materialised: contemporary dance, a diverse genre that continues to grapple with the complexities of a fast-moving world.

Many of the moderns' immediate successors, especially those coming up between the 1960s and 1980s, pivoted away from epic narratives and dramatic, personalised forms of expression to fashion sleek new relationships with motion, space and time. Take the Judson Dance Theater, a Greenwich Village collective energised by postmodern precepts around participation and process: they spurned drama and emotion in favour of a minimalist aesthetic, embracing pedestrian movement styles and unexpected performance spaces that blurred the boundaries between concert dance and the art of everyday life.

But amid such cool appraisals you can still spot the fiery influence of the moderns. The burning questions around sexuality and the male gaze that consumed Isadora Duncan, Loie Fuller and Maud Allan, for example, sent the female spearheads of Judson – Trisha Brown, Yvonne Rainer and Anna Halprin in particular – to a new ground zero of cultural renewal. They looked to ordinary movement to ground them amid the social upheaval of the sexual revolution, thrusting the objectification of women into a blunt new realm with their unisex costumes and unadorned, analytical compositions. Where the Judsons axed femininity from the aesthetic, fellow changemakers leaned into the performative power of dresses and high heels, including Pina Bausch, whose sensual, skirt-swinging productions probed the depths of female gender expression.

In the meantime, Ze'eva Cohen championed new interpretations of Jewish heritage, building on Pearl Lang's efforts to recentre marginalised histories; Alvin Ailey took the teachings of Katherine Dunham and Pearl Primus into bold new territories; Blondell Cummings married realism with the ferocities of the subconscious, a piercing escalation of the personal-is-political whistle sounded in the Graham era; and the troupe Pilobolus echoed the collectivist spirit of Anna Sokolow, Sophie Maslow and fellow 1930s protest dancers with lithe, eye-grabbing constellations intended to illustrate the beauty of human connection. The torch had passed to new hands, but its flame flickered on.

When I ensconce myself in the verve of modern dance, and especially when I apprehend it with my own body, I'm moved to something like faith, a quickening in my core that leaps between flashpoints of my womanhood; the pride and restlessness of a self in search of agency, answers, permission, freedom. When Graham contemplated grace in her work, she reached across to 'the sweep of life' that binds the person to the performer: 'I mean the grace resulting from faith – faith in life, in love, in people, in the act of dancing.'[1] Like Duncan, Fuller, Allan, Sokolow, Maslow, Dunham, Primus and Lang, she asked us to imagine an existence unhindered by society's blatant and unspoken expectations of graceful submission. Basking in the conviction of their art is an exhilarating, life-affirming experience.

Today's dance stage continues to foster thrilling work from forward-looking women: Crystal Pite, Fleur Darkin, Anne Teresa De Keersmaeker, Sharon Eyal, Jasmin Vardimon, Pam Tanowitz, Annabelle Lopez Ochoa. Despite the headway of their forerunners, these artists still have hills to climb, from narrow-minded commissioning processes to the pressures of balancing work and motherhood. Alert to the substance of self-expression, and to the power we build when we demand our stories are told, they persist, staging the issues that keep their blood pumping.

The moderns made this possible. The dynamism of bare feet, the galvanising force of consciousness, the virtues tied up in sex, nudity, beauty and desire – they not only prompted new conversations around these subjects but also gifted us a new language to advance them. The oceans of discontent that shaped their uprising still make waves today, including stigmas around how we live and who we love. As a woman, the onus to defend my own humanity still causes me to stumble. But it's with their bold voices in my ears and a furious muster of grace that I pull myself up and continue to stride ahead.

References

PROLOGUE

1 *Isadora Speaks: Uncollected Writings and Speeches of Isadora Duncan*, Franklin Rosemont (ed.) (City Lights Books, 1981), p. 48
2 Agnes de Mille, 'Artist or Wife,' *The Atlantic*, September 1958
3 Blurb for Isadora Duncan, *My Life* (W.W. Norton, 1996, first published by Boni and Liveright, 1927)
4 *Isadora Speaks*, p. 138
5 Martha Graham, *Blood Memory* (Doubleday, 1991), p. 7

ACT 1, CURTAIN

1 Isadora Duncan, *The Art of the Dance* (Theatre Arts Books, written *c.*1902 and first published 1928), p. 56
2 Mary Wigman, *The Language of Dance* (Wesleyan University Press, 1974), p. 8
3 *The Art of the Dance*, p. 63
4 Sarah Grand, 'The New Aspect of the Woman Question,' *The North American Review*, vol. 158, no. 448, March 1894, p. 270
5 *Four Great Plays of Henrik Ibsen* (Simon & Schuster, 2016), p. 83
6 Dee Garrison, *Mary Heaton Vorse: The Life of an American Insurgent* (Temple University Press, 1989), p. 77
7 *The Mary Wigman Book*, Walter Sorell (ed.) (Wesleyan University Press, 1975), p. 96

ACT 1, SCENE 1

1 'A Dance Poetess,' *Springfield Daily Republican*, 25 June 1905
2 Ann Daly, *Done into Dance: Isadora Duncan in America* (Indiana University Press, 1995), p. 101
3 *The Ezra Pound Encyclopedia*, (Bloomsbury Academic, 2005), p. 17
4 *Isadora Speaks*, p. 48
5 'New Acts of the Week,' *Variety*, 1 August 1908
6 Letter from 22 August 1908, published in Andrew J. Krivak's edition

of *The Letters of William Carlos Williams to Edgar Irving Williams*, 1902–1912 (Fairleigh Dickinson University Press, 2009), pp. 151–152

7 Jim Rasenberger, *America 1908* (Simon & Schuster, 2007), p. 11

8 *My Life* (Boni and Liveright, 1927), p. 14

9 Ibid., p. 22

10 Ibid., p. 19

11 Ibid., p. 27

12 Ibid., p. 33

13 Ibid., p. 46

14 Ibid., p. 27

15 Ibid., p. 164

16 Ibid., p. 21

17 Ibid., p. 75, 142

18 Ibid., p. 142

19 Ibid., p. 164

20 Ibid., p. 75

21 Ibid., p. 164

22 *The Art of the Dance*, p. 63

23 *My Life*, p. 28

24 Ibid., p. 3

25 Ibid., p. 44

26 Margaret Morris, *My Galsworthy Story* (Owen, 1968), p. 22

27 'To Isadora Duncan', *The Later Poetry of Charlotte Perkins Gilman*, Denise D. Knight (ed.) (University of Delaware Press, 1996), p. 141

28 'Isadora in Art', *Dance Index* (eds, Lincoln Kirstein, Paul Magriel, Donald Windham), 1946, p. 68

29 D.A. McComb, 'The Classroom Technique of the Isadora Duncan School of Dancing' (Isadora Duncan Archive, 1983) p. 3

30 *My Life*, p. 75

31 Sara Veale, 'She Dared to Be Seen,' *Fjord Review*, January 2020: https://fjordreview.com/blogs/all/isadora-now-viviana-durante

32 *The Art of the Dance*, p. 56

33 Sabrina Jones, *Isadora Duncan: A Graphic Biography* (Hill & Wang, 2008), p. 8

34 Dawn Mitchell, 'Retro Indy: That time a dancer and Indy mayor went at it', *IndyStar*, 24 March 2017: https://eu.indystar.com/story/news/history/retroindy/2017/03/24/battle-between-isadora-duncan-and-mayor-lew-shank-dancing/98364048/

35 *Isadora Speaks*, p. 129

36 Michelle Elizabeth Tusan, 'Inventing the New Woman: Print Culture and Identity Politics During the Fin-de-Siecle', *Victorian Periodicals Review*,

vol. 31, no. 2 (The John Hopkins Press, summer 1998), p. 174

37 *My Life*, p. 55

38 *Evening Telegraph*, 6 August 1900

39 Winnifred Harper Cooley, *The New Womanhood* (Broadway Publishing Company, 1904), p. 33

40 *My Life*, p. 85

41 *The Art of the Dance*, p. 57

42 Ibid., p. 63

43 *My Life*, p. 134

44 Ibid., p. 114

45 Edward Gordon Craig, *Index to the Story of My Days* (Viking Press, 1957), p. 246

46 Sewell Stokes, *Isadora Duncan: An Intimate Portrait, Brentano, 1928, p. 180*

47 Walter Terry, *Isadora Duncan: Her Life, Her Art, Her Legacy* (Dodd, Mead, 1963), p. 160

48 'Latest Amazing Love Affair of Isadora Duncan,' *Philadelphia Enquirer*, 25 June 1922

49 *My Life*, p. 152

50 *The Art of the Dance*, p. 63

51 *My Life*, p. 193

52 Ibid, p. 17

53 *Isadora Speaks*, p. 129

54 Ibid., p. 130

55 *My Life*, p. 17

56 *Isadora Speaks*, p. 104

57 *My Life*, p. 7

58 Ibid., p. 278

59 Ibid., p. 308

60 Ibid., p. 307

61 Ibid., p. 316

62 Irma Duncan and Allan Ross Macdougall, *Isadora Duncan's Russian Days* (Victor Gollancz, 1929), p. 164

63 Ibid., p. 171

64 *Isadora Speaks*, p. 48

65 Ibid., pp. 133–134

66 Peter Kurth, *Isadora: A Sensational Life* (Little, Brown, 2001), p. 555

67 *My Life*, p. 341

ACT 1, SCENE 2

1 Rhonda K. Garelick, *Electric Salome: Loie Fuller's Performance of Modernism* (Princeton University Press, 2009), p. 3

REFERENCES

2 Loie Fuller, *Fifteen Years of a Dancer's Life, With Some Account of her Distinguished Friends* (H. Jenkins, 1913), p. 72

3 Richard Nelson Current and Marcia Ewing Current, *Loie Fuller: Goddess of Light* (Northeastern University Press, 1997), p. 339

4 *Fifteen Years*, p. 70

5 Stéphane Mallarmé, *Oeuvres complètes* (Gallimard, 1945), p. 309

6 *Fifteen Years*, p. 32

7 Ibid., p. 33

8 *Fifteen Years*, p. 34

9 Sally R. Sommer, 'Loie Fuller,' *Drama Review*: vol. 19.1, March 1975, p. 57

10 Susan Chitwood, 'Special Effects Visionary: Loie Fuller,' 18 January 2022: https://dance-teacher.com/loie-fuller/

11 *Fifteen Years*, p. 34

12 Ibid., p. 272

13 Ibid., p. 46

14 Ibid., p. 50

15 Jean Cocteau, *Souvenirs* (Editions Flammarion, 1935), p. 5

16 *Fifteen Years*, p. 137

17 Ibid., p. 34

18 *Scientific American*, 20 June 1986, vol. 74, p. 392

19 Frank Kermode, 'Poet and Dancer before Diaghilev,' *Salmagundi*, 33–34 (1976), p. 40

20 *Fifteen Years*, pp. 63–64

21 Clare de Morinni, 'Loie Fuller: Fairy of Light,' *Dance Index*, vol. I, no. 3, March 1942, p. 47

22 Ibid., pp. 46–47

23 Ibid., p. 47

24 Jules Claretie, 'La Vie à Paris,' *Le Temps*, vol. 47, no. 16, 8 November 1907, p. 938 (Recounted in *Fifteen Years*, p. 286)

25 Giovanni Lista, *Danseuse de la Belle Époque*, Editions Somogy, 1995, p. 133

26 *Fifteen Years*, p. 165

27 'La Vie à Paris,' p. 938 (Recounted in *Fifteen Years*, p. 282)

28 Frederic Grunfeld, *Rodin: A Biography* (Henry Holt, 1987), p. 444

29 *Souvenirs*, p. 5

30 *Fifteen Years*, p. 19

31 'Fairy of Light,' p. 47

32 *My Life*, p. 95

33 Stéphane Mallarmé, (translated by Evlyn Gould), 'Ballets,' *Performing Arts Journal*, vol. 15, no. 1, 1993, p. 107

34 'Poet and Dancer before Diaghilev,' p. 41

35 *Fifteen Years*, pp. 64–65 (italics mine)

ACT 1, SCENE 3

1   Felix Cherniavsky, *The Salome Dancer: The Life and Times of Maud Allan* (McClelland & Stewart, 1991), p. 156

2   Maud Allan, *My Life and Dancing* (Everett & Co, 1908), p. 10

3   Joris-Karl Huysmans, *Against the Grain* (Three Sirens Press, 1931), p. 53

4   *My Life*, p. 125

5   Ibid., p. 127

6   *New York Sun*, 1908

7   *The Salome Dancer*, p. 143

8   Judith R. Walkowitz, *Nights Out: Life in Cosmopolitan London* (Yale University Press, 2012), p. 78

9   Felix Cherniavsky, 'Maud Allan, Part III: Two Years of Triumph 1908-1909,' *Dance Chronicle*, Vol. 7, No. 2, 1984, pp. 127–128

10 *The Salome Dancer*, p. 164

11 'Miss Maud Allan: Palace Crowded with Ladies to See New Dances,' *Daily Chronicle*, 13 June 1908

12 *My Life*, p. 112

13 *My Life*, p. 40

14 *New York Times*, 3 May 1908, p. 4

15 *Dance Magazine*, October 1977, p. 80

16 *My Life*, p. 53

17 Ibid., p. 54

18 Ibid., p. 36

19 Ibid, pp. 22–23

20 Ibid., p. 46

21 Toni Bentley, *Sisters of Salome* (University of Nebraska Press, 2005), p. 58

22 *Performing Objects and Theatrical Things*, Marlis Schweitzer and Joanne Zerdy (eds) (Palgrave Macmillan, 2014), p. 41

23 *My Life*, p. 79

24 Quoted in https://spartacus-educational.com/FWWallanM.htm

25 *My Life*, p. 36

26 Lucy Bland, *Modern Women on Trial: Sexual Transgression in the Age of the Flapper* (Manchester University Press, 2016)

27 Philip Hoare, *Oscar Wilde's Last Stand: Decadence, Conspiracy and the Most Outrageous Trial of the Century* (Arcade Publishing, 1998), p. 95

28 'Vision of Salome: Honour of a famous dancer impugned,' *News of the World*, 2 June 1918, pp. 3–4

29 Questioning recounted in Kevin Childs, 'A hundred years on from the "cult of the clitoris" libel trial, let's remember that fake news is nothing new,' *Independent*, 31 May 2018: https://www.independent.co.uk/news/long_reads/oscar-wilde-maud-allan-cult-of-the-clitoris-black-book-first-world-war-a8369811.html

30 *Sisters of Salome*, pp. 77–78

31 Recounted in *Sisters of Salome*, p. 79

32 Petra Dierkes-Thrun, *Salome's Modernity: Oscar Wilde and the Aesthetics of Transgression* (University of Michigan Press, 2011), p. 111

33 *Wilde's Last Stand*, p. 97

34 Ibid., p. 97

35 *Sisters of Salome*, p. 78

36 Maud Allan's *Memoirs*, serialised in *San Francisco Call and Post* in 1921 and recounted in *The Salome Dancer*, p. 244

37 *Verbatim Report of the Trial of Noel Pemberton Billing M.P.*, 'Vigilante' Office, 1918, p. 443

38 Ibid., p. 437

39 'A hundred years on'

40 *Oscar Wilde's Last Stand*, p. 184

41 Ibid., p. 183

42 'A Deplorable Scandal,' *Daily Telegraph*, 6 June 1918

43 *My Life*, p. 66

44 Ibid., p. 123, 128

45 Ibid., p. 78 -

46 Ibid., p. 19

ACT 2, CURTAIN

1 *Blood Memory*, p. 6

2 Marian Horosko, *Martha Graham: The Evolution of her Dance Theory and Training 1926–1991* (A Cappella Books, 1991), p. 51

3 *100 Years of the Nineteenth Amendment: An Appraisal of Women's Political Activism*, Holly J. McCammon and Lee Ann Banaszak (eds) (Oxford University Press, 2018), pp. 176, 182

4 *Martha Graham: The Early Years*, Merle Armitage (ed.) (Da Capo Press, 1978), p. 88

5 Marie Jenney Howe, 'A Feminist Symposium: Feminism', *Public Women, Public Words: A Documentary History of American Feminism: vol. 2: 1900–1960*, D. Keetley and J. Pettegrew (eds) (Rowman and Littlefield), p. 29–34

6 Walter Sorell, *Hanya Holm: the Biography of an Artist* (Wesleyan University Press, 1969), p. 17

7 William Korff and Mary Burns, 'History of the New Dance Group,' American Dance Guild: https://www.americandanceguild.org/ndghistory#:~:text=felt%20our%20appearance%20at%20the,power%20to%20change%20the%20world.

8 Ellen Graff, *Stepping Left: Dance and Politics in New York City 1928–1942* (Duke University Press, 1997), p. 151

ACT 2, SCENE 1

1 *Martha Graham: The Evolution*, p. 28
2 'Martha Graham Reflects on Her Art and a Life in Dance,' *New York Times*, 31 March 1985
3 *Martha Graham: The Evolution*, p. 48
4 *Blood Memory*, p. 118
5 Ibid., p. 213
6 Lamentations 1:12, *King James Bible*
7 *Blood Memory*, p. 75
8 'Martha Graham Reflects'
9 *Blood Memory*, p. 69
10 Ibid., p. 74
11 'The Dancer Revealed,' *American Masters*, season 8, episode 2, PBS, 13 May 1994
12 *Blood Memory*, p. 4
13 *Martha Graham: The Evolution*, p. 11
14 *Blood Memory*, p. 6
15 Agnes de Mille, *Martha: The Life and Work of Martha Graham* (Pennsylvania State University Press, 1991), p. 264
16 *Blood Memory*, p. 10
17 *Blood Memory*, p. 90
18 *The Evolution*, p. 51
19 Elizabeth Kendall, *Where She Danced: The Birth of American Art-dance* (University of California Press, 1979), p. 190
20 *Modernism, Gender, and Culture: A Cultural Studies Approach*, Lisa Rado (ed.) (Taylor & Francis, 1997), pp. 263–274
21 Michel Fokine, 'A Sad Art,' *Dance Magazine*, May 1931, p. 29
22 *Blood Memory*, p. 134
23 Ibid., p. 4
24 Ibid., p. 123
25 Ibid., p. 211
26 Lincoln Kirstein, 'Martha Graham at Bennington,' *The Nation*, 3 September 1938, p. 230

REFERENCES

27 Angelica Gibbs, 'The Absolute Frontier,' *The New Yorker*, 19 December 1947

28 *Blood Memory*, p. 44

29 *Stepping Left*, p. 24

30 *Blood Memory*, p. 123

31 *Orange Coast Magazine*, January 1991, p. 46

32 *Blood Memory*, p. 151

33 Gervaise Butler, '*American Document* Reviewed,' *Dance Observer*, 1938

34 Anna Kisselgoff, 'Martha Graham Dies at 96; A Revolutionary in Dance,' *New York Times*, 2 April 1991

35 *Martha Graham: The Evolution*, p. 79

36 Ibid., p. 63

37 Ibid., p. 81

38 John Martin, 'Dance: Clytemnestra; Martha Graham Work Offered by Her and Company at Broadway Theatre,' *New York Times*, 9 March 1962, p. 23

39 'Louis Horst, 80, Leader in Dance; Martha Graham's Former Musical Director Dies,' *New York Times*, 24 January 1964

40 *Blood Memory*, p. 79

41 Miguel Covarrubias, 'Sally Rand and Martha Graham,' *Vanity Fair*, December 1934

42 *The Life and Work of Martha Graham*, p. 264

43 *Blood Memory*, p. 181

44 Ibid., p. 8

ACT 2, SCENE 2

1 Lisa Jo Sagolla, 'Reminiscing With a Rebel,' *Backstage*, *c*.1999: https://www.backstage.com/magazine/article/reminiscing-rebel-19337/

2 Larry Warren, *Anna Sokolow: The Rebellious Spirit* (Princeton Book Company, 1991), p. 26

3 Anna Sokolow, 'The Revolutionary Dance,' lecture delivered at the New School for Social Research, 1936

4 Margaret Murphy and Lucille Rhodes (prod. and dir.), *Anna Sokolow, Choreographer*, 1980, First Dance Horizons Video, 1991

5 *You Work Tomorrow: An Anthology of American Labor Poetry 1929–41*, Josh March (ed.), p. 217

6 Barbara Newman, *Interview with Anna Sokolow*, Oral History Project of the Jerome Robbins Dance Division, the New York Public Library for the Performing Arts, Dorothy and Lewis B. Cullman Center, December 1974–May 1975

7 Ibid.

8 *Frances Hellman's Diary: With Anna Sokolow in Mexico*, 1939: https://sokolowtheatredance.org/archives/frances-hellmans-diary-with-anna-

REFERENCES

sokolow-in-mexico-1939/

9   Anna Kisselgoff, 'In Anna Sokolow's Dance, Her Beliefs,' *New York Times*, 2 December 1975, p. 46

10 'Reminiscing With a Rebel'

11 Billie Mahoney (prod.), *Dance on: Anna Sokolow*, 1981

12 *Blood Memory*, p. 135

13 *Martha Graham: The Evolution*, p. 46

14 Dorothy Bird and Joyce Greenberg, *Bird's Eye View: Dancing with Martha Graham and on Broadway* (University of Pittsburgh Press, 1997), p. 49

15 Kelly and Leslie Morris, 'An Interview with Anna Sokolow,' *TDR 14*, vol. 14, no. 1 (1969), p. 100

16 Deborah Jowitt, 'Kill Mama,' *Village Voice*, 4 April 2000

17 Lewis Segal, 'Anna Sokolow; Modern Dance Pioneer,' *Los Angeles Times*, 31 March 2000

18 John Martin, *New York Times*, 2 December 1934

19 *Rebellious Spirit*, p. 16

20 Newman, *Interview with Anna Sokolow*

21 *Rebellious Spirit*, p. 69

22 Ibid., p. 142

23 Anna Sokolow, 'The Rebel and the Bourgeois,' *The Modern Dance: Seven Statements of Belief*, Selma Cohen (ed.) (Wesleyan University Press, 1965), pp. 63–75

24 Elie Wiesel, *Night*, (transl. Marion Wiesel) (Hill and Wang, 1958) p. 58

25 'The Rebel and the Bourgeois'

26 Clive Barnes, 'Dance: Powerful "Dreams: Anna Sokolow Shows Man, Unable to Communicate, Reduced to Fear",' New York Times, 1966

27 *Rebellious Spirit*, p. 279

28 Ibid., p. 125

29 Hannah Kosstrin, *Honest Bodies, Revolutionary Modernism in the Dances of Anna Sokolow* (Oxford University Press, 2017), p. 20

30 Clive Barnes, 'Dance: Anna Sokolow, Poet of Chaos,' *New York Times*, 14 November 1968

31 'Kill Mama'

32 Clive Barnes, 'Dance: Pity Without Sentimentality,' *New York Times*, 12 March 1967

33 'Obituary: Anna Sokolow,' *Guardian*, 12 April 2000

34 Elizabeth McCausland, 'Sokolow Accents Contemporary Mood: Young Dancer Interests New York Audience Present at Her First Program Last Sunday,' *Springfield Morning Union*, 21 November 1937

35 Margery Dana, 'Anna Sokolow and Dance Unit in Prominent Debut: Young

Modern Dancer and Group Sponsored by New Masses at Guild,' *Daily Worker*, 20 November 1937, p. 7

36 John Martin, 'The Dance: Romanticism – A Venerable Tradition With Light to Shed On Modern Trends—Coming Events,' *New York Times*, 3 March 1939

37 Henry Gilfond, 'Workers' Dance League, Civic Repertory Theater, November 25, 1934,' *Dance Observer*, December 1934, p. 89

38 Owen Burke, 'The Dance,' *New Masses*, 16 March 1937, p. 28

39 Louise Mitchell, 'New Dance Unit is Tops,' *Daily* Worker, 3 March 1937

40 Owen Burke, 'Anna Sokolow and Other Dancers,' *New Masses*, 7 December 1937, p. 28

41 Nathan Mishori, 'Anna Sokolow, The Lyric Theatre and Israel,' *Israel Dance*, 1978/79, p. 40

42 Ibid., p. 41

ACT 2, SCENE 3

1 'Sophie Maslow Interview' (dir. Nick Havinga, prod. Dan Gallagher), Creative Arts Television, 2007

2 Woody Guthrie, 'Singing, Dancing, and Team-work,' *Dance Observer*, January 1943, pp. 104–105, quoted in *Pastures of Plenty: A Self-Portrait*, Dave Marsh and Harold Leventhal (eds) (HarperCollins, 1990), pp. 72–76

3 Margaret Lloyd, *The Borzoi Book of Modern Dance*, A. A. Knopf, 1949, p. 183

4 Josh Perelman, 'I'm the Everybody Who's Nobody, I'm the Nobody Who's Everybody,' *Seeing Israeli and Jewish Dance*, Judith Brin Ingber (ed.), (Wayne State University Press, 2011), p. 89

5 *Borzoi Book*, p. 184

6 'Interview with Doris Hering,' *Dance Magazine*, May 1946

7 'Sophie Maslow', Jewish Women's Archive: https://jwa.org/encyclopedia/article/maslow-sophie

8 *Dance Today*, no. 36, September 2019, p. 81

9 'Sophie Maslow', Jewish Women's Archive

10 *Borzoi Book*, p. 191

11 Woody Guthrie, 'Dusty Old Dust', *Dust Bowl Ballads* (Victor Records, 1940)

12 *Stepping Left*, p. 139

13 Nora Guthrie, 'Sophie Maslow and Woody Guthrie,' *Monthly Review*, 7 November 2006: https://mronline.org/2006/07/11/sophie-maslow-and-woody-guthrie/

14 *Stepping Left*, p. 143

15 'Sophie Maslow and Woody Guthrie'

16 'Singing, Dancing and Team-work'

17 'I'm the Everybody Who's Nobody,' p. 90

18 John Martin, 'The Dance: Americana', *New York Times*, 6 December 1942

REFERENCES

19 Rebecca Rossen, *Dancing Jewish: Jewish Identity in American Modern and Postmodern Dance* (Oxford University Press, 2014), p. 148

20 Deborah Jowitt, 'In Memoriam: Sophie Maslow (1911–2006),' *Village Voice*, 4 July 2006

21 'Sophie Maslow and Woody Guthrie'

22 'Ageless Movement,' *Jewish Week*, 7 June 1996

23 'In Memoriam'

24 *Martha Graham: The Evolution*, p. 53

ACT 3, CURTAIN

1 As noted in 'Proceedings of the Twenty-second Biennial Conference', International Council of Kinetography Laban (compiled by Marion Bastien and printed in Paris, 2001), p. 247

2 *Blood Memory*, p. 6

3 T. S. Eliot, *Four Quartets* (Harcourt Brace, 1943), p. 5

4 *The Art of the Dance*, p. 62

5 Frederick Orme, 'The Negro In Dance, As Katherine Dunham Sees Him', *American Dancer*, March 1938, p. 46

6 'The Cover,' *The Crisis*, vol. 47, no. 23, March 1940

ACT 3, SCENE 1

1 Horace R Cayton and St Clair Drake, *Black Metropolis: A Study of Negro Life in a Northern City* (Jonathan Cape, 1946), p. xvii

2 Katherine Dunham, *A Touch of Innocence* (Harcourt, Brace and Company, 1959), p. 179

3 Langston Hughes, *The Collected Poems of Langston Hughes* (Knopf, 1994), p. 336

4 Ibid., p. 23

5 Blurb for 'Black History Dance Series: Katherine Dunham's Legacy': https://www.alvinailey.org/extension/black-history-dance-series/katherine-dunhams-legacy

6 Film footage accessible at https://www.patheos.com/blogs/voodoouniverse/2015/10/foremama-said-wit-and-wisdom-of-katherine-dunham/

7 Katherine Dunham, *Island Possessed* (Doubleday & Company, 1969), p. 7

8 Katherine Dunham, Public Broadcasting Service (NewsHour Productions, 1978), retrieved from https://video.alexanderstreet.com/watch/katherine-dunham

9 *Katherine Dunham on Dunham Technique*, Library of Congress: https://www.loc.gov/item/ihas.200003814/

10 'Katherine Dunham Helped Teach the World to Dance,' *All Things Considered*, 27 May 2006

11 *Daily News*, 8 November 1946

12 'Notes on Dunham's Work: Rites de Passage', Library of Congress: https://www.loc.gov/collections/katherine-dunham/articles-and-essays/notes-on-dunhams-work/rites-de-passage/

13 'Notes on Dunham's Work: Southland', Library of Congress: https://www.loc.gov/collections/katherine-dunham/articles-and-essays/notes-on-dunhams-work/southland/

14 'Hottest Thing on Broadway,' *Sunday News*, 8 December 1940

15 Joanna Dee Das, *Katherine Dunham: Dance and the African Diaspora* (Oxford University Press, 2017), p. 83

16 'Katherine Dunham Timeline', Library of Congress: https://www.loc.gov/collections/katherine-dunham/articles-and-essays/katherine-dunham-timeline/

17 Ibid.

18 Robert Coleman, 'Katherine Dunham's Dancing is Torrid,' *New York Daily Mirror*, 20 September 1943

19 *Dance and the African Diaspora*, p. 89

20 Dan Burley, 'Dan Burley's Back Door Stuff,' *New York Amsterdam News*, 25 September 1943, p. 22

21 'Dunham Dancing While Rome Pays,' *Chicago Daily News*, c.March 1949

22 Katherine Dunham, 'Comment to a Louisville Audience,' 19 October 1944, reprinted in Clark and Johnson, *Kaiso!: Writings by and About Katherine Dunham* (University of Wisconsin Press, 2005), p. 255

23 James Baldwin, *Go Tell It on the Mountain* (Penguin, 1991), p. 252

24 'Katherine Dunham on dance anthropology,' Library of Congress: www.loc.gov/item/ihas.200003840/

25 'Katherine Dunham's *Tropical Revue*', *The Harvard Crimson*, 8 December, 1944

ACT 3, SCENE 2

1 Abel Meeropol, 'Strange Fruit', reprinted in David Margolick, *Strange Fruit: The Biography of a Song* (Ecco Press, 2001), p. 22

2 Peggy and Murray Schwartz, *The Dance Claimed Me: A Biography of Pearl Primus* (Yale University Press, 2011), p. 36

3 *The Dance Claimed Me*, p. 10, also reprinted as 'My Statement' in the Black Theater Alliance newsletter vol. 4, no. 9, 1979

4 Ibid., p. 10

5 David Gere, 'Dances of Sorrow, Dances of Hope,' *Los Angeles Times*, 24 April 1994

REFERENCES

6 Pearl Primus, *Five Evenings with American Dance Pioneers: Pearl Primus*, lecture delivered at Hess Studio, 29 April 1983

7 John Martin, 'The Dance: Five Artists; Second Annual Joint Recital Project of the Y.M.H.A. – Week's Programs,' *New York Times*, 21 February 1943

8 *The Dance Claimed Me*, p. 67

9 Ibid., p. 55

10 'Dances of Sorrow, Dances of Hope'

11 *The Dance Claimed Me*, p. 46

12 Ibid., p. 46

13 Ibid., p. 51

14 *Dance and the African Diaspora*, p. 91

15 Langston Hughes, 'Here To Yonder,' *Chicago Defender*, 3 July 1943

16 Quoted in *The Dance Claimed Me*, p. 65

17 Langston Hughes, 'My Early Days in Harlem,' 1963

18 *Borzoi Book*, p. 271

19 *The Dance Claimed Me*, p. 115

20 John Perpener, *African-American Concert Dance: The Harlem Renaissance and Beyond* (University of Illinois Press, 2005) p. 168

21 *The Dance Claimed Me*, p. 47

22 'Pearl in Our Midst: Pearl Primus (November 29, 1919-October 29, 1994)', *Dance Research Journal*, vol. 27, no. 1, 1995, p. 80

23 Ibid., p. 47

24 *The Dance Claimed Me*, p. 96

25 Ibid., p. 37

26 *African-American Concert Dance*, p. 169

27 Richard Wright, *Native Son* (HarperCollins, 1989), p. 367

28 *The Dance Has Many Faces*, Walter Sorell, (ed.) (World Publishing Company, 1951), p. 256

29 *The Dance Claimed Me*, p. 72

30 Ibid., p. 70

31 'Africa Dances: a letter from Pearl Primus,' *Observer*, December 1949, quoted in *The Dance Claimed Me*, p. 76

32 John Perpener, 'Dance of the African Diaspora: Pearl Primus', Jacob's Pillow Dance Interactive: https://danceinteractive.jacobspillow.org/themes-essays/african-diaspora/pearl-primus/

33 'Dances of Sorrow, Dances of Hope'

34 *The Dance Claimed Me*, p. 102

ACT 3, SCENE 3

1 Mark Franko, *Oxford Handbook of Dance and Reenactment*, p. 106

REFERENCES

2 Ze'eva Cohen, 'Tribute to Pearl Primus,' speech delivered at the 92nd Street Y, 5 November 2009

3 Clive Barnes, 'Dance: Pearl Lang and Her Company,' *New York Times*, 3 February 1971

4 Judges 5:7, *King James Bible*

5 Jean-Paul Sartre, *Anti-Semite and Jew*, Schocken Books, 1965, p. 48

6 *Dancing Jewish*, p. 76

7 Ibid., p. 62

8 Billie Mahoney (prod.), *Dance on: Pearl Lang*, 1989

9 Ibid.

10 Masha Leon, 'Remembering Pearl Lang – A National Jewish and Dance Treasure,' Forward, 11 March 2009: https://forward.com/israel/103890/remembering-pearl-lang/

11 Ibid.

12 *Dance on: Pearl Lang*

13 *Martha Graham: The Evolution*, p. 78

14 Anna Kisselgoff, 'Pearl Lang's "Possessed" Has World Premiere at "Y"', *New York Times*, 8 January 1975

15 Deborah Jowitt, 'Parts Can Blur the Whole,' *Village Voice*, 20 January 1975

16 *Dance on: Pearl Lang*

17 *Blood Memory*, p. 200

18 *Dance on: Pearl Lang*

19 Anna Kisselgoff, 'Dance: The True Pearl Lang', *New York Times*, 15 April 1977

20 Emma Lazarus, *An Epistle to the Hebrews* (Jewish Historical Society of New York, 1987), p. 31

21 'Pearl Lang and the Choreography of Prayer,' *The Jewish Week*, 13 March 2009

22 Marian Horosko, *Martha Graham: The Evolution of her Dance Theory and Training* (revised edition, University Press of Florida, 2002), p. 78

23 'Remembering Pearl Lang'

24 *Martha Graham: The Evolution* (revised edition), p. 79

25 'Remembering Pearl Lang'

26 *Martha Graham: The Evolution* (revised edition), p. 79

27 'Dance: The True Pearl Lang'

CODA

1 Martha Graham, 'I Am a Dancer,' *The Routledge Dance Studies Reader*, Alexandra Carter and Janet O'Shea (eds) (Routlege, 2010), p. 96

252

Acknowledgements

Writing a book, I discovered in the six years it took to get *Wild Grace* from first notion to final draft, is a staccato exercise, with as much agonised backtracking as there is forward momentum. There were many days when the thought of getting to this very page was my sole source of steam.

My endless thanks to Fiona Baird, my stellar agent and starbright friend: you championed this project when it was still a scramble of ideas and never let me lose faith that it would see the light of day.

Thanks also to the brilliant Ka Bradley, for encouraging me to attempt it in the first place and offering invaluable guidance as it started to take shape.

I'm beyond grateful to the wise and warm team at Faber, particularly Belinda Matthews, for taking a chance on me, and Fred Baty, whose conscientious editing marshalled this text beautifully. Hannah Knowles has also been a beacon of insight and positive energy. Thank you to Laura Hassan, Alex Bowler, Josephine Salverda, Anna Swan, Jo Stimfield, Kate Burton and Emmie Francis too, as well as the many other team members doing the silent but vital work behind the scenes.

A huge thank you to the arts editors who've given me column inches and other platforms to develop my dance criticism over the years, especially the stupendous Penelope Ford of *Fjord Review*; and to the many dance teachers of my past for their diligent instruction and mentorship, including Sybil Huskey, whose passion for dance is an art in and of itself.

My heartfelt thanks go to my superb friends and colleagues, Sarah Worth in particular, for giving me the space and encouragement to write while the duties of life and work stormed around me.

Martina Ferrera, thank you for all the lovely headshots.

A moment of recognition for the biographers, academics and archivists who've dedicated their careers to safeguarding the stories of modern dance: I appreciate you and your critical work. Thanks also to the librarians who helped me access these precious resources, including the staff at the British Library; to Marie-Christine Dunham Pratt, for her insightful corrections and clarifications; and of course to my subjects themselves, for their extraordinary contributions to both art and humanity.

'Grateful' doesn't quite cover how appreciative I am of my unbelievably big-hearted family, including my siblings, in-laws and especially my parents, Jay and Patti Veale, the best cheerleaders an author could dream of. What a different journey this would have been without your support. I treasure you all.

To my husband, Will Greaves, who held my hand throughout the rollercoaster of fretting and revelling and nail-biting that was publishing this book: thank you for carrying my heart. Your love is blinding in the very best way.

And finally, all my love and gratitude to my gorgeous boys, Jesse and Rafferty, who make my days brighter and my world infinitely more knowable.

List of Illustrations

Isadora Duncan in Edenic repose, *c.*1917.
Photograph by Arnold Genthe. Heritage Image Partnership Ltd/Alamy Stock Photo.

Studio portrait of Duncan in her London days, *c.*1906–12.
Photograph by Charles Ritzmann. GL Archive/Alamy Stock Photo.

Loie Fuller conjuring a butterfly with a sweep of her wingspan, 1902.
Photograph by Frederick W. Glasier. Library of Congress, item 96514367.

Watercolour painting of Fuller in her 'Archangel' routine, 1902.
Painting by Koloman Moser. The Yorck Project via Wikimedia Commons.

Patented design for a theatrical dancing garment by Fuller with specifications for wands, a skirt and a crown, 1894.
United States Patent and Trademark Office.

Maud Allan as the sinuous Salome, *c.*1923.
Photographer unknown. University of Washington Libraries, Special Collections, item JWS26200.

Anna Sokolow instructing at a dance company in New South Wales, Australia, 1976.
Photograph by Robert Pearce/Fairfax Media via Getty Images.

Martha Graham in *Letter to the World*, dedicated to the poet Emily Dickinson, 1940.
Photograph by Barbara Morgan. Published with permission from Barbara and Willard Morgan photographs and papers, UCLA Library Special Collections.

Graham surrounded by her early company in her breakout work, *Heretic*, c.1929.
Photograph by Soichi Sunami. Courtesy of Martha Graham Resources.

An ecstatic utterance from Pearl Lang, pictured at age 50, in 1971.
Photograph by Jack Mitchell/Getty Images.

Lang and Robert Cohan as the Couple in Red in Martha Graham's *Diversion of Angels*, c.1954.
Photographer unknown. Courtesy of Martha Graham Resources.

Pearl Primus swinging low in *Hard Time Blues*, a critique of share-cropping in the American South, 1943.
Photograph by Carl Van Vechten. Jerome Robbins Dance Division, The New York Public Library. Published with permission from © Van Vechten Trust.

Primus striking one of her famous five-foot-high leaps for *Strange Fruit*, 1951.
Photograph by Baron/Hulton Archive/Getty Images.

Sultry cigarette smoke from Katherine Dunham in 'Le Jazz Hot', 1939.
Photographer unknown. Katherine Dunham Photograph Collection, Special Collections Research Center, Morris Library, Southern Illinois University, Carbondale. Published with permission from Marie-Christine Dunham Pratt.

An outflung Sophie Maslow in 'On Top of Old Smokey', from *Folksay*, 1942.

Photograph by Barbara Morgan. Published with permission from Barbara and Willard Morgan photographs and papers, UCLA Library Special Collections.

Index

for New York Metropolitan Opera, 175, 190; costumes, 179, 181, 185; dance school in New York, 188, 189–90; dance troupe, 180, 189–90; death, 191; family background, 176, 177; funding, 180, 182; Hollywood films, 184; hunger strike, 191; identities, 191; in Brazil, 187; in England, 186; in Haiti, 179–80; in Mexico, 186; in New York, 183–4; in Senegal, 190; influence, 164, 236; *Island Possessed* (anthropological text), 180; Kentucky curtain call, 187, 198, 201; *L'Ag'Ya*, 180–1, 182, 190; marriage, 185, 187; memoir, 176, 177; Negro Dance Group, 178; *Negro Rhapsody*, 178; *Pins and Needles* choreography, 184; politics, 167–8, 169, 190–1; portfolio, 183–4; programme notes, 183; racist environment, 170; restaging of *La Guiablesse*, 178; reviews, 182, 185–6, 191, 201; *Rites de Passage*, 179, 182, 183, 185; round-the-world tours, 186; *Shango*, 186; Southern Illinois University post, 190; *Southland*, 182, 183, 187–8; teaching, 162, 178; technique, 179, 181; theatrical approach, 179, 199; training, 176, 177; *Tropical Revue*, 184, 185, 187, 191, 201; *Tropics and Le Jazz Hot*, 179, 183, 184, 185, 186; US State Department cultural adviser, 190; *Veracruzana*, 186; view of Black dance, 169–70
Durante, Viviana, 30–1
Dutch National Ballet, 229

Edison, Thomas, 25, 55
Edward VII, King, 65
Epstein, Hadassah Spira, 166, 168, 170, 216, 217
Epstein, Jacob, 127
Erdman, Jean, 115, 166, 226
eurhythmics, 14
Evans, Redd, 166
Eyal, Sharon, 237

Faust, Lotta, 67
Federal Dance Project (FDP), 97
Feist, Hertha, 13

feminism: Britain, 79; consciousness-raising, 135, 158; France, 46, 57; Jewish feminists, 170, 216, 225, 228; new currents, 6; New Woman, 15–19, 32, 36, 57–8, 93; role of personal reflection, 95; United States, 34, 40, 92–3, 135; women's rights, 93, 94; women's suffrage, 92
femininity: ballet version of, 27; Duncan's work, 24, 31, 32, 33; Fuller's work, 46, 48, 62; Judson attitude to, 236; Lang's work, 231; modern attitudes, 2–3; new courses of, 5; perceptions of, 18
First World War, 39, 55, 79, 92
Flammarion, Camille, 55
Fokine, Michel, 29, 110
Fonteyn, Margot, 117
Fort, Syvilla, 189
Franko, Mark, 107
Freud, Sigmund, 104
Froelich, Bianca, 68
Fuller, Loie: appearance, 45, 48, 58–60, 62; Bernhardt's influence, 27n; *The Butterfly*, 53; career, 4, 19, 48–9, 52–3, 56, 74; celebrity, 56–7; choreography, 48, 49, 51; company, 29, 60; costume, 13, 45, 49–51, 53–4, 55, 59–60; dancing, 46, 49, 62; family background, 48; *Fire Dance*, 54; imitators, 51, 52; in Europe, 120; in Germany, 52; in London, 48; in New York, 50, 51, 52; in Paris, 45, 52–3; lighting effects, 48, 49–50, 53–4, 56, 60; *Lily Dance*, 51n, 61; marriage, 58; memoir, 46, 56, 59; performances, 29, 59–60; questions around sexuality and the male gaze, 235; *Radium Dance*, 55; reconstructions of her dances, 61; relationship with Duncan, 53, 60; reputation, 53; reviews, 49, 53; *Salome*, 57, 67; scientific interests, 54–6, 59; 'Serpentine Dance', 45, 49–50, 51, 52, 55; sexuality, 19, 58; skirt dancing, 49, 50; stage presence, 45–6; technique, 58; view of ballet, 12; *The Violet*, 53; *The White Dance*, 53

Geltman, Fanya, 95
George VI, King, 209
Georgi, Yvonne, 87n